MODE ILLUSTRATION

WILLEMINA HOENDERKEN (Hg./Ed.)

Für Alexander

EIN HANDBUCH
*Fashion Illustration
A Manual*

ARNOLDSCHE

6 GRATWANDERUNG
Einleitung

9 **TECHNIK**

12 DER AUSGANGSPUNKT
Materialerklärung

14 ERSTE SCHRITTE
Zeichentechniken

18 BEWEGUNGSÜBUNGEN
Materialexperimente

36 DIE RICHTIGE RICHTUNG
Collagen

45 EIN EIGENER WEG
Hintergründe

52 SCHRITT FÜR SCHRITT
Zeichnen am Computer

BALANCING ACT [294]
Introduction

TECHNIQUE [294]

STARTING OUT [294 – 295]
Explaining your materials

FIRST STEPS [296 – 297]
Drawing techniques

EXERCISES IN ANIMATION [297]
Experimenting with materials

THE RIGHT DIRECTION [298]
Collage

YOUR OWN WAY [298]
Backgrounds

STEP BY STEP [298 – 299]
Drawing on the computer

71
GESTALTUNG
72
INNEHALTEN
Skizzenbuch
84
STOLPERN UND AUFSTEHEN
Figürliche Zeichnungen
130
SCHNURGERADE
Werkstattzeichnungen
134
ZIELGERICHTET
Köpfe
160
AUF DER SPITZE
Stylingzeichnungen
180
STEINE BESEITIGEN
Kreativität
185
DIE GROSSE FREIHEIT
Illustrationen
214
ESSAY
Bilder der Mode. Einige Anmerkungen
Anna Zika

223
PRAXIS
225
AM ZIEL
Die Praxis
248
INTERVIEW
Willemina Hoenderken im Gespräch mit Annette Görtz
252
DER GIPFEL
Illustration einer Winterkollektion
274
GESCHAFFT
Interviews mit Profis
286
BILDNACHWEIS
293
ENGLISCHE ÜBERSETZUNG
316
KONTAKTE
317
IMPRESSUM
318
DANK

CREATION [299]

PAUSING TO TAKE STOCK [299]
Sketch book

STUMBLING AND [299 – 301]
STANDING UP AGAIN
Figure drawing

STRAIGHT AS A DIE [302]
Workshop drawings

FOCUSED [303]
Heads

TO THE POINT [303 – 304]
Styling drawings

REMOVING STUMBLING [304]
BLOCKS
Creativity

FREEDOM KNOWS NO [305]
BOUNDS
Illustrations

ESSAY [305 – 308]
Fashion images. Some observations
Anna Zika

WORKING LIFE [308]

THE FINISHING LINE [308 – 309]
How to get there

INTERVIEW [309 – 310]
Willemina Hoenderken in conversation
with Annette Görtz

THE SUMMIT [310 – 311]
Illustrating a winter collection

I DID IT! [311 – 315]
Interviews with professionals

CREDITS [286]

CONTACTS [316]

IMPRINT [317]

ACKNOWLEDGEMENTS [318]

Einleitung

Willemina Hoenderken

Man spürt, ob man ein Zeichner ist oder nicht. Ich glaube, ein (Mode)Zeichner kann nicht anders, als zu zeichnen. Etwas ruft, etwas lässt einen nicht los. Wenn man unterwegs ist, zu Fuß in der Stadt, aus dem Fenster eines Zuges schaut, in der Kneipe sitzt, gibt es überall Motive, die man sofort als Zeichnung umsetzen möchte. Die markante Nase im Profil des Nachbarn, ein Kleid, welches irgendwo hochweht, die optische Verkürzung des eigenen Beines. (Übrigens ein Grund, weshalb viele Zeichner ein Skizzenbuch in der Tasche haben.)

Es gibt aber unendlich viele Gründe, diesem Drängen kein Gehör zu schenken: „Ach, ich bin doch nicht gut genug" oder „Ich weiß nicht, wie ich es machen soll" oder „Kind, damit kannst du doch kein Geld verdienen." Wirklich schade – so gibt man sich, bevor man überhaupt angefangen hat, keine Chance. Vielleicht darf ich deshalb etwas überspitzt sagen, dass man zu einer kleinen Gruppe privilegierter Menschen gehört und dass man von irgendwoher ein besonderes Talent bekommen hat, das man nutzen sollte!

Ein Zeichner geht keinem geregelten Job nach, niemand wartet, kein Mensch kommt auf einen zu. Aber trotzdem ... Wenn man zeichnen kann, sollte man sich für den steinigen Weg entscheiden.

Trenne dich nicht von deinen Illusionen.
Wenn sie verschwunden sind,
wirst du weiter existieren,
aber aufgehört haben zu leben.

MARK TWAIN

Aus eigener Erfahrung kenne ich das Gefühl von Stolz und Zufriedenheit, wenn eine Zeichnung gut gelungen ist. Der Weg dahin ist aber nicht immer einfach. Dieses Buch ist ein wenig wie eine Wanderung. Es gibt ebene Strecken, einfach zu bewältigen. Es gibt aber auch Steigungen, und manchmal ist man außer Atem. Dann wiederum kommen Momente, in denen man innehalten kann. Unterwegs gibt es viel zu sehen, zu entdecken. Nicht jeder Schritt wird vorgemacht. Die Wegweisung fehlt hier und da. Dann muss man den Pfad selbst entdecken, vielleicht sogar einige Steine aus dem Weg räumen. Aber wenn man die große Freiheit erlangt und den Gipfel erreicht, wird man mit Stolz und Zufriedenheit belohnt.

Ich möchte Mut machen. Mode ist Faszination, Kult, Schutz und Schmuck. Mode kann alles und noch viel mehr sein. Von der Haute Couture bis zur zweckdienlichen Bekleidung erfahren wir Mode am eigenen Körper und nehmen sie wahr in den vielfältigsten Erscheinungsformen der Werbung, im Internet und in Magazinen, raffiniert, erotisch, provokant und superästhetisch umgesetzt in verführerischen Bildern.

Die Modeillustration hat vor einigen Jahren ein Comeback gefeiert, und das ist gut so. Heute bietet die digitale Fotografie die Möglichkeit, eine Realität zu zeigen, die mit der Wahrheit nichts zu tun hat. Die Zeichnung aber ist das Medium par excellence, um Illusionen zu verbreiten. Und von Illusionen lebt die Mode. Eine Modezeichnung visualisiert die vielen Gesichter der Mode. So kann sie provokativ sein oder eher still und träumerisch, sie kann opulent und barock sein oder eher puristisch.

GRATWANDERUNG 7

Eine Modeillustration ist ein Produkt der Fantasie. Warum? Weil sie Ideale vermittelt, weil sie Begehrlichkeiten schaffen soll. Fantasie, Ideale und Begehrlichkeiten werden durch die Mode beeinflusst und ändern sich somit ständig.

Wenn man die besten Modezeichnungen der letzten 100 Jahre nebeneinander legt, sieht man diesen Wandel der Geschmäcker. Und eines fällt auf: In unserer Zeit gibt es keinen eindeutigen Trend mehr. Die Bandbreite einer Modezeichnung erstreckt sich heute von einer fast naturalistischen Zeichnung bis hin zu einer Art fremder, außerirdischer Wesen. Es gibt anscheinend keine goldenen Regeln mehr – oder nur noch wenige.

Warum dann dieses Buch, warum in dieser Form? Wie ich eines Tages feststellte, hatte mein Archiv mit Modezeichnungen ein beachtliches Ausmaß angenommen. Schade eigentlich, dass die Arbeiten nur von wenigen Leuten gesehen worden waren, diese Bilder von enormer Kraft. Hier sind sie jetzt – sortiert, in Reihenfolge gebracht, somit „sichtbar" gemacht und mit kleinen Texten versehen.

Wer viele Bilder sieht, lernt das Sehen. In dieser Publikation geht es darum, verschiedene Stile und Ausdrucksformen kennenzulernen.

Das Buch soll Anregung sein und das eine oder andere vermitteln. Nicht mit erhobenem Zeigefinger, sondern eher in lockerer Form. Viele Bilder veranschaulichen die Vielzahl der Wege, das Ziel zu erreichen. Es gibt keinen Königsweg.

Ich möchte Begeisterung wecken für Linien, Formen, Farben und Flächen. Leidenschaft für eine spannende Haltung, für Erotik, die Passion teilen für das Zeigen oder das Weglassen, ein Hochgefühl wecken beim Betrachten ungebremster Fantasie.

Ich möchte aber auch Verständnis fördern für die Logik der Schatten oder des Layouts, für die Vernunft eines Konzeptes, die intelligente Umsetzung einer Inspiration oder die Konsequenz einer Botschaft.

Es gibt Bücher, die das Modezeichnen von der Pike auf lehren, es gibt Bücher, die ohne Kommentar auskommen. Dieses Buch stellt sich in die Mitte. Ohne bei null anzufangen, aber doch mit wertvollen Tipps aus der Praxis. Vielleicht sollte man es betrachten als eine Wanderung durch ein Museum. Es gibt zwar eine Führung, aber diese lässt Raum für eigene Beobachtungen und Selbsterkenntnis. Dies ist ein Buch mit Arbeiten von Studierenden, aber doch auf einem hohen Niveau. Ein Buch für Leute, die das Fach lernen möchten, aber auch geeignet für diejenigen, welche schon fortgeschritten sind. Oder für solche, die ein Herz für schöne Zeichnungen haben.

Ich möchte Lust und Leidenschaft wecken für eine Zeichenkunst, die es längst verdient hat, wieder mehr beachtet zu werden.

→ ENGL: [294]

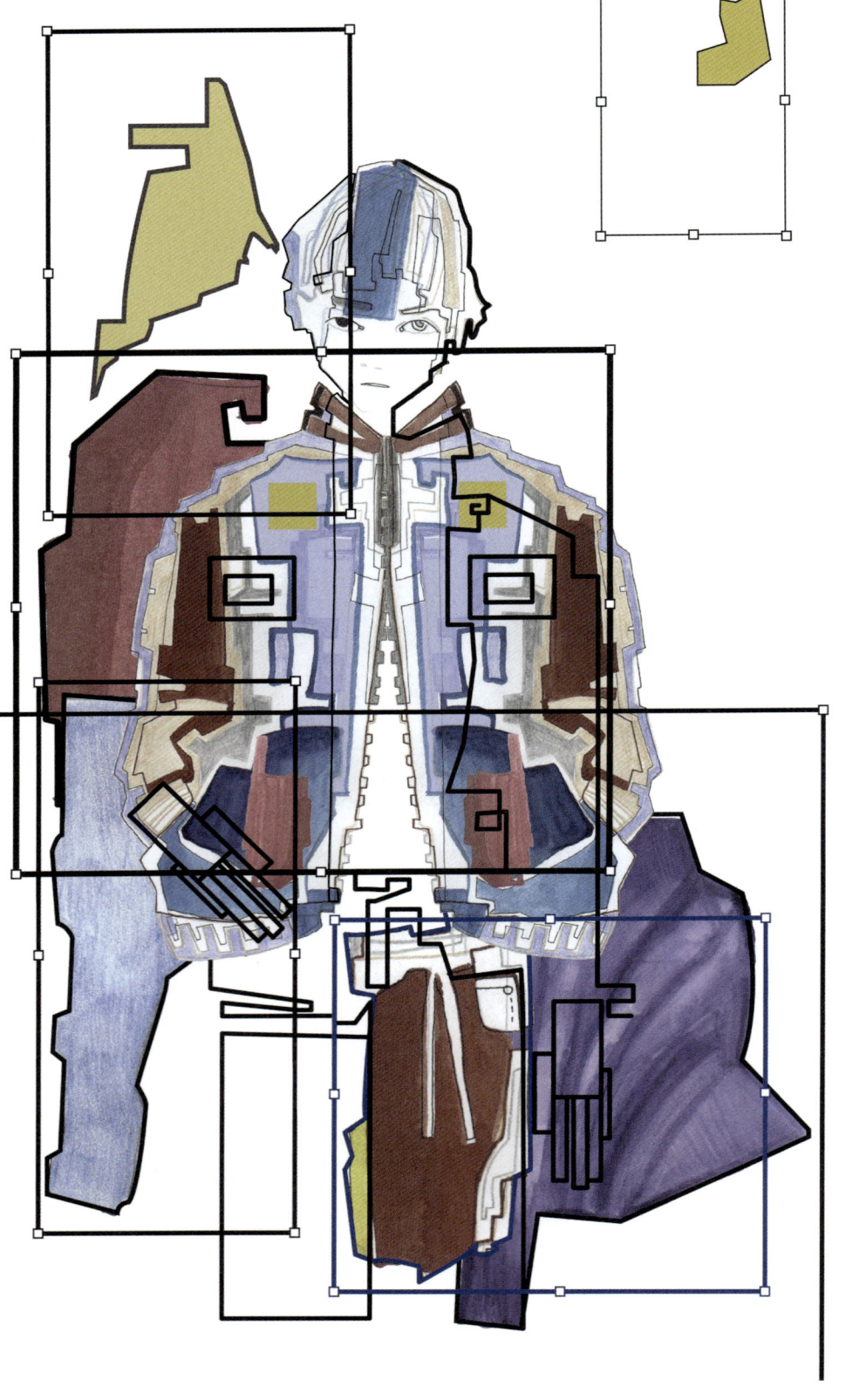

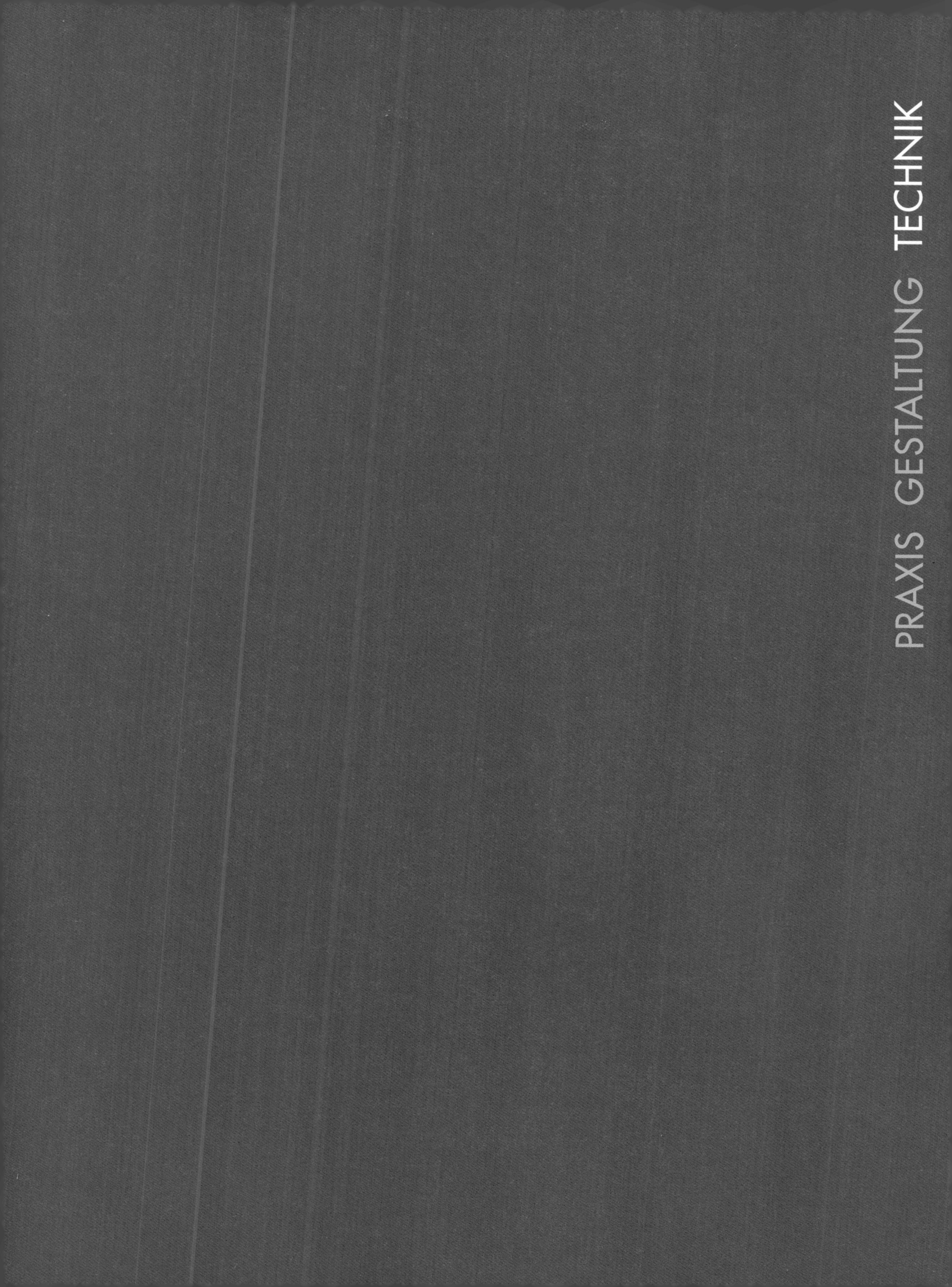

TECHNIK - DER AUSGANGSPUNKT

Materialerklärung

In diesem Buch werde ich die Materialien ansprechen, die speziell für Modezeichner wichtig sind. Das sind in erster Linie verschiedene Stifte und einfache Farbmaterialien. Die Eigenschaften und Resultate eines Materials wie Ölfarbe erklären zu wollen, wäre hier nicht angebracht. Das Arbeiten in Öl verlangt viel Zeit, man arbeitet in mehreren Schichten und jede Schicht muss mehrere Stunden trocknen. Die Mode ist schnell, eine Modezeichnung ebenso. Also arbeitet man mit schnelltrocknenden Farben.

Als Starterpaket ist Folgendes zu empfehlen:

■ VERSCHIEDENE BLEISTIFTE IN DEN STÄRKEN H, HB, B BIS 6B

Erfahrungsgemäß reichen diese aus, um eine gewisse Bandbreite zu zeigen. H steht für den härtesten Stift und hiermit erzeugt man die hellste Linie. B steht für einen weichen Stift. Je höher die Zahl, desto dunkler die Linie. Noch dunkler allerdings arbeitet man mit einem Graphitstift. Für sehr dunkle Linien lässt sich auch ein Buntstift benutzen.

■ KUGELSCHREIBER IN VERSCHIEDENEN FARBEN

Mit einem Kugelschreiber kann man wunderbar skizzieren. Je weniger Druck man ausübt, desto heller die Linien. Natürlich kann man Kugelschreiber nicht wegradieren, aber somit lernt man, dass es nicht schlimm ist, auch mal einen Fehler zu machen.

■ BUNTSTIFTE (MINDESTENS 24 FARBEN)

Es gibt eine Auswahl an harten und weichen Stifte. Empfehlenswert sind die weicheren. Hiermit lassen sich sowohl helle als auch dunkle Linien setzen (je nach Druck) und größere Flächen können übergangslos koloriert werden. Außerdem gibt es Aquarellstifte. Man gibt ein wenig Wasser auf die Linie und kann dann die Farbe ausstreichen.

■ SCHWARZE FILZSTIFTE IN VERSCHIEDENEN STÄRKEN

Ganz feine Stifte benutzt man für Konturlinien oder Details wie zum Beispiel eine Stepperei in Kleidung, etwas dickere, um einen Kontrast anzubringen, und ganz dicke Stifte kann man statt Tusche für größere Flächen verwenden. Die Fläche mit Filzstift hat eine regelmäßigere Oberfläche als eine Fläche aus Tusche.

■ FINELINER (MINDESTENS 12 FARBEN)

Diese Stifte benutzt man für Konturlinien oder Details.

■ ÖLKREIDE (MINDESTENS 12 FARBEN)

Eine fetthaltige Kreide, die sehr gut haftet. Da es eine grobe Struktur hat, ist dieses Material in erster Linie für große Flächen oder große Arbeiten zu empfehlen. Man kann jedoch auch einzelne Flächen innerhalb einer Zeichnung mit Ölkreide bearbeiten, um eine Stofflichkeit wie von Leder oder Tweed hervorzuheben.

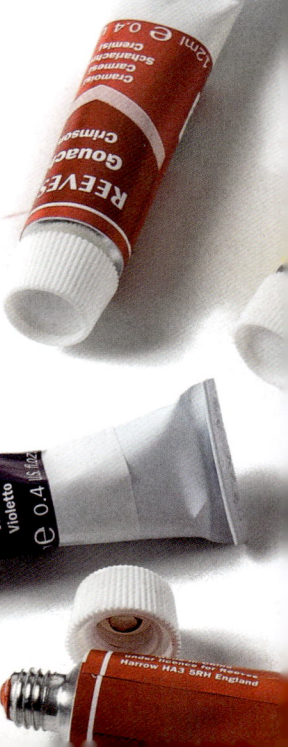

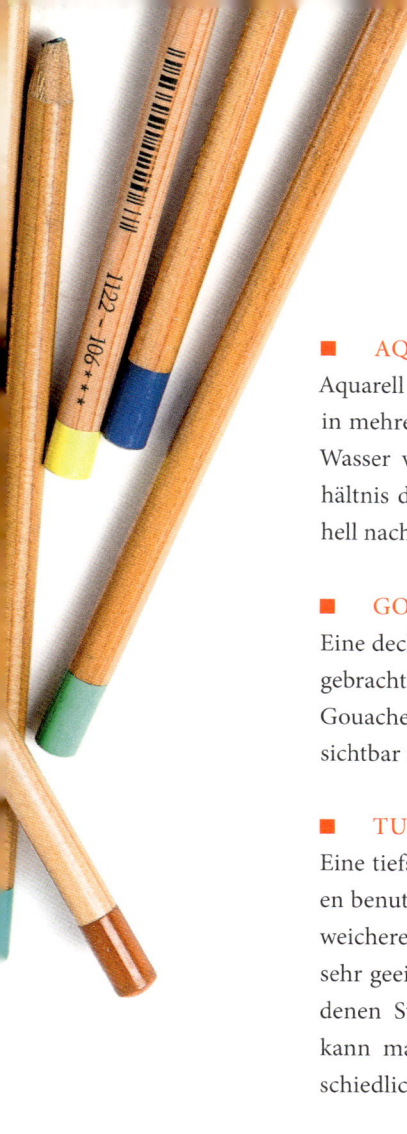

■ AQUARELLFARBEN (MINDESTENS 18 FARBEN)
Aquarell ist eine transparente Farbe, die man mit einem Pinsel in mehreren Schichten aufbringt. Die Farbe wird immer mit Wasser verdünnt. Durch Ausprobieren lernt man, das Verhältnis der Mischung einzuschätzen. Man sollte immer von hell nach dunkel arbeiten, weil die Farbe nicht deckend ist.

■ GOUACHEFARBEN (MINDESTENS 18 FARBEN)
Eine deckende Farbe, die mit Pinsel und wasserverdünnt aufgebracht wird. Die Farbigkeit ist brillanter als Aquarell. Weiße Gouachefarbe ist durch seine Deckkraft sehr gut geeignet, um sichtbar über andere Farben gesetzt zu werden.

■ TUSCHE
Eine tiefschwarze Farbe, die mit einer Feder für scharfe Linien benutzt werden kann. Mit einem feinen Pinsel lassen sich weichere Linien setzen. Für große Flächen ist Tusche auch sehr geeignet. Die Fläche ist sehr lebendig, zeigt an verschiedenen Stellen eine unterschiedliche Farbintensität. Tusche kann man sehr gut mit Wasser verdünnen und so unterschiedliche Grautöne erzielen.

■ FARBIGE TUSCHE ODER ECOLINE
Eine mit viel Wasser verdünnte und somit äußerst flüssige Farbe, die sehr transparent erscheint. Die Farben sind brillant.

■ FEDERHALTER
FEDERN IN 2 VERSCHIEDENEN STÄRKEN
Man braucht eine sehr spitze Feder für feine Linien und eine mit etwas breiterer Spitze für stärkere Linien.

■ EIN SET FLACHER PINSEL
Anfänglich reicht es aus, ein Set zu kaufen. Diese werden angeboten in den Stärken 2 bis 14 (je höher die Zahl, desto breiter der Pinsel). Man kann die Pinsel sowohl in der Breite als auch mit der schmalen Seite benutzen. Die schmale Seite eignet sich zum Beispiel gut für das Setzen von Haaren. Wenn man eine große Fläche mit einem flachen Pinsel einfärbt, wirkt sie allerdings ein wenig gestreift.

■ RUNDPINSEL IN VERSCHIEDENEN STÄRKEN
Diese Pinsel sind besser geeignet für größere Flächen. Ein runder Pinsel nimmt mehr Farbe auf als ein flacher Pinsel; dadurch lässt sich die Farbe besser verteilen und fließt stärker ineinander. Auch hier kann man ein fertiges Set kaufen. Sowohl für flache Pinsel als auch für runde Pinsel gilt, dass sie nicht sehr teuer sein müssen. Man sollte durch Übungen erst die Eigenschaften der verschiedenen Pinsel entdecken. Wenn man weiß, mit welchen Pinseln man am besten zurechtkommt, kann man mehr Geld investieren. Eine Beratung im Fachgeschäft ist sehr zu empfehlen. Es gibt zu viele unterschiedliche Pinsel, um alle an dieser Stelle vorstellen zu können.

■ ZEICHENBLOCK DIN A3
ELFENBEIN- ODER EIERSCHALFARBEN
Die Voraussetzung für eine gelungene Arbeit ist ein qualitativ gutes Zeichenpapier von mindestens 80 Gramm, am besten in einem Eierschal- oder Elfenbeinton. Auf schneeweißem Papier sieht eine Zeichnung schnell zu hart aus. Nur für Entwurfsskizzen darf man auch mal ein einfaches Kopierpapier benutzen.

■ SKIZZENBUCH DIN A4
ELFENBEIN- ODER EIERSCHALFARBEN
Es empfiehlt sich, ein gebundenes Skizzenbuch zu nehmen. Bei einem Buch mit einer Ringbindung ist leicht die Spirale im Weg.

■ LOSE BLÄTTER AQUARELLPAPIER
Es gibt Aquarellpapier in den Stärken fein, mittel und grob. Man sollte alle drei ausprobieren, um zu sehen, welche einem am besten gefällt. Auf grobem Aquarellpapier kann man auch sehr gut mit Bleistift oder Buntstift arbeiten; das ergibt einen tollen Effekt, weil die Struktur des Papiers zum Vorschein kommt.

Pastellkreide fehlt in der Liste, da ich es als nicht zeitgemäß empfinde, dieses Material großflächig einzusetzen. Kleinere Schattierungen oder Konturen kann man auch mit Pastellbuntstiften erzeugen.

Mit den Materialien aus der Liste kann man auf jeden Fall alles zeichnen: von einer einfachen, linearen Stylingzeichnung bis hin zur hochkomplizierten Illustration. Wenn man später seine Palette ausdehnen möchte, empfehlen sich zum Beispiel Acrylfarbe, Lackfarbe (auch als Sprühfarbe gut einzusetzen) oder Wandfarbe.

→ ENGL: [294-295]

Zeichentechniken

Es gibt verschiedene Zeichen-, Mal-, und Drucktechniken. Hier werden die Techniken erklärt, die für einen Modezeichner am wichtigsten sind. Man sollte die einzelnen Methoden ausprobieren, damit man ein Gespür für die unterschiedlichen Vorgänge entwickelt.

■ LINIEN

Die Linie ist ein wichtiges Merkmal. Oftmals erkennt man an der Linie schon die Handschrift eines Zeichners. Eine Linie kann weich sein, suchend mit mehreren Strichen, kann klar sein, kräftig, hell oder dunkel, unregelmäßig oder mit einem Lineal gezogen. Wenn man eine lineare Zeichnung erstellt, kommt es sehr darauf an, was das Ziel ist. Für eine lebendige Zeichnung empfehle ich, Konturlinien abhängig von Licht und Schatten zu setzen. Da, wo es einen Schatten gibt, kann man die Linie dunkler setzen, dort wo es hell ist, sollte auch die Linie hell sein. Mit einem Stift erzielt man diese Effekte, indem man einmal mehr und einmal weniger Druck ausübt.

■ SCHRAFFIEREN

Schraffieren bedeutet das Setzen von vielen kleinen, parallel verlaufenden Linien, die gemeinsam eine Fläche bilden. Man benutzt diese Technik, um einen Schatten anzudeuten. Am ruhigsten ist eine Schraffur, wenn man die Linien in einer Richtung setzt. Man kann aber auch als Kontrast einen Teil der Zeichnung in eine Kreuzschraffur setzen. Die Abstände der Linien können variieren. Setzt man eine Fläche ein, um einen Schatten anzudeuten, erscheint eine Fläche mit sehr nah aneinandergesetzten Linien natürlich dunkler als eine Fläche, auf der die Linien weiter auseinanderstehen. Diese Technik ist nicht materialabhängig. Oft ist eine Materialkombination, zum Beispiel eine Buntstiftschraffur über einer Aquarellfläche, sehr reizvoll. Auch lassen sich verschiedene Farben miteinander kombinieren.

■ SCHUMMERN

Mit einem Bleistift oder einem Buntstift macht man kleine, kreisende Bewegungen übers Papier. Wird konstanter Druck ausgeübt, so entstehen regelmäßige graue oder farbige Flächen ohne Streifen. Wenn man an bestimmten Stellen etwas stärker aufdrückt, erzielt man einen Schatten.

■ FROTTAGE

Wenn man ein strukturiertes Papier (z.B. Raufasertapete) oder einen Gegenstand mit Relief unter ein Blatt Papier legt und anschließend mit einem Bleistift oder Buntstift schummert, entsteht ein Muster. Man kann auch in eine nasse Farbfläche ein Stück zerknittertes Papier oder Stoff drücken. Wenn man es anschließend abzieht, entstehen interessante Muster.

■ AQUARELLIEREN

Bei der klassischen Methode klebt man das Aquarellpapier so stramm wie möglich mit einem breiten Papierklebestreifen von oben nach unten auf einen Untergrund, am besten aus Holz. Diese Maßnahme sorgt dafür, dass das Papier keine Wellen schlägt, wenn man es mit viel Wasser bearbeitet. Nun gibt es zwei verschiedene Arbeitsmethoden. Man kann „trocken" arbeiten, also sofort mit dem Pinsel Flächen anbringen. Bei dieser Methode hat man eine gewisse Kontrolle über die Flächen. Mit ein bisschen Geduld beim Antrocknen kann man klar abgegrenzte Flächen übereinanderlegen. Das ergibt eine Arbeit, in der man die einzelnen Schichten gut erkennen kann. Für die Schattierung eines Gesichts können beispielsweise vier bis fünf pastellige Töne übereinandergelegt werden, um so eine spannungsreiche Fläche zu schaffen. Wichtig ist es, sich immer bewusst zu machen, dass man nur von hell nach dunkel arbeiten kann.

Man kann aber auch „nass" arbeiten. Hierzu macht man das aufgespannte Papier mit einem Schwamm ganz nass und bringt anschließend Farbflächen auf. Bei dieser Methode hat man keine Kontrolle über die Flächen. Die Farbe läuft aus. Aber gerade das ist das Merkmal dieser Technik. Es ist sehr reizvoll, wenn man verschiedene Farben kombiniert und das Papier zur Mischpalette wird. Viel Übung hilft, ein Gespür für die Farben zu entwickeln. Natürlich kann man auch einzelne Stellen, die man vorher festgelegt hat, nass machen.

Große, regelmäßige Flächen sollte man immer von oben nach unten auftragen; der Pinsel zieht das Wasser mit. Wenn man mal etwas zu viel Farbe auf dem Pinsel hat, hilft ein Taschentuch oder ein Stückchen Küchenpapier. Hiermit lässt sich der Überschuss auf dem Aquarellpapier sofort aufsaugen. Sowieso ist es zu empfehlen, am Rand der Zeichnung eine Stelle als Probierstelle zu nutzen. Hier kann man sehen, ob die Farbintensität die richtige ist. Die Farbe sollte man nicht direkt aus der Tube nehmen. Es ist besser, eine Portion auf einem Teller vorzubereiten. Wasser, das immer in einem Glas oder Becher bereitsteht, sollte man regelmäßig austauschen, sonst beeinflusst es die Farbe des Aquarells.

Gouache- und Acrylfarbe werden auch mit Wasser verdünnt. Beide Farben eignen sich aber in erster Linie, wenn man etwas deckender arbeiten möchte als mit Aquarellfarben.

■ LASIEREN

Bei dieser Technik wird Farbe stark mit Wasser verdünnt auf Papier aufgetragen. Hierfür empfehlen sich Aquarell oder Acryl. Das Ergebnis ist eine stark transparente Fläche. Nachdem die Farbe gut getrocknet ist, wird eine weitere Schicht aufgetragen. Die erste Schicht scheint nun durch die zweite hindurch. Man kann diese Methode immer wiederholen; es entsteht ein glänzender Effekt.

■ SPRITZEN

Spritzen kann man, indem man mittelflüssige Farbe auf ein feines Sieb gibt und diese Farbe mit einer alten Zahnbürste durchpresst. Diese Methode ist einigermaßen zu kontrollieren. Wenn man die Farbe direkt mit einem Pinsel auf das Papier „schmeißt", hat man weniger Kontrolle.

BLASEN
Vor allem bei einer flüssigen Farbe wie Aquarell, Tusche oder Ecoline kann man die Farbe mit einem Strohhalm in eine gewisse Richtung blasen und so den Effekt eines Verlaufs erzeugen.

STUPSEN
Mit einem Stupspinsel kann man Farbe stupsen oder tupfen. Dieser Pinsel hat kurze, robuste Borsten. Man streicht die Farbe nicht über das Papier, sondern bringt sie mit kleinen Stößen auf. Diesen Pinsel benutzt man auch, um Schablonen mit Farbe zu füllen.

IMPASTO
Bei dieser Technik wird die Farbe mittels eines Spachtels oder Malmessers sehr dick aufgetragen. In dieser dicken Schicht sieht man die Spuren des Arbeitsmaterials. Man kann aber auch direkt aus der Tube arbeiten und die Farbe in einem Muster auftragen.

MASKIEREN
Wenn man bestimmte Stellen in einer Zeichnung abklebt oder mit Papier bedeckt, kommt hier keine Farbe auf das Blatt. Diese Methode benutzt man für Hintergründe oder Muster. Die gleiche Methode kann man auch mit Fotokleber anwenden. Man „zeichnet" mit dem Kleber Linien, koloriert anschließend und kann dann den Kleber mit einem Radiergummi entfernen. Diese Technik eignet sich sehr gut für das Erstellen von Mustern oder für das Zeichnen von Haaren.

KLECKSOGRAFIE (RORSCHACH)
Wenn man eine Farbe willkürlich auf ein Papier aufbringt und dieses anschließend faltet, entsteht ein symmetrisches Muster. Oftmals eignet sich das Muster als Kleidungsstück oder als Entwurf für ein Stoffdessin. Sowohl sehr flüssige Farben als auch Gouache- oder Acrylfarben können bei dieser Technik eingesetzt werden.

■ FÄDEN ZIEHEN

Man bringt Farbe auf ein Papier auf. Anschließend taucht man einen Baumwollfaden von mindestens der doppelten Länge des Papiers in flüssige Farbe wie Tusche, Ecoline oder Aquarell, legt diesen Faden doppelt auf das Papier, faltet das Blatt und zieht langsam den Faden von oben nach unten. Man kann den Faden sowohl gerade nach unten ziehen als auch in unregelmäßigen Bewegungen. Es entsteht ein spannendes Muster. Dieser Vorgang lässt sich beliebig und mit unterschiedlichen Farben wiederholen.

■ TON IN TON

Eine schwierige Technik ist das Ton-in-Ton-Arbeiten. Man entscheidet sich für eine Farbe und deren Abstufungen, zum Beispiel Schneeweiß, Elfenbein, Eierschale und Off-White. Zuvor werden die Flächen bestimmt, die man für eine Figur oder ein Porträt braucht. Nachdem man die Flächen gesetzt hat, bearbeitet man die Zeichnung mit einer transparenten Farbe, um gewisse Stellen oder Details zu verdeutlichen. Nur durch Experimentieren entdeckt man, welche Abstufungen nötig sind, um die Darstellung deutlich zu machen.

■ COLLAGIEREN

In einer Collage klebt man verschiedene Materialien zusammen zu einer neuen Fläche. Gut geeignet sind Fotos aus Magazinen oder Teile von Zeitungsartikeln. Auch alle möglichen anderen flachen Materialien kann man nutzen, wie zum Beispiel Tesafilm, Malerkrepp, Aufkleber oder Geschenkpapier.

■ COMPUTER

Der Computer ist auch für Zeichner ein wichtiges Arbeitsgerät. Einige Arbeitsmethoden werden in einem gesonderten Kapitel erklärt.

■ INDIVIDUELLE TECHNIKEN

Neben klassischen Techniken mit Farbe und Papier gibt es besondere Techniken, die sich eher konzeptuell erklären lassen.

Ein tolles Beispiel ist das Zerschneiden. Die hier gezeigten Arbeiten erinnern an Puzzlestücke und gliedern die Figuren neu. Es entstehen anders gelagerte Gewichtungen. Details entfallen oder wecken gerade eine besondere Aufmerksamkeit. Ein bestimmtes Thema kann als Leitfaden für die zeichnerische Umsetzung dienen.

Der Computer mit seinen Pixeln und Platinen kann solch eine Inspiration sein. Die Figuren erscheinen in einer besonderen und sehr modernen Atmosphäre. Man sollte sich viel mit Kunst auseinandersetzen und regelmäßig Ausstellungen besuchen. Sowohl die Kunst der Vergangenheit als auch die Kunst der Gegenwart bieten viele Anregungen, die für die eigene Arbeit eine enorme Bereicherung sein können.

→ ENGL: [296-297]

Materialexperimente

Im vorigen Kapitel sind die klassischen Methoden des Farbauftrags beschrieben. Dennoch gibt es viele sehr freie Arten, Farben anzulegen. Es macht großen Spaß, mit den verschiedensten Materialien zu experimentieren. Man sollte sich bei den ersten Versuchen frei machen von innerlichen Verboten und einfach vieles ausprobieren. Experimente gelingen nicht immer, aber man lernt mit der Zeit, wie sich Materialien verhalten.

Zuerst breitet man alle Zeichen- und Malmaterialen aus und geht mit offenen Augen durch die Wohnung: Was gibt die Küche her? Salz, Zucker, Spülbürste oder Topfkratzer? Im Wohnzimmer findet man vielleicht eine Heizungsabdeckung oder eine raue Tapete, im Garten ein wenig Sand. Reicht das alles nicht, gibt es noch den Baumarkt, das Schreibwaren- oder Farbenfachgeschäft.

Nun geht es darum zu entdecken, was Wasser mit Aquarell macht, ob man viel oder wenig zufügt, ob man steuert oder laufen lässt. Und was ist der Effekt von Salz, wenn man es mit Aquarell kombiniert? Plötzlich erinnert man sich noch aus dem Kindergarten, wie es sich mit Aquarell und Ölkreide verhält.

Tusche und Wasser, Tusche und Seife, Tusche und Kerzenwachs. Hart und weich, weich und glänzend, hart und matt. Farbe und Seidenpapier, Farbe und Papiertaschentücher, Farbe und Tesafilm, Farbe und Malerkrepp. Verschiedene Schichten, Materialkombinationen, fremde Arbeitsgegenstände.

Auf einmal sind Experimente entstanden, die man sofort als Stoffe erkennt. Herrliche, luftige Seidenstoffe oder ein winterlicher robuster Tweed. Und man erkennt die Möglichkeit, Kleidung anders darzustellen, frecher, ungewöhnlicher. Wenn man die Erkenntnisse in eine Arbeit einfließen lassen möchte, gibt es zwei Varianten der Machart.

Bei der ersten Methode arbeitet man direkt auf dem Papier. Das setzt eine Planung voraus. Schon im Vorfeld sollte man bedenken, mit welchen Materialien man arbeitet und wie die Form sein soll. Dennoch kann es natürlich sein, dass das Experiment nicht so gelingt, wie gedacht. Oft kann man aber durch zusätzliche Eingriffe ein zufriedenstellendes Resultat erzielen. Wenn es sich um sommerliche Stoffe handelt, sollte man etwas Luft lassen.

Das heißt, innerhalb der Fläche sollten leere Stellen stehen bleiben; die Papierfarbe wirkt wie eine Glanzpartie oder eine helle Stelle.

Bei einer winterlichen Kollektion braucht man das weniger. Dennoch sieht die Arbeit auch hier spielerischer aus, wenn man beispielsweise die Farbe nicht exakt bis an die Kontur aufbringt.
Bei der zweiten Methode erstellt man zuerst einige Blätter mit Experimenten. Auch hier sollte man vorher einen Plan haben. Dieser bezieht sich aber nicht auf die Form, sondern auf Licht, Schatten und Farbverlauf. Diese Experimente werden ausgeschnitten und anschließend neu zusammengeklebt. Ein tolles Vorbild ist „Die kleine Raupe Nimmersatt" von Eric Carle.

Das Untergrundmaterial spielt auch eine große Rolle beim Experimentieren und es kann sehr reizvoll sein, mit ungewöhnlichen Papieren zu arbeiten. Braunes Packpapier (Achtung, es gibt eine glatte und eine stumpfe Seite!), Seidenpapier, beides glatt oder zerknittert, Tonpapier, gemustertes Geschenkpapier, Zeitungspapier, kariertes Papier aus dem Matheheft, grauen oder braunen Karton ...

Vieles eignet sich, um einen ungewöhnlichen Effekt zu erzielen. Wenn man eine Zeichnung auf einem farbigen Hintergrund anlegen möchte, sollte man die Finger von grellen Farben lassen. Ein neongrüner oder pinkfarbener Hintergrund zieht alle Blicke auf sich und lässt die Zeichnung verschwinden. Und die sollte doch die Hauptsache sein. Eine Ausnahme ist eine Arbeit in kräftigem Schwarz.

→ ENGL: [297]

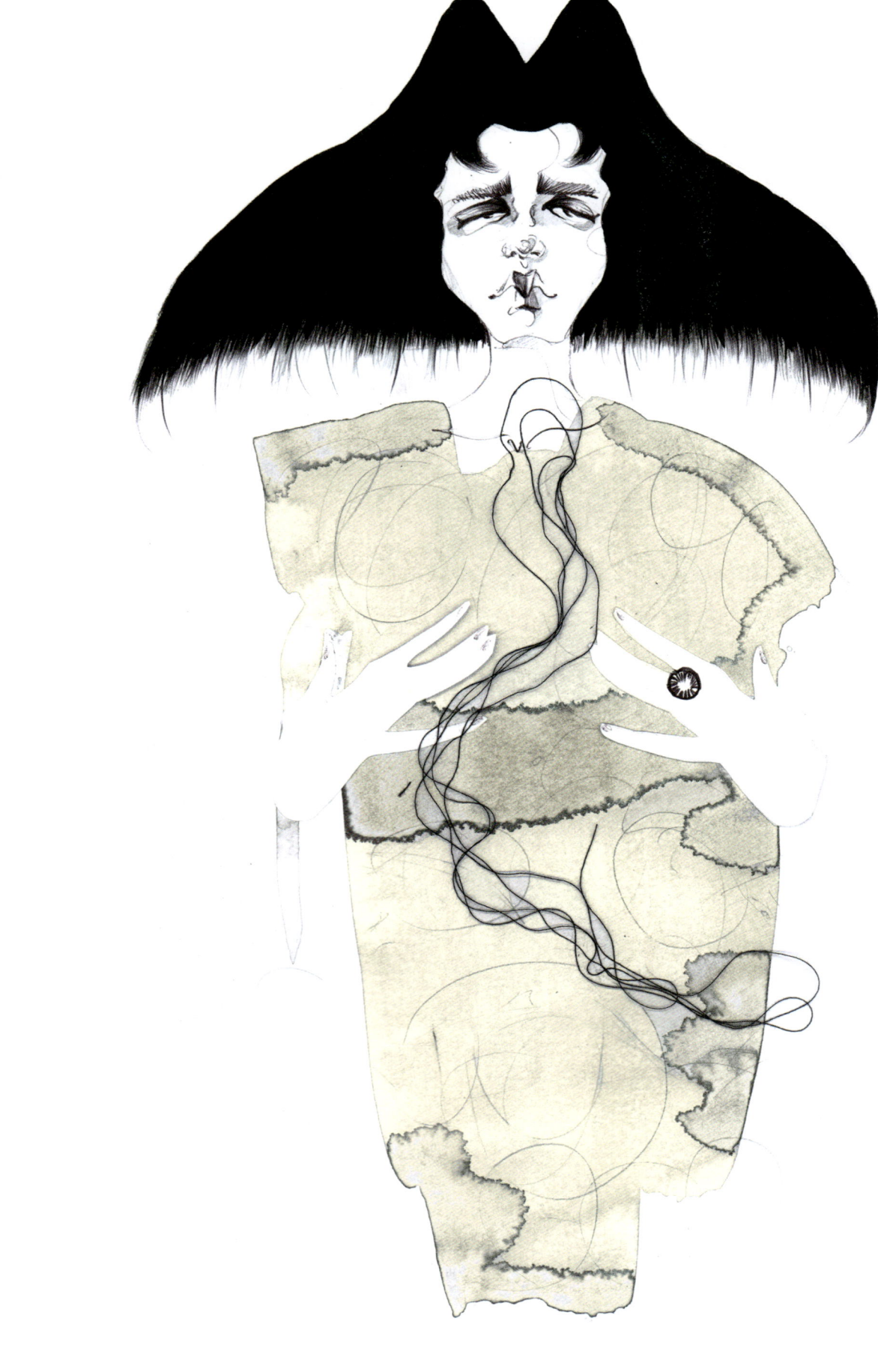

COLLAGEN

Das Wort „Collage" kommt vom französischen Wort für kleben („coller"). In einer Collage klebt man verschiedene Materialien zu einer neuen Fläche zusammen. Gut geeignet sind Fotos aus Magazinen oder Teilen von Zeitungsartikeln. Auch diverse andere flache Materialien kann man nutzen, wie zum Beispiel Tesafilm, Malerkrepp, Aufkleber oder Geschenkpapier.

Lege eine Kollektion von Sammelmappen an. Eine für rote Flächen, eine für grüne ... Eine für Haare, Äste und andere Linien, eine für Kieselsteine, Felsen, eine für Himmel, für Erde, eine für Tiere, eine für Gebäude und noch vieles mehr. Später kann man genau das auch mit dem Computer machen.

Wichtig: Wenn man Menschen in einer Collage zeigt, darf diese Person nie erkennbar sein. Dies würde die Persönlichkeitsrechte verletzen. Auch sehr bekannte Motive aus der Printwerbung sollten nicht verwendet werden. Hier wird es schwierig mit dem Copyright und außerdem beeinflusst man den Betrachter viel zu sehr.

Eine Collage hat nie etwas Willkürliches, sondern sollte immer von einer Richtung geprägt sein: horizontal, vertikal oder diagonal. Ist man unzufrieden mit seiner Collage, ist es

TECHNIK - DIE RICHTIGE RICHTUNG 37

immer die Richtung, die fehlt! Das gilt für die Gegenstände in der Collage, aber auch für die Farbe. Es sollte ein verständlicher Verlauf sein. Bei schwarzweißen Collagen bestimmen Hell und Dunkel die Richtung.

Aber wie so oft bestätigen Ausnahmen die Regel. Es kann besonders langweilig sein, wenn alles stimmt. Deswegen: einen Störfaktor einbauen! Eine Abwechslung zwischen möglichst gerade gerissenen Flächen und präzise ausgeschnittenen Gegenständen oder zwischen Fotos und Zeichnungen macht die Arbeit noch interessanter.

Die Collagetechnik kann man sehr gut für den Hintergrund verwenden. Oft lässt sich durch eine einfache Fläche die Aufmerksamkeit auf ein Detail der Kleidung lenken. Sehr interessant wird es, wenn Teile des Vorder- und Hintergrundes zusammengeführt werden.

→ ENGL: [298]

TECHNIK - EIN EIGENER WEG 45

Hintergründe

Die ersten Zeichnungen entstehen meistens ohne Hintergrund. Man ist schon froh, wenn die Arbeit einigermaßen gelungen ist. Es dauert eine Weile, bis man ein Gefühl für Proportionen und Ausdruck entwickelt und das Papierformat im Griff hat, also die Figur nicht zu groß oder zu klein zeichnet.

Es ist aber wichtig, sich weiterzuentwickeln und der Zeichnung eine Geschichte mitzugeben. Ein absolutes „Muss" für Illustratoren ist es, in seiner Arbeit etwas zu erzählen, die Fantasie des Betrachters anzuregen und nicht einfach nur „schön" zu zeichnen.
Das geht am einfachsten, indem man einen Raum kreiert. Ein gutes Beispiel für Einfachheit und Ausdrucksstärke ist auf dieser Seite zu sehen. Es ist empfehlenswert, am Anfang mit einfachen Quadraten oder Rechtecken zu arbeiten.

In dieser Form kann man einen Mehrwert oder eine Information verarbeiten, beispielsweise eine Farbe, Worte oder Motive, und so die Stimmung unterstützen.

Wichtig: Ein Hintergrund darf nie prominenter sein als der Vordergrund. Achte also darauf, dass er ruhig bleibt und die Figur im Vordergrund nicht erschlägt.
Eine weitere Stufe ist das Entwickeln eines Hintergrundes ohne festen Rahmen. Hier muss man das ganze Format immer im Auge behalten, um zu sehen, ob das Layout stimmt. Und auch hier sollte die Figur oder das Porträt im Vordergrund bleiben.
→ ENGL: [298]

Es ist eine tolle Übung, eine Figur vor verschiedenen Hintergründen zu platzieren und so zu entdecken, wie sich die Stimmung jeweils verändern lässt.

TECHNIK - SCHRITT FÜR SCHRITT

Zeichnen am Computer

Wenn man das Zeichnen einigermaßen beherrscht, ist es an der Zeit, sich mit dem Computer zu beschäftigen. Es geht nicht mehr ohne. Es gibt verschiedene Programme, die für Illustratoren sehr geeignet sind. Photoshop (zur Bildbearbeitung von Pixelgrafiken), InDesign (zur Layouterstellung) oder Illustrator (zur Erstellung und Bearbeitung von Vektorgrafiken). In diesem Kapitel werden zwei Arbeiten, die mit Illustrator gemacht wurden, ausführlich erklärt.

Der Computer ist ein Werkzeug, genau wie ein Pinsel oder ein Bleistift. Man sollte keine Angst haben, etwas falsch zu machen. Wenn etwas nicht auf Anhieb gelingt, kann man immer zurück und es noch einmal probieren. Vielleicht denkt man zu Anfang: „Dieses Ding ist nichts für mich", aber hier ist Durchhaltevermögen gefragt. Nach einer Phase des Übens offenbaren sich die vielen Möglichkeiten und Vorteile.

Am Anfang ist es eine gute Übung, eine Bleistiftzeichnung einzuscannen, diese in Illustrator durch interaktives Abpausen in eine Vektorgrafik umzuwandeln und die Flächen mit Farbe auszufüllen. In einer zweiten Stufe sollte man sich mit dem Erstellen von Vektorgrafiken, zum Beispiel dem Nachzeichnen einer gescannten Freihandskizze beschäftigen.

Gescannte Handzeichnungen können durch das Vektor-Malen nachträglich auf vielfältige Art und Weise gestaltet werden. Durch das Arbeiten mit dem Computer hat man die Möglichkeit, verschiedenste Kolorierungen und Effekte auszuprobieren, ohne auf der Originalzeichnung zu arbeiten. Wann immer ein Strich oder eine Farbe nicht gefällt, kann man den Arbeitsschritt rückgängig machen und etwas Neues probieren. Eine Funktion, die man sich beim analogen Zeichnen schon so oft gewünscht hat!

TECHNIK - SCHRITT FÜR SCHRITT   53

Beim intensiven Arbeiten am Computer merkt man schnell, wie eine Zeichnung durch einfache Eingriffe eine andere Atmosphäre ausstrahlen kann. Manchmal ist es sehr reizvoll, eine Stylingzeichnung mit den entsprechenden Stoffen auszufüllen, für ein Trendtableau reicht oftmals eine Farbfläche. Text kann in vielerlei Formen und Farben problemlos eingesetzt werden. Eine weitere Möglichkeit bietet die Kombination von Zeichnungen und Fotografien. Man kann eine Zeichnung auf einen fotografierten Hintergrund stellen oder auch Zeichnungen mit Fotomaterial füllen.

Wichtig: Man sollte ein umfangreiches Archiv anlegen mit selbst entwickelten Mustern, Used-Effekten, Hintergrundmaterial und mit Gegenständen aus verschiedenen Themenbereichen.

Allen Illustratoren, die intensiv mit Grafikprogrammen umgehen, ist anzuraten, mit einem Grafiktablett zu arbeiten. Dieses erleichtert das schnelle und exakte Zeichnen ungemein und lässt die Hand des Zeichners weniger schnell ermüden als das Arbeiten mit der Maus. Ein weiterer Vorteil ist, dass der Stift zusammen mit der Oberfläche des Tabletts ähnlich wie Papier und Bleistift bzw. Filzstift reagiert: Je nach Druck auf die Spitze werden schmalere oder dickere Linien erzeugt.

Photoshop: Bearbeitung von Bitmaps (Pixelbildern), Bildkorrektur und -retusche, Bildbearbeitung und -montage, digitales Malen, Erstellung von Montagen.
InDesign: Layouterstellung, Druckvorbereitung.
Illustrator: Bearbeitung und Erstellung von Vektorgrafiken, Abpausen (Umwandlung von Bitmap in Vektoren), Erstellung von Montagen.
Alle Programme können Vektor- und Bitmapgrafiken anzeigen.
→ ENGL: [298-299]

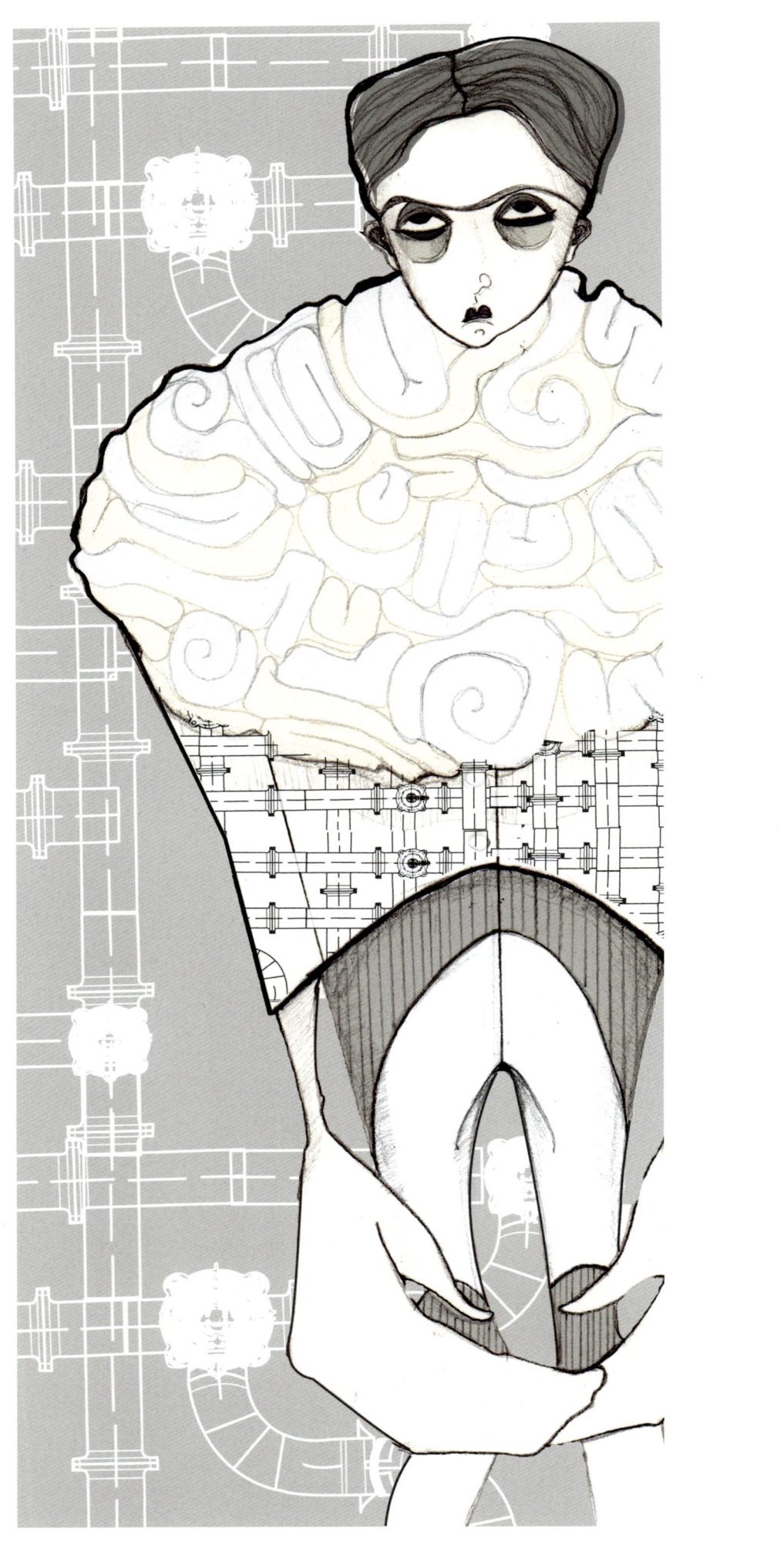

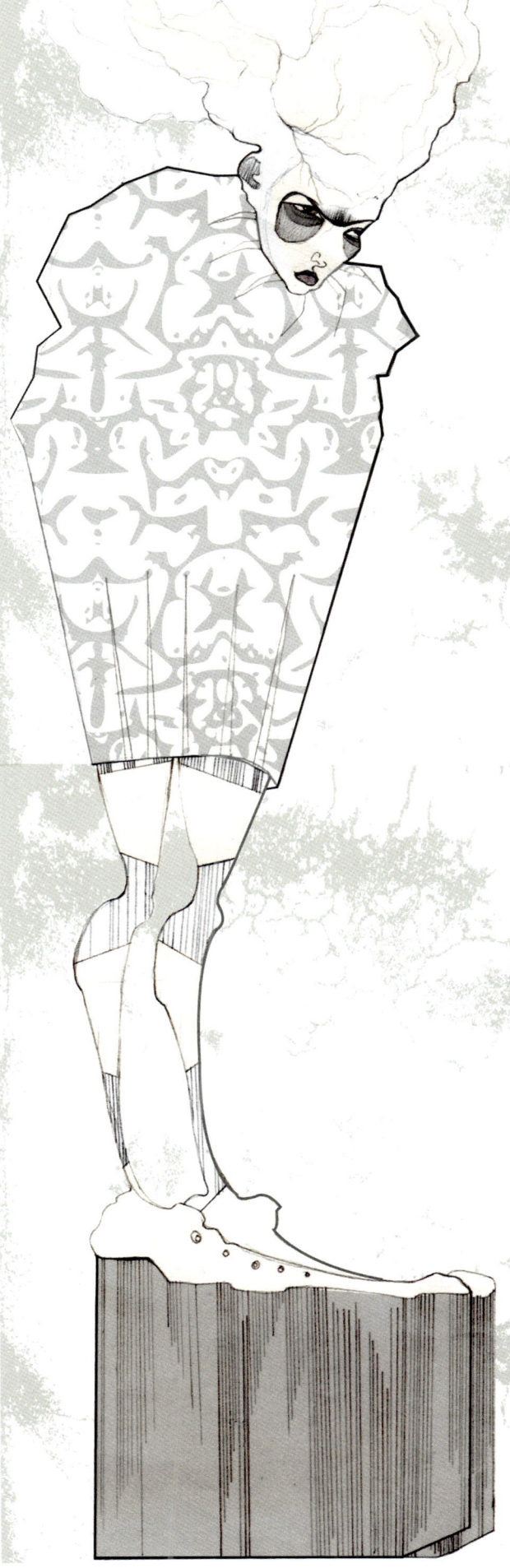

1. Die Vorskizzen werden eingescannt und im Programm Illustrator erst platziert und dann eingebettet. Danach werden sie interaktiv nachgezeichnet. Im nächsten Schritt macht man sich Gedanken um die Anordnung auf dem Blatt, die einzelnen Skizzen können auf jede beliebige Größe skaliert werden. Damit einzelne Elemente aufeinander liegenbleiben und nicht aus Versehen voneinander getrennt werden, gruppiert man diese. Das Arbeiten an einer Illustration wird dadurch vereinfacht, dass auf mehreren Ebenen gearbeitet wird, in diesem Fall wurde für jede Figur eine eigene Ebene angelegt. Sehr hilfreich ist auch ein im Voraus auf Papier aufgezeichneter „Bauplan", in dem grob festgelegt wurde, wie die Illustration am Ende aussehen soll – ein Leitfaden, um den Überblick zu behalten und nach dem sich die Vorgehensweise richtet.

TECHNIK - SCHRITT FÜR SCHRITT

2. In diesem Beispiel wird zunächst ein Hintergrund festgelegt. Ein Teil der Figuren ist mit weißer Farbe gefüllt, bei den anderen wurde die Farbe entfernt, so dass nur noch die Kontur sichtbar ist.

3. Wurde beim Vorzeichnen darauf geachtet, dass die einzelnen Flächen geschlossen sind, kann nun durch einfaches Anklicken Farbe hineingegeben werden. Die Farbe der Kontur ist auf dieselbe Weise zu ändern.

4. Allover-Prints können wie folgt erstellt werden: Man setzt ein Muster in einem rechteckigen Kasten zusammen, gruppiert alles und zieht diesen Kasten in die Farbpalette. Vorheriges Skalieren des Kastens bestimmt, in welcher Größe das Muster schließlich erscheinen soll.

5. Nun kann das Muster wie jede andere Farbe verwendet werden. Dieser Kasten wird dann innerhalb der zu befüllenden Fläche automatisch wiederholt und aneinandergereiht.

6. Es gibt neben dem Allover-Print auch die Möglichkeit, Flächen mit Grafiken, Fotos etc. zu füllen. Hierzu fügt man ein Bild in die Datei ein und legt die Form, die befüllt werden soll, darüber. Anschließend wählt man „Schnittmaske erstellen". Dabei muss beachtet werden, dass die Form aus einem zusammengesetzten Pfad besteht und nicht aus einzelnen Elementen. Die Option „Zusammengesetzter Pfad" befindet sich im Programm in der oberen Leiste unter dem übergeordneten Reiter „Objekt". Die Schnittmaske wird schließlich mit dem Pfeilcursor wieder in die Figur gelegt. Mit Rechtsklick können die einzelnen Elemente angeordnet werden, d.h. man kann wählen, was im Vordergrund stehen und somit alles andere überlappen soll, oder auch einzelne Stücke schrittweise nach hinten verschieben. Beispielsweise soll in diesem Bild die karierte Schnittmaske unter den Augen und unter der Kontur liegen. Dazu wird sie wird in den Hintergrund verschoben, die vorherige weiße Farbe wird rausgelöscht, nur deren Kontur bleibt erhalten.

7. Spannende Effekte lassen sich erzeugen, indem mehrere Konturen übereinander gelegt werden, oder auch, wenn die Farbfläche von der Kontur getrennt und etwas versetzt daruntergelegt wird. Durch die Benutzung verschiedener Pinsel kann mit der Kontur gespielt werden, man kann ihr beispielsweise einen Bleistift- oder auch einen Aquarellcharakter geben. Reichen die in der Programmbibliothek gespeicherten Pinsel nicht aus, kann ein individueller Pinsel selbst angelegt werden.

8. Jederzeit können neue Ebenen erstellt und weitere Gegenstände hinzugefügt werden. Die Reihenfolge der Ebenen lässt sich ändern, die Elemente der einzelnen Ebenen liegen so übereinander, wie von der Arbeitsfolge vorgegeben. Je weiter oben die Ebene in der Übersicht, desto weiter im Vordergrund befinden sich die Gegenstände dieser Ebene. Oft wird zum Ende erst sichtbar, ob der Illustration noch etwas fehlt. Durch viel Ausprobieren, Änderungen der Größe, Hinzufügen und Entfernen wird schließlich das Bestmögliche aus jeder Illustration herausgeholt.

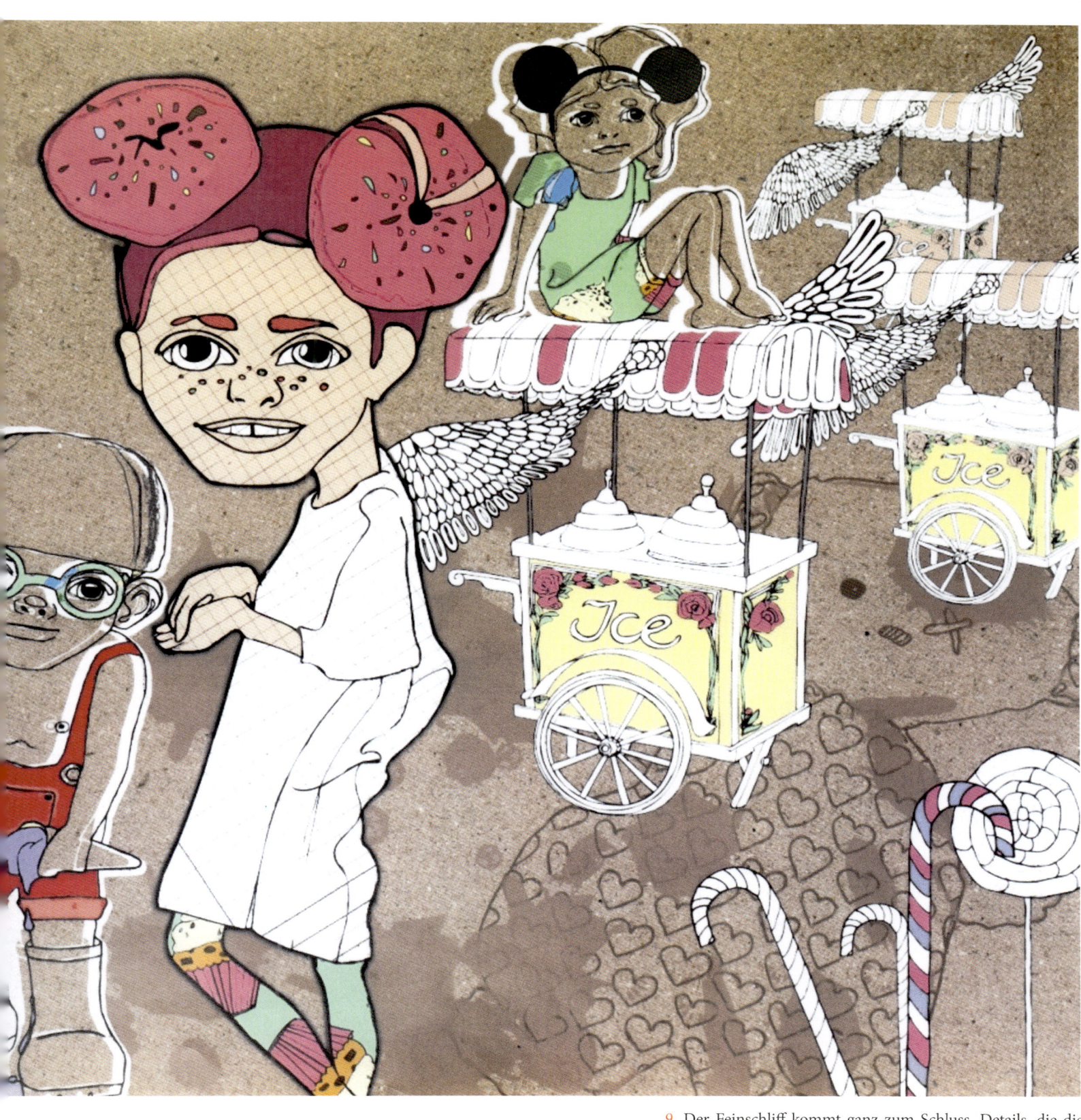

9. Der Feinschliff kommt ganz zum Schluss. Details, die die Illustration dynamischer und spannender machen, können hinzugefügt werden. Um dem ganzen einen zeichnerischen Charakter zu geben, wurde hier ein Pinsel aus der Kategorie „Künstlerisch - Tinte" gewählt, um Kleckse zu erzeugen.

→ ENGL: [299]

Skizzenbuch

Ein Ort der Ideen, etwas Intimes, eine Möglichkeit, Fehler zu machen, ein Fundus, etwas Vertrautes, ein Inspiration, lebenswichtig. Ein Skizzenbuch sollte unverzichtbar werden. Man muss sich vielleicht erst einmal an das Ritual gewöhnen, immer alle Ideen zu skizzieren, aber nach einer Weile kann man nicht mehr ohne. Ein Zeichner sieht am Tag tausend Dinge und es ist erstaunlich, wie schnell man vergisst. Farben, Materialkombinationen, Formen, Haltungen, Verkürzungen, ein Profil, eine außergewöhnliche Frisur, das Skizzenbuch ist eigentlich nichts anderes als ein visuelles Tagebuch. Hier kann man nur für sich arbeiten, ausprobieren, experimentieren, und auch „misslungene" Arbeiten haben einen Platz darin. Vielleicht dienen diese Zeichnungen später doch als Anregung. Kein Mensch urteilt über oder beurteilt den Inhalt des Skizzenbuchs, es ist ein Raum nur für einen selbst.

Inspiration holt man sich an vielen Stellen. Eigentlich kenne ich keinen Zeichner ohne eine Pinnwand zuhause. Ein Zeichner ist ein Sammler. Ansichtskarten von einer Ausstellung, die man besucht hat, Fotos aus Magazinen, die unwiderstehlich sind, Stückchen Papier, weil die Farbe so schön ist, ein Stoff mit einem besonderen Muster, ein Zitat. Die Pinnwand ist, wie das Skizzenbuch, eine ganz persönliche Sammlung.

Wenn man einen Auftrag bekommt, geht man genauso vor. Um sich über die Atmosphäre der Arbeit klarzuwerden, sollte man eine transportable Pinnwand (auch Moodboard genannt) herstellen. Depafit eignet sich als Trägermaterial besonders gut; es ist ein weicher Schaum, bekleidet mit Karton. Mit Stecknadeln lassen sich Fotos, Zeichnungen und Materialien darauf immer wieder neu anordnen.

→ ENGL: [299]

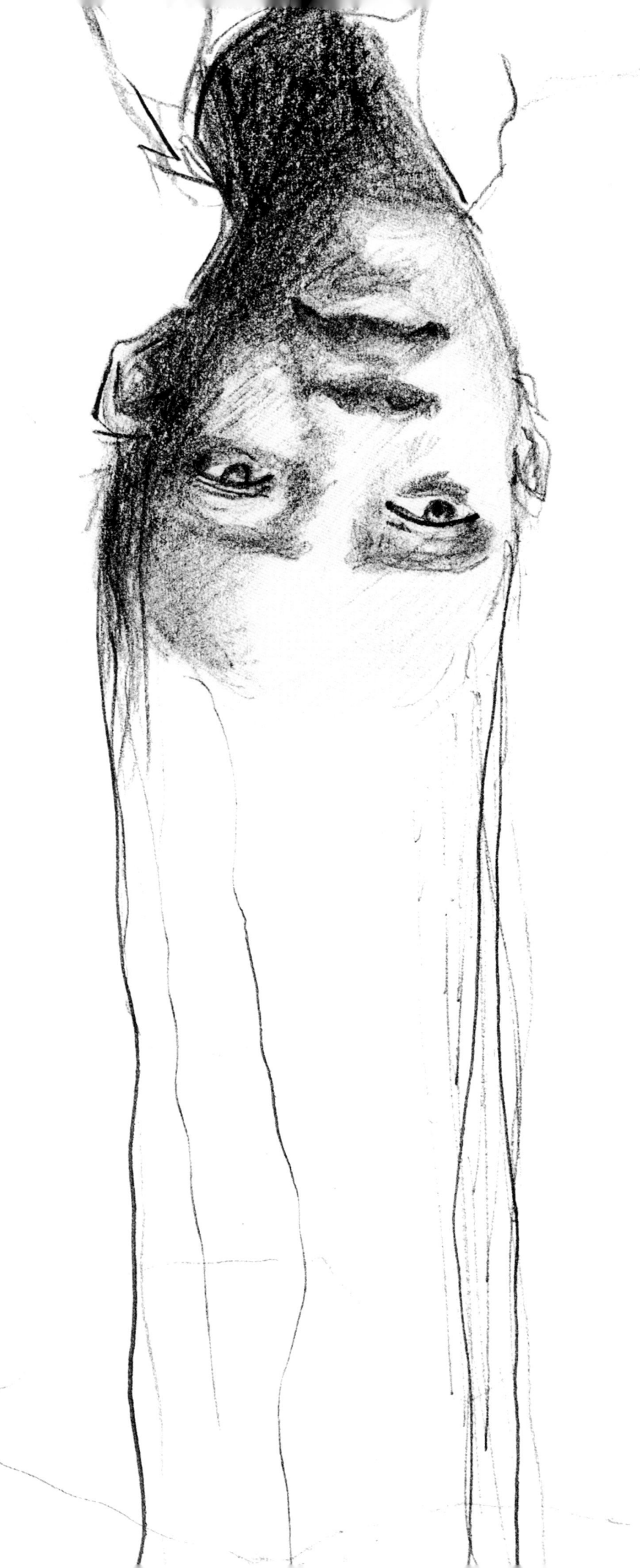

Figürliche Zeichnungen

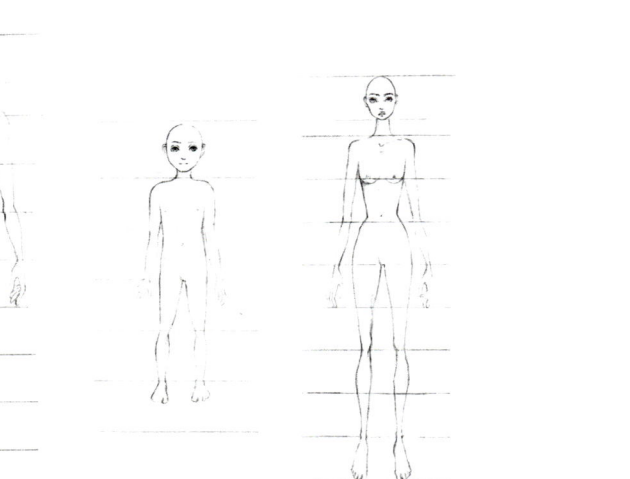

Eine Modefigurine ist die Verkörperung des gängigen Trends. Unsere heutige Idealvorstellung eines menschlichen Körpers ist eine von Gesundheit und Beweglichkeit, und das bedeutet: schlank sein. So ist eine Modefigur heute immer länger und schlanker, als es die Wirklichkeit vorgibt.

Beobachtung ist die wichtigste Voraussetzung für eine gute figürliche Modezeichnung. Viel zu oft fängt man zu zeichnen an, ohne sich vorher die Zeit zu nehmen, intensiv hinzuschauen. Zeichnen hat viel mit Sehen zu tun. Also muss man es trainieren. Wissenschaftler sagen, dass der Höhepunkt unseres Sehens mit sechs Jahren erreicht ist, danach geht es bergab. Es geht hier nicht darum, wie scharf oder unscharf man sehen kann, sondern um die Art des Sehens. Kinder können viele Details gleichzeitig sehen, Erwachsene dagegen sind nur fähig, ein Detail zu betrachten und erst danach das zweite. Man kann aber üben. Schauen, schauen, sich immer mehr mit einem Sujet beschäftigen, immer tiefer eindringen.

Die figürliche Zeichnung bildet die Basis für das Modezeichnen. Nicht nur Illustratoren, sondern auch Designer sollten wissen, wie ein Körper „funktioniert" und wie Kleidung sich zum Körper verhält. Durch immer neues Üben, auch wenn man später schon in der Praxis arbeitet, schult man sein Auge. Es gibt etliche körperliche Details, die von großem Einfluss auf die Kleidung sind. Schlüsselbeine, Brüste, Hintern, Knie, Waden, Muskeln. Es gibt einige gute Anatomiebücher für Künstler. Am besten hat man immer eines griffbereit.

Was sind die unterschiedlichen Bausteine einer gelungenen Figur?

■ PROPORTIONEN

Die Proportionen ergeben sich aus dem Maß des Kopfes. Ausgehend von einen Frauenkörper wird die Kopflänge in einer naturalistischen figürlichen Zeichnung mit einem Maßstab von 1:8 berechnet. Für eine modische figürliche Zeichnung berechnet man heute einen Maßstab von 1:9. Diese Überlänge entsteht in der Beinpartie. Anders als in der Wirklichkeit zeichnet man die Unterschenkel genau so lang wie die Oberschenkel. Es gibt einige körperliche Unterschiede zwischen Männern und Frauen, die man in einer Zeichnung berücksichtigt: Frauen haben ein breiteres Becken, Männer breitere Schultern und größere Schulterblätter. Eine männliche Figur ist idealerweise etwas größer als eine Frau. In der Realität haben Männer längere Unterschenkel im Verhältnis zu ihren Oberschenkeln, als es bei Frauen der Fall ist.

In einer Modezeichnung vereinfacht man die Maße. Ober- und Unterschenkel der Männer werden gleichlang gezeichnet wie bei den Frauen. Bei männlichen Figuren zeichnet man den Oberkörper überlang. Bei Kindern ist es schwierig, ein Maß anzugeben. Die Proportionen sind stark abhängig vom Alter des Kindes. Bei einem etwa zwei Jahre alten Kind ist der Maßstab 1:3, bei einem zirka achtjährigen Kind 1:5.

■ LINIEN

Man zeichnet am besten auf einem großen Blatt Papier. Ich bevorzuge ein DIN-A2-Format. So hat man die Möglichkeit, auch Details erkennbar zu zeichnen.
In der Mitte des Blattes zieht man eine vertikale Linie und teilt diese horizontal in neun Flächen ein. Oben und unten sollte dabei etwas Platz gelassen werden. Innerhalb dieser Flächen wird die Figur gezeichnet. Man vermeidet durch die Einteilung, dass die Figur zu groß oder zu klein wird. Wenn man die Längen einigermaßen im Griff hat, braucht man nur noch in der Mitte des Blattes einen – kleinen Strich zu setzen. Dieser markiert die Mitte des Körpers, die Stelle der Hüften, das reicht als Anhaltspunkt völlig aus.
Um die Richtigkeit der Zeichnung zu kontrollieren, sollte man regelmäßig messen. Die Längenmaße stehen fest, aber die Breiten nicht. Dafür nimmt man einen Bleistift und misst die Länge des Kopfes. Man sollte immer mit einem geraden, gestreckten Arm messen, so bleiben alle Messungen gleich. Wenn man den Arm auch nur etwas biegt, entstehen falsche Maße. Die Spitze des Bleistiftes ist auf das obere Ende des Kopfes gerichtet, der Daumen markiert am Bleistift die Position des Kinns. Mit dieser Einheit kann man nun die anderen Maße ermitteln, zum Beispiel die Breite der Taille oder den Winkel des Armes. Man kann auch andere Einheiten nehmen, etwa bei einer sitzenden Figur. Das Maß von der Schulter bis zur Unterkante der Sitzfläche ist so eine Einheit. Bei einer seitlichen Position kann man hiermit ermitteln, wie weit das Knie vom Körper entfernt ist oder in einer frontalen Position lässt sich messen, wie lang die Beine sind.

■ STAND

Am Anfang ist es wichtig, sehen zu lernen, wie ein Model steht. Am einfachsten ist es, wenn es sein Gewicht auf beide Beine gleichmäßig verteilt. Der Körper steht dann in der Regel gerade. Die vertikale Linie, die in der Mitte des Blattes gezogen wurde, bildet die Richtung des gesamten Körpers und verläuft vom Halspunkt (der Einbuchtung unter dem Kehlkopf) durch die Mitte der Brust über den Nabel, den Schritt bis mittig zwischen beide Füße. Der Körper wird symmetrisch in gleichen Teilen links und rechts der Richtungslinie gezeichnet. Wenn das Model aber sein Gewicht auch nur minimal verlagert, redet man über ein Standbein und ein Spielbein. Ein Standbein trägt das Gewicht, der Knöchel steht *immer* unter dem Halspunkt und sorgt somit dafür, dass man nicht umfällt. Ein Spielbein ist das Bein, das kein oder kaum Gewicht tragen muss. Das hat weitreichende Folgen für die Figur. Diese Folgen nenne ich das *Harmonikaprinzip*. Ein Harmonika funktioniert durch Zusammendrücken und Auseinanderziehen, und genau das kann man auch beim Körper beobachten. Das Standbein schiebt die Hüfte nach außen und drückt den Oberkörper an der Seite quasi zusammen. Auf der Seite des Spielbeins wird der Oberkörper dadurch auseinandergezogen. Die Richtung von Ober- und Unterkörper ändert sich. Es entsteht eine schräge Linie. Wenn man gedanklich die Hüften miteinander verbindet oder die Taille betrachtet, sieht man das ganz deutlich.

Es gibt mehrere Körperteile, die eine eigene Richtung haben können: der Kopf, der Oberkörper von den Schultern bis zur Taille (wenn man ganz genau hinschaut, ist ersichtlich, dass die Mittellinie von den Schultern bis zur Brust sogar in einer anderen Richtung verlaufen kann als die Mittellinie von der Brust bis zur Taille), der Unterkörper von der Taille bis zu den Hüften, die Oberschenkel, die Unterschenkel, die Füße, die Oberarme, die Unterarme und die Hände. Wenn man mit dem figürlichen Zeichnen anfängt, sollte man in jedem Körperteil die einzelnen Richtungen angeben. Später wird man mit nur wenigen dieser Linien auskommen. Es ist sehr hilfreich, bestimmte Punkte im Körper auf das Verhältnis zueinander zu untersuchen. Man schaut etwa, wo der äußerste Schulterpunkt im Verhältnis zur Hüfte steht oder wo die Füße stehen, wenn man gedanklich eine gerade Linie von den Schultern nach unten zieht. So bildet man einen Rahmen, in dem die Figur gezeichnet werden kann. Man sollte sich angewöhnen, vor dem Loszeichnen die folgenden Punkte zu betrachten: Stand- und Spielbein, die Entfernung der beiden Beine, den äußersten Hüftpunkt im Verhältnis zu den Schultern, die Linie der Schultern, die Linie der Taille. Erst dann hat man den Rahmen entdeckt, in dem sich die Figur bewegt.

Schaue genau die Freiräume an, die man bei einem Stand sehen kann. Also das Loch zwischen Arm und Rumpf oder die Lücke zwischen beiden Knöcheln. Das hilft enorm bei der Erfassung der Figur.

■ SCHATTIERUNGEN

Die ersten figürlichen Zeichnungen werden nur linear sein, für mehr fehlt oft die Zeit. Aber irgendwann wird man schneller und möchte der Arbeit einen Mehrwert hinzufügen. Schattierungen sind sehr geeignet, um die Zeichnung lebendiger zu machen und ihr eine räumliche Wirkung zu geben. Die Figur erscheint plastisch. Wie ein dreidimensionaler Gegenstand, zum Beispiel ein Zylinder, hat auch ein Mensch Rundungen und Seiten. Durch das Setzen von dunklen Stellen kann man dies verdeutlichen. Wie in der Realität sollte ein Schatten von oben nach unten durchlaufend gesetzt werden. Nichts ist unruhiger als ein Schatten, der seitlich am Kopf anfängt, bei den Armen und dem Rumpf aufhört und plötzlich an den Hüften wieder anfängt, um dann auf Höhe der Schuhe zu verschwinden.

Wenn die Lichtverhältnisse unklar sind, sollte man gedanklich eine starke Lampe zur Hilfe nehmen. Alle der Lampe zugewandten Teile sind hell und alle abgewandten liegen im Dunkeln. Vergiss dabei nicht, dass „voluminöse" Körperteile, wie eine Wade oder eine Brust, trotzdem Licht auffangen.

Schattierungen haben mehrere Abstufungen. Für eine Modezeichnung sollte man die Schatten vereinfachen und nicht mehr als drei bis fünf Stufen berücksichtigen. Mit verschiedenfarbigen Aquarellschichten ergibt das ein sehr schönes Resultat. Wenn man nur linear arbeiten möchte, kann man den Schatten andeuten, indem man die Konturlinie an den entsprechenden Stellen stärker macht.

■ KONTRASTE

Wenn eine Zeichnung durchgehend in einer Farbintensität gehalten wird, fehlt die Spannung. Das gilt insbesondere für eine schwarzweiße Arbeit. Dieses Problem lässt sich durch das bewusste Einsetzen von Kontraste lösen. Es gibt viele Möglichkeiten, kontrastreich zu arbeiten. So kann man sich entscheiden, die Zeichnung linear zu halten, den Pullover aber flächig zu bearbeiten. Oder man skizziert den Körper in einfachen Linien und arbeitet den Kopf detailliert aus. Es sollte immer einen Punkt in der Zeichnung geben, der das Auge des Betrachters anzieht.

■ DETAILS

Wenn eine figürliche Zeichnung zu viele Details aufweist, kann sie schnell zu naturalistisch werden. Als Modezeichner sollte man sich für bestimmte Details entscheiden. Das kann der Kopf sein oder ein besonders schöner Schal. Auch Stiefel oder Turnschuhe können spannend sein, wenn man daran jedes Detail sieht.

Wenn man sich unsicher ist, ob eine Zeichnung gelungen ist, gibt es einige Möglichkeiten, dies zu kontrollieren. Man kann die Zeichnung an die Wand hängen und den Raum verlassen. Man spült oder geht einkaufen. Wenn man dann wiederkommt, hat man nach der Pause einen „frischen" Blick und entdeckt schnell mögliche Fehler.
Man kann auch das eigene Gehirn überlisten; man dreht die Zeichnung um 180 Grad oder hält sie vor den Spiegel. Es ist erstaunlich, wie schnell man durch das „andere" Sehen die Fehler erkennt.

Eine figürliche Modezeichnung hat etwas Unnatürliches. Die Figur ist zu lang und zu dünn. Viele müssen sich beim Zeichnen daran gewöhnen und möchten sich mit dieser Art der Umsetzung nicht anfreunden. Ich finde aber, man sollte imstande sein, das gängige Schönheitsideal darzustellen. Später kommt die Zeit, seine eigene Figur zu entwickeln.
In der Ebenmäßigkeit wird die Schönheit empfunden. Gerade eine Modezeichnung läuft aber Gefahr, schnell als „zu glatt" wahrgenommen zu werden. Um das zu vermeiden, empfehle ich, absichtlich eine kleine Asymmetrie oder Disharmonie einzubauen. Das Auge des Betrachters soll schließlich innehalten und das lässt sich hiermit erreichen.
Sexualität oder Erotik spielen eine große Rolle in der Modezeichnung. Wie sie auszusehen haben, ist von Fall zu Fall unterschiedlich. Das kann eine tolle Körperhaltung sein, die Intensität einer Farbe oder auch die fantastische Linie einer Brust. Schließlich visualisiert die Modezeichnung unsere Begierden und unsere Träume.

→ ENGL: [299-301]

Um eine Figur zu erfassen, sollte man am Anfang nur Silhouetten in Aquarell erstellen. So lernt man, den Stand genau zu entdecken, und muss sich auf die wesentlichen Merkmale konzentrieren. Bedenke, dass Übertreibung angesagt ist; eine Modezeichnung überspitzt die Wirklichkeit. Die ersten Arbeiten sollte man einfarbig anlegen. Später kann man dann eine zweite oder sogar dritte Farbe verwenden.
Eine Silhouette kann zur eigenständigen Arbeit werden, vor allem, wenn man gelernt hat, das eine oder andere wegzulassen. Ein Meister hierin ist MATS GUSTAFSON.

Es gibt Menschen, die immer wieder radieren, wenn sie eine Zeichnung machen. Nie kommen sie zur perfekten Linie. Um diese viel zu hohen Anspruch zu überlisten, nimmt man ein Material, das sich nicht einfach auswischen lässt. Toll geeignet ist Tusche, mit einer Feder oder einem Pinsel zu benutzen, oder ein Kugelschreiber. Man macht vielleicht Fehler oder das Resultat ist nicht so, wie man es geplant hatte. Das gehört zu jeder künstlerischen Arbeit. Man sollte es wieder und wieder probieren, irgendwann entstehen gute Zeichnungen.

Streaming

Edited by FRANCES TAYLOR

SOCIETY SWANS
Clockwise from top left: Chloë Sevigny, Naomi Watts, Molly Ringwald, Calista Flockhart, Diane Lane and Demi Moore play elite New Yorkers

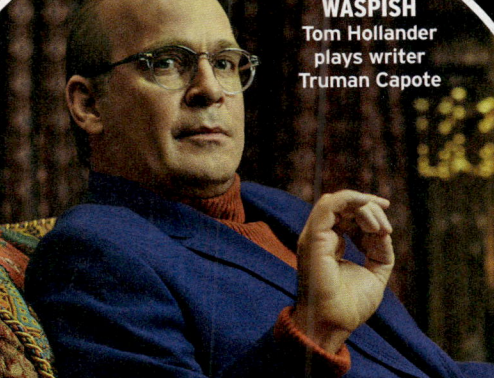

WASPISH
Tom Hollander plays writer Truman Capote

HISTORICAL DRAMA
Feud: Capote vs the Swans
All 8 episodes available from Wednesday on Disney+
Tom Hollander makes for a formidable Truman Capote — mannered and monstrous, without tipping over into unbelievable caricature — in a corkingly gossipy drama based on real events. We hop between various timelines to tell the story of the fabled writer befriending a group of female socialites in the 1960s, only to destroy the relationship in the 1970s by transparently basing a novel on their secrets and heartbreaks. The portrait of a bygone elite, riven with drugs, booze, betrayal and insecurity, is delicious and the cast is indulgently stellar: Diane Lane, Demi Moore, Chloë Sevigny and Naomi Watts all dial up the vicious glam. **JACK SEALE** *See feature: page 18*

Smart TV

CAROLINE FROST

THANK YOU FOR THE MUSIC

Never mind the songs, the way they handled Shep and *Swap Shop* shows Abba were a class apart

POP LEGENDS From left: Bjorn Ulvaeus, Frida Lyngstad, Agnetha Faltskog and Benny Andersson in 1976

THE THINGS POP stars will do to plug their songs. Never mind the glorious walk down musical memory lane that formed part of last Saturday's Abba Night on BBC2 marking 50 years since the Swedes' victory at the Eurovision Song Contest, the bits I enjoyed most were the clips of the group following up their success in Brighton with the hard graft of pop promotion in the UK, surrendering to the rites of what used to pass for mainstream British entertainment with impressive Scandi sangfroid.

Thus the unassuming quartet kept smiling as they were interviewed on *The Mike Yarwood Show*, their host impersonating Larry Grayson all the while. This came after they'd sat down on the *Blue Peter* sofa, Bjorn answering the questions while Agnetha stroked Shep, and, beamed live from the "tea bar of the BBC TV Centre", appeared alongside Noel Edmonds and Keith Chegwin on *Multi-Coloured Swap Shop*. Their last ever joint TV appearance also came courtesy of Edmonds on *The Late, Late Breakfast Show* in 1982. In a memorably awkward interview, they united in denying they would split, but perhaps that was what decided it for them.

So far, so David Cassidy and the Osmonds. But from day one, there was something special about Abba. The romance of two couples, of two wholesome boys who'd won the hearts of their contrasting goddesses and whose songwriting talents were matched by the ladies' silky voices, was like something out of a Swedish fairy tale.

For a long time, their simplicity disguised the craft in every chord. Frida once recounted how Benny had come home and played her his first, unpolished version of *Dancing Queen*: "I cried," she said. For five years it seemed effortless, until the relationships foundered and the songs stopped being pop and became poetry.

'Abba's is a tale of talent and togetherness that transcends the music'

Record producer Pete Waterman has remarked that fans stopped liking Abba when they started writing about their heartbreak. What planet is he on?

For this piece, I asked people for their favourite Abba song, and their diverse, passionate replies tell their own story. My more musically technical friends wax lyrical about the accomplishment of *SOS*, saying something about syncopation and arpeggios, and have similar praise for *The Day Before You Came*. I received a three-minute voice message from a DJ friend Australia describing the impact *Voulez-Vous* on the dancefloor, and why. My school pals s soak up the drama of *Knowing Me, Knowi You*; others enjoy the enigma of *Waterloo*; da well up for *Slipping Through My Fingers*. me, it's the generosity of *My Love, My Life*.

IT'S MORE THAN any one song, though. It's t contrast between their understated Swedi selves and the huge hearts on display in th songs – their willingness, to coin one of th later offerings, to "let the music speak". The fa that Bjorn wrote *The Winner Takes It All* f Agnetha when they were divorcing, and she sa it for him, still fills me with wonder at their cre tive courage; Frida's farewell to Benny, *When Is Said and Done*, equally so.

Watching them finding their way back to ea other after a 40-year gap with 2021's *I Still Ha Faith in You* makes me want to hug anyone I' ever loved. Despite the tunes' tireless glor Abba's is a tale of talent and togetherness th transcends the music. What a joy, what a li what a chance. Aren't we lucky they chose us?

BBC2's Abba Night, including the documentary When Abba Came to Britain, is available now on iPlayer. For more on Abba's 1974 Eurovision victory, see page 12

RADIO TIMES & SMART TV PODCASTS

■ Catch up with *Radio Times Podcast* host **Kelly-Anne Taylor's** chat with *QI* Elf and *No Such Thing as a Fish* podcaster **Dan Schreiber**.

■ Join **Kelly-Anne Taylor** and **Caroline Frost** for **Smart TV** – *RT's* bonus podcast previewing the TV week. Available every Friday.

YOUR TV WEEK STARTS HERE

STREAMING The latest TV and film picks from Netflix, Amazon Prime, Disney+ and more **p30**

DAILY CHOICES AND LISTINGS 70 packed pages for the week ahead **p40**

Im Laufe der Zeit wird man weniger abhängig vom Model. Natürlich braucht man das Model, um zu sehen, wie die Kleidung sich am Körper verhält, aber Gesicht, Haare und Make-up sind sekundär. Man ist jetzt in der Lage, einen eigenen Typus zu entwickeln.

Manchmal ist es spannend, einige Flächen oder Linien wegzulassen. Man sollte aber kritisch sein und nicht auf irgendetwas Wesentliches verzichten. Das Gehirn des Betrachters muss die fehlenden Elemente erkennen und vervollständigen können.

Materialkombinationen erzielen spannende Effekte. In diesen Beispielen sorgen Aquarell oder Tusche in Kombination mit Ölkreide für eine interessante Textur.

Man sollte aufpassen, dass man beim Zeichnen nicht den „Autopilot" einschaltet. So nenne ich es, wenn man gar nicht mehr so richtig hinschaut und das zeichnet, was man immer zeichnet. Zeit für eine erzwungene Änderung! Eine gute Übung mit überraschenden Resultaten ist das Zeichnen, ohne den Stift abzusetzen. Oft entdeckt man hierbei Elemente, die man bei anderen Arbeiten gezielt einsetzen kann.

Eine Weiterführung ist das Ausfüllen entstandener Flächen mit Farbe oder das Hinzufügen von Details.

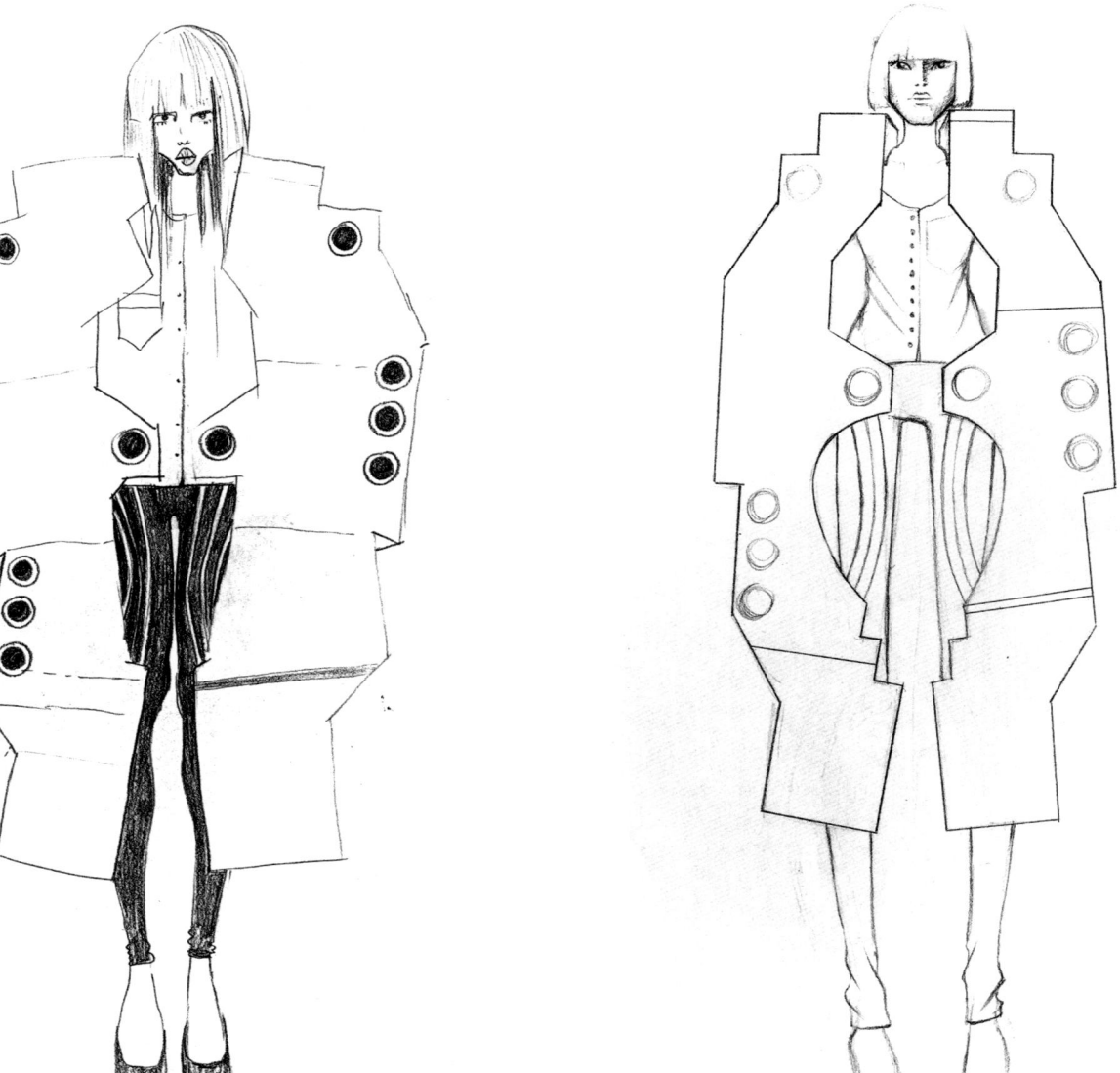

Einige Beispiele für unterschiedliche Umsetzungen eines Fotos. Es ist wichtig, eine eigene Handschrift zu entwickeln. Das bedeutet aber nicht, dass man sich zu schnell zufriedengeben und sich nicht an neuen Stilen versuchen soll. Die Suche und das Experimentieren sollten einen ein Leben lang begleiten.

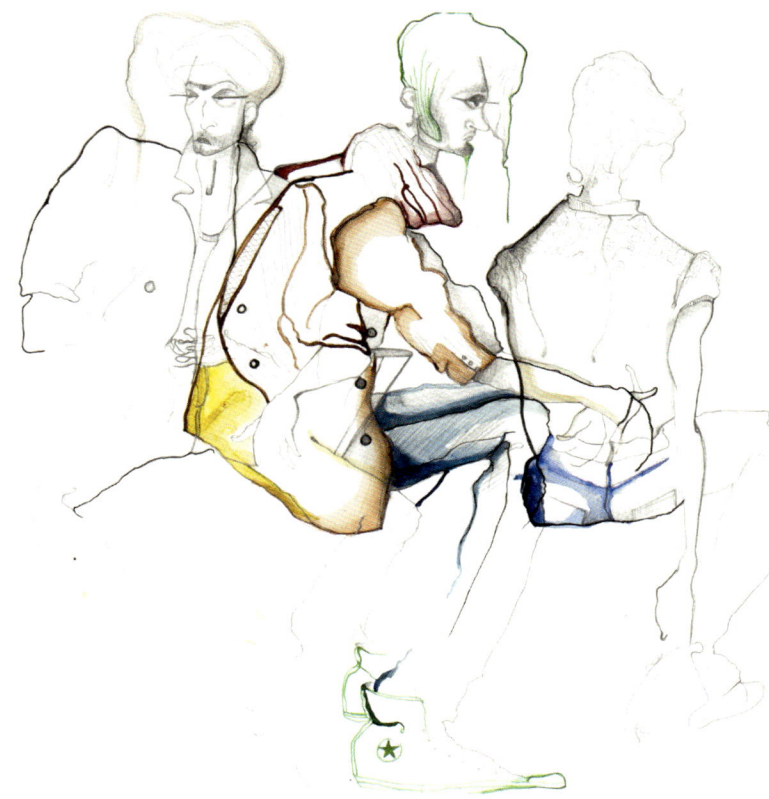

Wenn man mehrere Figuren sich überschneiden lässt, ist es besonders wichtig, eine klare Linie zu haben. Durch Farbflächen lassen sich Akzente setzen, die für Ruhe sorgen. MOLLY GRAD kann das übrigens hervorragend.

Es sind nicht immer die makellosen Models, die am meisten Spaß bringen beim Zeichnen. Im Gegenteil, gerade unerwartete „Schönheitsfehler" kann man überspitzen und somit die Figur zum Charakter werden lassen. Üppige Models sind ein Highlight; da gibt es herrliche Formen zu zeichnen, man kann richtig aus sich herausgehen.

Füllige Frauen sind zu Transvestiten umgezeichnet worden oder eignen sich als Models für sinnliche Stylingzeichnungen.

Ein Model im Clownkostüm.

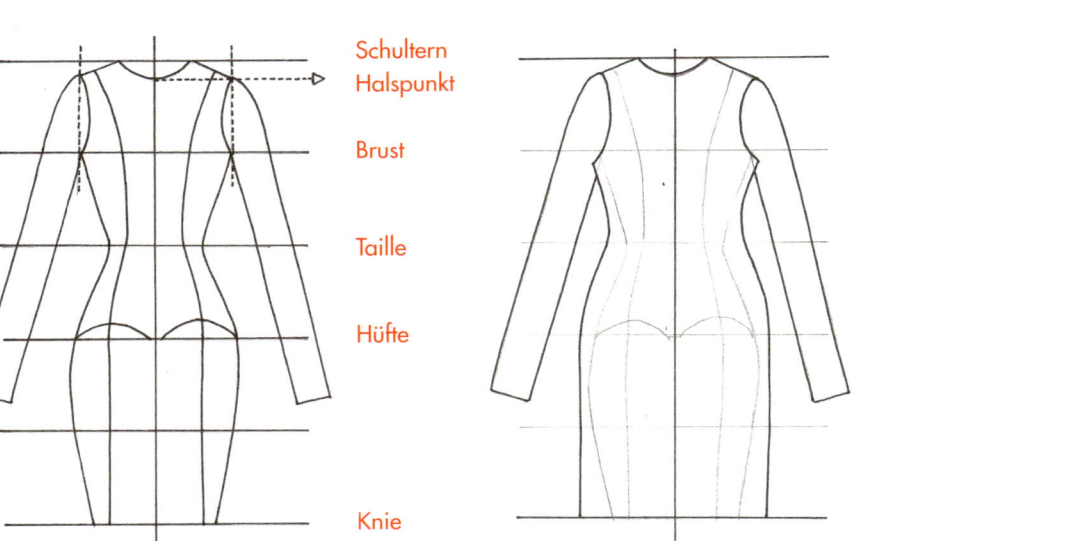

Werkstattzeichnungen

Werkstattzeichnungen sind die Baupläne eines Kleidungsstücks. Anhand dieser Zeichnungen können die Schnittmacher einer Modefirma Entwürfe in einem Schnitt umsetzen. Bei dieser Art des Zeichnens kommt es in erster Linie nicht auf Kreativität an, sondern auf ein hohes Maß an Konzentration und Genauigkeit. Jede Linie wird so übernommen, wie sie gezeichnet wurde. Wenn man nicht genau ist und beispielsweise einen Kragen zeichnet, der an der einen Seite eine Spitze aufweist und an der andere Seite eine kleine Rundung, wird der Schnittmacher einen asymmetrischen Kragen machen. Vielleicht war das aber nicht beabsichtigt, man hat nur nicht sorgfältig genug gearbeitet.

Um überhaupt ein Gefühl für die Proportionen eines Kleidungstücks zu bekommen, sollte man ein Lieblingsteil auswählen und dieses flach auf einem Tisch ausbreiten. Versuche, das Kleidungsstück so symmetrisch wie möglich hinzulegen. Wenn es Ärmel hat, sollten diese schräg neben das Teil gelegt werden. Auch Hosenbeine ordnet man schräg an. Dann lässt sich besser feststellen, wie tief das Armloch ist oder wie tief der Schritt sitzt. Am Beispiel eines knielangen, geraden, einfachen Mantels durchläuft man nun folgende Schritte:
Als erstes zeichnet man eine vertikale Linie in der Mitte des Blattes. Dann setzt man eine horizontale Linie, die den höchsten Punkt der Schultern markiert. Man bestimmt dann die Länge, indem man ein Maß für den Abstand zwischen Schultern und Brust festlegt, zum Beispiel 4 cm. An diese Stelle wird wieder eine horizontale Linie gesetzt. Nach weiteren 4 cm setzt man eine horizontale Linie, welche die Taille andeutet, 4 cm darunter eine für die Hüften und 8 cm unterhalb die Linie, die das Knie bestimmt. Nun hat man den oberen und den unteren Teil des Kleidungsstückes.

Die Breitenmaße stehen nicht fest. Diese sind stark abhängig vom Modell des Kleidungsstückes. Ausgehend von der Schulterbreite hat man aber einen ersten Anhaltspunkt. Hierzu beobachtet man ganz genau, wie das Halsloch aussieht. Es ist besonders wichtig, dass diese Partie nicht nur in der Form, sondern auch proportional passend gezeichnet wird. Dann zeichnet man die Länge und die Schräge der Schultern. Der Anfang ist das Halsloch. Als nächstes schaut man sich das Armloch an, die Tiefe, die Rundung und die Breite. Dann zeichnet man eine vertikale Linie vom äußersten Schulterpunkt und bestimmt die Tiefe. Danach zeichnet man die Rundung des Armloches. Oft ist das Armloch an der Unterseite etwas breiter, als die Schulter. Im Fall des Mantels können nun die Seiten mit einer leichten Rundung nach innen für die Taillierung bis zur Hüfte gezeichnet werden. Von der Hüfte bis zum Knie wird die Seitenlinie gerade nach unten gezogen. Jetzt bestimmt man die Länge der Ärmel, indem man beobachtet, wie groß der Unterschied zwischen dem Ende des Mantels und dem Ende der Ärmel ist. Auch sollte man schauen, wie der Ärmelkopf geformt ist. Gibt es eine deutliche Rundung oder ist er eher flach? Die Breite des Ärmelsaumes bietet ein weiteres Maß. Nun kann man die Form zeichnen. Das Außengerüst des Kleidungsstückes steht.

Jetzt geht es um die Details. Der einfache Mantel hat einen Knopfverschluss. Die Knöpfe sind *immer* in der Mitte. Man bestimmt die Zahl und den Abstand zwischen den Knöpfen und zeichnet diese auf der Mittellinie. Dabei entdeckt man, dass das Ende des Vorderteils einige Zentimeter neben der Mittellinie liegt. Das nennt man den Übertritt, dieser ist wichtig für die Positionierung der Knopflöcher. Ein Knopf rutscht immer zum Ende des Knopfloches, so dass man dies auch korrekt zeichnen soll. Unmittelbar unterhalb des Kragens sitzt der erste Knopf. Im Falle eines Reverskragens (üblich bei den gängigen Mantelmodellen) bestimmt man zuerst die Tiefe des Halslochs, dann die Breite des Oberkragens und des Unterkragens. Danach beobachtet man die Spitzen von Ober- und Unterkragen. Ein Reverskragen hat eine sogenannte Spiegelnaht (die Naht, die die beiden Kragen verbindet). Man sollte genau schauen, wie diese verläuft. Nun zeichnet man den Kragen. Die Knöpfe werden jetzt in regelmäßigem Abstand gezeichnet. Meistens befindet sich ein Knopf auf Brusthöhe und ein Knopf auf der Höhe der Taille. Falls es im Mantel Nähte, Taschen, Riegel oder besondere Steppereien gibt, werden diese jetzt gezeichnet.

Die gleiche Prozedur wiederholt sich nochmal für die Rückansicht. Für die Deutlichkeit empfehle ich, die Vorderansicht *immer* links zu zeichnen und die Rückansicht in einer etwas verkleinerten Form rechts daneben. Wenn es unsichtbare Details gibt, zum Beispiel einen Reißverschluss unter einer Taschenklappe, sollte man eine Detailzeichnung anfertigen. Die Klappe wäre in diesem Fall hochgeschlagen, wodurch man einen Teil des Reißverschlusses sieht.

Werkstattzeichnungen werden linear gezeichnet. Für die Außenkontur und für die Nähte benutzt man einen Filzstift, für die Steppereien einen Fineliner. Ich empfehle, die Stepperei als durchgehende Linie zu zeichnen. Wenn die Linie durchbrochen ist, sieht die Stepperei proportional viel größer aus, als sie in Wirklichkeit ist. Man sieht den Unterschied zwischen Nähten und Stepperei gut durch die verschiedenen Stärken der Linie. Eine Werkstattzeichnung darf eine minimale Bewegung zeigen, indem man zum Beispiel einige Hauptbewegungsfalten zeichnet. Auch kann man Farbe einsetzen, indem man die Fläche koloriert oder die Außenkonturen farbig setzt. Muster zeigt man normalerweise nicht. Der Schnitt wird durch Farbe oder Muster nicht verändert. Wird eine Werkstattzeichnung gleichzeitig als Präsentationszeichnung benutzt ist es aber erlaubt.

Wenn man verschiedene Kleidungsstücke gezeichnet hat und die Materie gut beherrscht, kann man Werkstattzeichnungen am besten mit dem Programm „Illustrator" machen. Werkstattzeichnungen setzen immer einen persönlichen Kontakt zum Schnittmacher voraus. Man muss beispielsweise die Maße des Kleidungsstückes mitteilen. Ist das nicht möglich, arbeitet man mit technischen Zeichnungen.

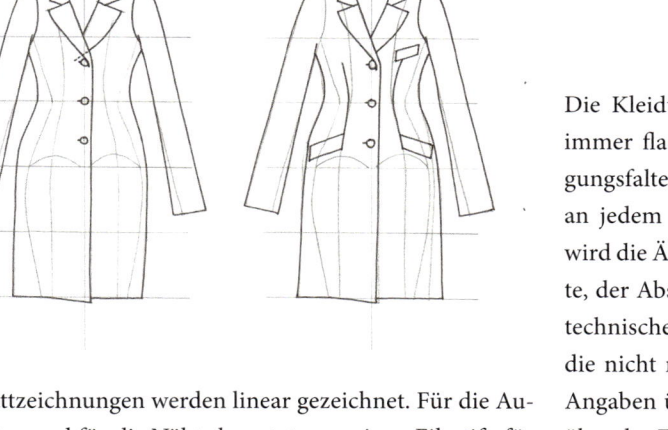

Vorderansicht

Rückenansicht

Die Kleidungsstücke in einer technischen Zeichnung sind immer flach dargestellt. Sie haben keine Farbe oder Bewegungsfalten. Im Gegensatz zu einer Werkstattzeichnung steht an jedem wichtigen Punkt eine Maßangabe. Zum Beispiel wird die Ärmellänge benannt, die Rumpflänge, die Saumbreite, der Abstand zwischen den Knöpfen und vieles mehr. Die technischen Zeichnungen sind Teil einer Produktionskarte, die nicht nur jedes Detail schriftlich festhält, sondern auch Angaben über das Garn, mit dem das Teil genäht wird oder über das Futter macht. Diese Produktionskarten können von Firma zu Firma leicht unterschiedlich sein, die Art des Zeichnens in der Regel nicht.

→ ENGL: [302-303]

- ⌇ Kordel
- ◊ Knopfloch
- durchscheinendes Teil
- ------ Stepp
- —— Falte
- ○ Druckknopf
- —— transparentes Kleidungsstück

Köpfe

Der Kopf ist die Visitenkarte der Modezeichnung. Die einzelnen Elemente Augen, Augenbrauen, Nase, Mund, Ohren und Haare erzählen eine Geschichte. Stimmt die Geschichte, weiß der Betrachter sofort, um welche Atmosphäre es sich handelt.
Das ist besonders wichtig, wenn es darum geht, die Intention der Kleidung zu vermitteln. Wenn man beispielsweise eine sportliche Kollektion zeichnet, aber die Köpfe romantisch anlegt, ist die Botschaft nicht klar. Klarheit darüber, was man als Zeichner kommunizieren möchte, ist oberstes Gebot. Also: *nachdenken, bevor man anfängt zu arbeiten!*

Es gibt niemanden, der ein symmetrisches Gesicht hat. Trotzdem versuchen Viele, ein perfekt symmetrisches Gesicht zu zeichnen, sobald es sich um eine Modeillustration handelt. Ich empfinde das Ergebnis als relativ langweilig.
Eine einfache Übung, das Auge zu schulen, ist die Betrachtung von schwarzweißen Fotos. Wenn der (Mode)Fotograf das Gesicht nicht total überblendet hat, entdeckt man, dass die Schatten *nie* gleich sind. Das sollte man in der Zeichnung unbedingt berücksichtigen. Und wenn man schon dabei ist: Ein Schatten im Gesicht besteht aus Flecken, die miteinander verbunden sind. Entdecke, wie spannend es ist, dass zum Beispiel die Schattierungen von Nase und Augen ineinander übergehen. Aber berücksichtige auch, dass diese Flecken auf der linken Seite des Gesichtes anders sind als auf der rechten.

Nasen: keine Steckdosen, keine Schweinchen.
Augen: Reduziere die Wimpern zu einem Strich. Wenn ein Kopf nur drei Zentimeter groß ist, kann man nicht jedes Wimperchen zeichnen.

Eine Schattierung im Gesicht besteht aus vielen unterschiedlichen Nuancen. Klug ist es, diese auf höchstens drei oder vier Stufen zu reduzieren. Zeichnet man ein farbiges Gesicht, ist die Papierfarbe die hellste Stufe. Wenn jemand einen roten oder grünen Pullover trägt, spiegelt sich das im Gesicht wider. Das sollte man auf jeden Fall einbeziehen. Es gibt der Zeichnung etwas Eigenes.

Die einzelnen Elemente eines Gesichtes bieten die Möglichkeit, einen Charakterkopf darzustellen. Manchmal reicht es schon, der Nase einen kleinen „Huckel" zu geben oder die Ohren etwas abstehen zu lassen. Die Hauptsache ist, das Porträt so zu gestalten, dass der Blick des Betrachters hängenbleibt. Auch kann man eine gute Wirkung erzielen, indem man ein einzelnes Element besonders hervorhebt. Vergiss nicht, ein Gesicht wirklich aufmerksam zu betrachten, und vermeide allzu häufige Wiederholungen.

Bevor man anfängt, ein Gesicht nach Modell oder nach einen Foto zu zeichnen, sollte man die Augen zusammenkneifen und durch die Wimpern schauen. Alle Details verschwinden und man erkennt sofort die Hauptmerkmale. Für ein Modeporträt ist es wichtig, ein Element des Gesichtes besonders hervorzuheben.

Eine super Übung ist es, wenn man versucht, demselben Gesicht durch Materialvariationen eine andere Atmosphäre zu geben. Es macht viel aus, ob man ein Porträt nur bis zur Schulter zeichnet oder aber bis zur Taille. Dies ermöglicht es, ein wenig mehr Geschichte zu erzählen. Auch Hintergründe spielen eine große Rolle. Achte aber darauf, dass das Gesicht das wichtigste Element in der Zeichnung bleibt.
Die Haare sollten mit großer Aufmerksamkeit gezeichnet werden. Oft sehe ich Arbeiten, bei denen das Gesicht konzentriert gezeichnet wurde, das Ganze aber keine Wirkung hat, weil man anstelle von Haaren etwas Undefinierbares produziert hat.

Haare: kein Wischmopp, kein komisches Kopftuch.

Es ist eine gute Übung, anhand einer schwarzweißen Porträtfotografie alle Haare zu zeichnen, die man sieht. Das setzt Geduld voraus, aber man entdeckt, wie wichtig die Außenform und die Richtung der Haare sind. Später kann man die gleiche Frisur immer und immer wieder reduzieren, um zu sehen, welchen Effekt dieses Weglassen hat. Eine Expertin für fantastische Haare ist übrigens LAURA LAINE.

Wenn man nicht jedes Haar zeichnen und eher flächig arbeiten möchte, sollte man sich die hellen und dunklen Partien ganz genau anschauen. Auch hier sieht man sofort, dass es keine Symmetrie gibt. Die hellste Farbe ist die des Papiers, die anderen Flächen bestehen aus höchstens drei Stufen. Um die einzelnen Flächen zusammenzuziehen, sollte man einige wenige Strähnen zeichnen.
Natürlich gibt es auch andere Möglichkeiten, die Haare darzustellen, zum Beispiel einen Scherenschnitt oder lediglich einen Umriss.
Sehr gute Effekte erzielt man, indem man mit einem trockenen Pinsel und minimal angefeuchteter Aquarellfarbe arbeitet. Auch einen leeren, großen Edding sollte man nicht wegwerfen. Er gibt immer noch ein bisschen Farbe, mit der man tolle Haare zeichnen kann.

Fazit: Ein Gesicht sollte eine markante Ausstrahlung haben, egal ob aggressiv, verträumt, cool oder extravagant. Es soll den Betrachter fesseln und die Atmosphäre der Zeichnung unmissverständlich klarmachen.

→ ENGL: [303]

Wieder eine Übung, bei der man entdeckt, wie wichtig es ist, nicht immer gedankenlos zu zeichnen. Durch andere Materialien oder Farben kann man die Atmosphäre gewaltig beeinflussen.

Es ist sehr wichtig, sich mit aktuellen Trends in der Mode auszukennen. Manchmal kann es aber auch richtig Spaß machen, das gängige Schönheitsideal zu verneinen und einen eigenen Typ zu entwickeln. Diese Köpfe sind inspiriert durch Königin Elisabeth I. von England. Schönheit und Hässlichkeit liegen nah beieinander. Beides kann uns rühren.

GESTALTUNG - AUF DER SPITZE

Stylingzeichnungen

Manchmal werde ich gefragt: „Was ist genau der Unterschied zwischen einer Stylingzeichnung und einer Illustration?" Die Antwort ist nicht eindeutig, oft verschwimmen die Grenzen. Grob gesagt muss eine Stylingzeichnung erkennbare Kleidung zeigen, eine Illustration nicht unbedingt.

Es gibt zwei Arten von Stylingzeichnungen. Die erste wird angefertigt, wenn eine Kollektion schon fertig ist. Oftmals werden diese Zeichnungen in der Produktion benutzt und müssen deshalb absolut fehlerfrei gezeichnet werden. Diese Zeichnungen weisen immer eine Reduktion auf, eine Konzentration auf das Wesentliche. Das gilt für den Stand; er sollte einfach sein und gerade von vorne und von hinten gezeichnet werden. Das gilt auch für die Haare und das Makeup; hier ist Zurückhaltung geboten. Die Formen sollte man absolut treffend darstellen. Es ist sehr wichtig, die Proportionen innerhalb des Kleidungsstückes sorgsam zu übertragen. Man muss sehen können, aus welchem Stoff ein Kleidungsstück hergestellt ist. Das trifft auch auf Strichzeichnungen zu. Farbe und Muster sind in diesem Fall nicht zu zeichnen. Sie haben keinen Einfluss auf die Schnittgestaltung. In einer Stylingzeichnung muss man alle Details erkennen können: Wie lang ist das Kleidungsstück? Wie weit? Welche Arten von Taschen gibt es? Wie sieht der Kragen aus? Hat es vier oder

sechs Knöpfe? Sind sie verdeckt oder nicht? Hat es Falten, und wenn ja, welche? Bügelfalten, Kellerfalten, Falten nach links oder rechts? Oder ist es doch nur angekräuselt? Jeder Knopf, jede Saumbreite muss der Wirklichkeit entsprechen. Diese Zeichnungen dienen auch dazu, die Kleidungsstücke, die aus der Produktion kommen, zu kontrollieren.

Die zweite Art des Stylingzeichnens nennt man auch das Trendzeichnen. Diese Zeichnungen sind für Designer gedacht und geben Informationen über kommende Looks. Hier sind vor allem der Look, die Silhouetten, die Farben und die Materialien wichtig. Die Atmosphäre wird ausgedrückt in der Haltung, aber der Stand muss unbedingt zu dem Stil der Kleidung passen. Also keine introvertierte Pose, wenn die Kleidung sportlich ist oder keine extravertierte Haltung, wenn die Kleidung puristisch und zurückhaltend ist. Die Silhouetten werden übertrieben gezeichnet um den Look deutlich zu machen. Die Farben sollen hauptsächlich der Wirklichkeit entsprechen. Man hat aber eine gewisse künstlerische Freiheit. Trotzdem darf ein Kleidungsstück nicht braun erscheinen, wenn es eigentlich schwarz ist. Die Darstellung von Stoffen in ihrer Haptik ist eine besondere Herausforderung. (Man sollte sich noch einmal auf die Materialexperimente besinnen.) Hier ist es wichtig vorhandene Muster unbedingt zu zeichnen. Informationen über die Details sind auch hier von großer Bedeutung. Eventuelle Accessoires sollten sorgfältig gezeichnet werden. Sie sind eine wichtige Information für den Look. Vor allem das Gesicht, die Haare und das Make-up darf man künstlerisch übertreiben. Diese Stylingzeichnungen werden auch als Werbematerial von Modefirmen benutzt (hier sollte man sich über den Kundenkreis im Klaren sein und den richtigen Typus treffen) oder als erklärende Zeichnung in Modemagazinen (hier gibt es die größte künstlerische Freiheit). Dann kann es auch einen Hintergrund geben. Die Aussage der Kleidung oder der Typus soll so unterstützt werden.

→ ENGL: [303-304]

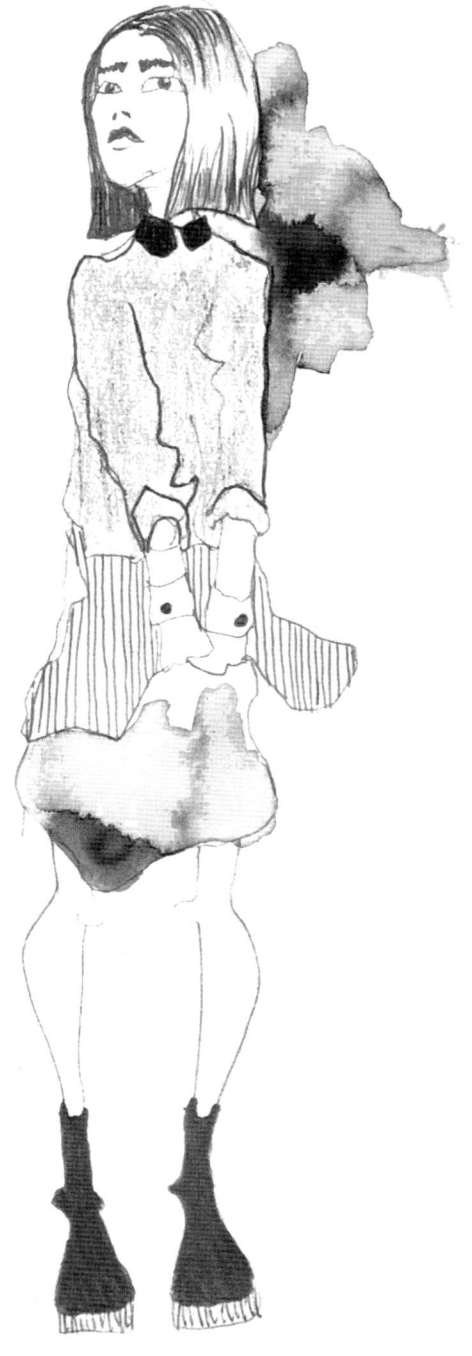

Kreativität

Kreativität kann man nicht benennen, kann man nicht berechnen. Es gibt keine Formel für sie. Die Kreativität ist ein Paket. Wir bekommen es bei der Geburt. Der eine macht seines auf, der andere lässt es liegen. Manche erfreuen sich daran und spielen mit ihm ein Leben lang, manche wissen damit nicht so recht etwas anzufangen. Man braucht Neugierde, Offenheit, Toleranz. Man sollte keine Angst haben, Fehler zu machen. Neue Dinge ausprobieren wollen. Nicht aufgeben, wenn etwas nicht auf Anhieb klappt. Bekannte Lösungen hinterfragen. Über Grenzen gehen. Wege beschreiten, die vielleicht noch niemand vorher gegangen ist.

Kreativität ist ein sensibles Ding. Schnell ist sie abgelenkt und wenn jemand ihr zu nahe tritt, zieht sie sich ganz schnell zurück. Auch mag sie es nicht, wenn sie belächelt wird; verteidigen kann sie sich kaum. Sie ist ja nicht messbar. Manchmal braucht sie Hektik, Spannung und Drama. Manchmal braucht sie Ruhe, große Ruhe, und viel Platz. Kreativität braucht Raum. Aber kann man berechnen, wieviel Raum die Kreativität braucht? Und wie sieht dieser Raum aus? Ist es ein Innenraum oder ist es ein Außenraum?
Ach, man soll sie einfach lassen, die Kreativität. „Vertrauen" ist das Stichwort. Nur dann kann man neue Wege beschreiten. Nur dann kann man suchen. Mal nach links, mal nach rechts gehen. Und wenn es holperig wird, einfach weiterlaufen. Steine beseitigen oder einfach umgehen. So ist man als Kreativer, man kann nicht anders.

GESTALTUNG - STEINE BESEITIGEN | 181

Bevor man nun endgültig als harmloser Spinner abgetan wird, sollte man lernen, nicht in der eigenen Kreativität zu ertrinken. Dieser Prozess, zu lernen, wie man schwimmt, ist vielleicht das einzige, das man sich erarbeiten kann. Es gibt viele Untersuchungen, ob man Kreativität lernen kann oder nicht. Die Wissenschaftler sind sich uneinig.

Als jemand mit einer schöpferischen Begabung sollte der kreative Mensch sich auszeichnen durch Problemsensibilität, durch Ideenreichtum, Flexibilität und Originalität. Ein kreativer Mensch sollte neugierig sein, bereit selbstständig zu denken und in der Lage sein, in verschiedene Richtungen zu schauen. Er sollte Dinge miteinander kombinieren, die eigentlich nicht zusammenpassen. Er sollte das Vertraute verfremden.

Er sollte nichts als selbstverständlich hinnehmen. Er sollte den Mut haben, sich gegen die herrschende Norm aufzulehnen, nicht die gängige Meinung hinnehmen. Er sollte keine Angst vor Konflikten haben, und auch die Frustration gilt es zu überwinden. Er sollte den inneren Schweinehund jeden Tag vor die Tür setzen, nicht aufgeben, weitermachen, ohne zu erstarren oder sich zu fixieren. Selbstkritisch sollte er sein, nicht schnell zufrieden.

Das ist ein hartes Stück Arbeit. Das ist, als ob man in einem riesigen Meer schwimmt. Die Wellen sind unkontrollierbar. Manchmal drohen sie sogar, einen zu überspülen oder in die Tiefe zu ziehen. Da sollte man schwimmen lernen.

Nach meiner Erfahrung ist dies das wichtigste: Schwimmreifen auswerfen, behutsam lernen, den Kopf über Wasser zu halten. Als Hochschullehrerin kann ich nur versuchen, das herauszukitzeln, was schon vorhanden ist, und hoffen, dass die Studierenden mich als Schwimmlehrerin annehmen, dass wir ein Stück gemeinsam schwimmen.

Die erste Übung nach einer Problemstellung ist es, zu fragen: „Erzähle mal, was du in deinem Bauch fühlst. Versuche dein Bauchgefühl zu beschreiben."
Kommunikation ist nämlich die Voraussetzung, um andere einbeziehen zu können in den Prozess der Kreativität oder sie von einer Idee zu überzeugen. Wenn man diese erste Übung vervollständigt, das heißt in einen gesellschaftlichen, kulturellen und/oder historischen Kontext einbettet und anschließend mit einem eigenen Lösungsansatz ergänzt, hat man ein Konzept. Und schon weiß man, in welche Richtung man schwimmen kann.

Die zweite Übung behandelt das „Wie". Nach einer Phase, in der der Fantasie keine Grenzen gesetzt werden und es von Ideen nur so sprudelt, ist meine Frage: „Was passiert, wenn du einen Schritt zurücktrittst? Was ist gut und was ist schlecht?" Dieses Abstandnehmen ist notwendig, um nicht nur selbstkritisch Ideen zu hinterfragen und zu überprüfen, ob Originalität vorhanden ist, sondern auch, um zu kontrollieren, ob die Richtung immer noch vorhanden ist.

Die letzte Übung ist die Metamorphose. Meine Frage lautet: „Wie wird deine Idee zum Produkt, welche Voraussetzungen musst du erfüllen?" Gerade in dieser Phase ist es sehr wichtig, sich nochmals auf die Richtung zu konzentrieren, sich Techniken anzueignen oder sich helfen zu lassen von Dritten, welche diese beherrschen. Jetzt kann man formvollendet schwimmen.

So lautet meine These:
Kreativität ist nicht lehr- oder lernbar. Sie kann aber gefördert oder behindert werden.

→ ENGL: [304-305]

GESTALTUNG - DIE GROSSE FREIHEIT 185

ILLUSTRATIONEN

Neben der Information, die eine Modezeichnung vermitteln soll, wenn es um die Silhouette und die Details geht, soll eine Modezeichnung vor allem präsentieren. Hier hat der Illustrator eine große Freiheit. Er kann seine persönliche Sichtweise vermitteln, seine persönliche Arbeitsmethode ausbauen und so seine Handschrift entwickeln. Wiederum muss ich sagen: tillstehen sollte man aber nicht. Die Mode ändert sich ständig, ein Illustrator darf nicht einschlafen, sich zufriedengeben mit dem momentanen Stand der Dinge.

Man sollte so viele Modezeichnungen anschauen wie möglich. Sich an Details aufhalten, analysieren, welche Materialien genutzt wurden, ergründen, welche Besonderheiten einen bestimmten Illustrator ausmachen. Manchmal ist es gut, einen Illustrator zu kopieren, einfach, um den Blick zu schärfen und das Gefühl in den eigenen Händen zu bekommen. Die Hand soll sich erinnern können.

Irgendwann aber ist es genug. Dann hat man ausreichend experimentiert und kopiert. Es entsteht eine eigene Handschrift, auch wenn sie flexibel bleiben und nie als abgeschlossen betrachtet werden sollte.
Die freieste Form des Modezeichnens ist die Illustration. Hier geht es nicht im Detail um die Erkennbarkeit der Kleidung, sondern um die Atmosphäre. Man entscheidet, ob die Silhouette das Wichtigste ist oder die Farbigkeit, der Look oder vielleicht die Trägerin. Man kann eine Illustration in unendlich vielen Ausführungen umsetzen. Weil es hier um die eigene Fantasie, die eigene Kreativität und die eigenen Ansprüche geht, gibt es eigentlich keine Regeln.
Es geht nicht darum, die Wirklichkeit perfekt darzustellen; es geht darum, die Essenz zu treffen. Man darf bei aller Freiheit das Ziel nicht aus den Augen verlieren. Die Atmosphäre der Kleidung bleibt das Wichtigste. Es geht hierbei aber weniger um kommerzielle Information, als vielmehr darum, dass der Betrachter sich mit dieser Aussage identifizieren kann, seine Träume und Begehrlichkeiten geweckt werden.

→ ENGL: [305]

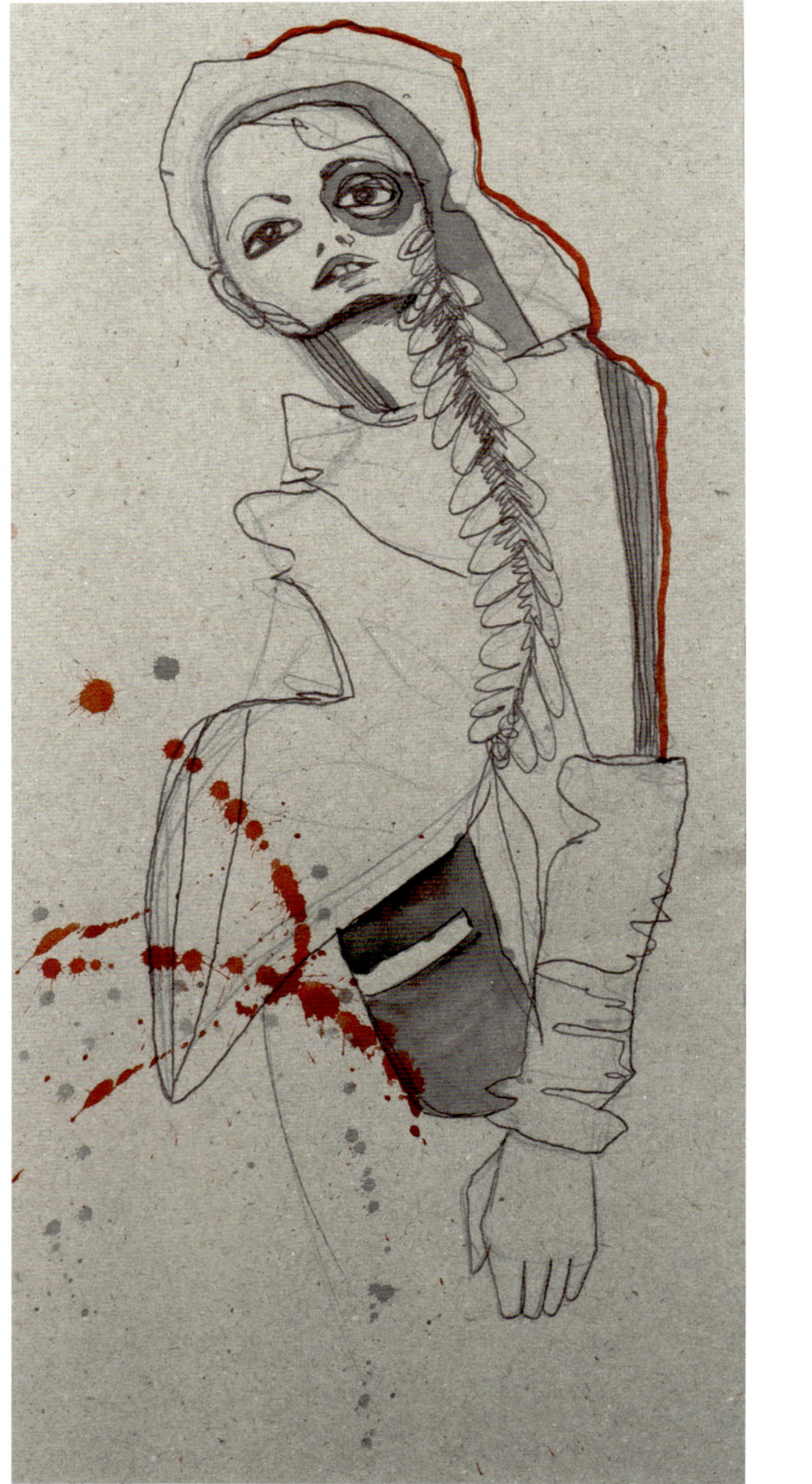

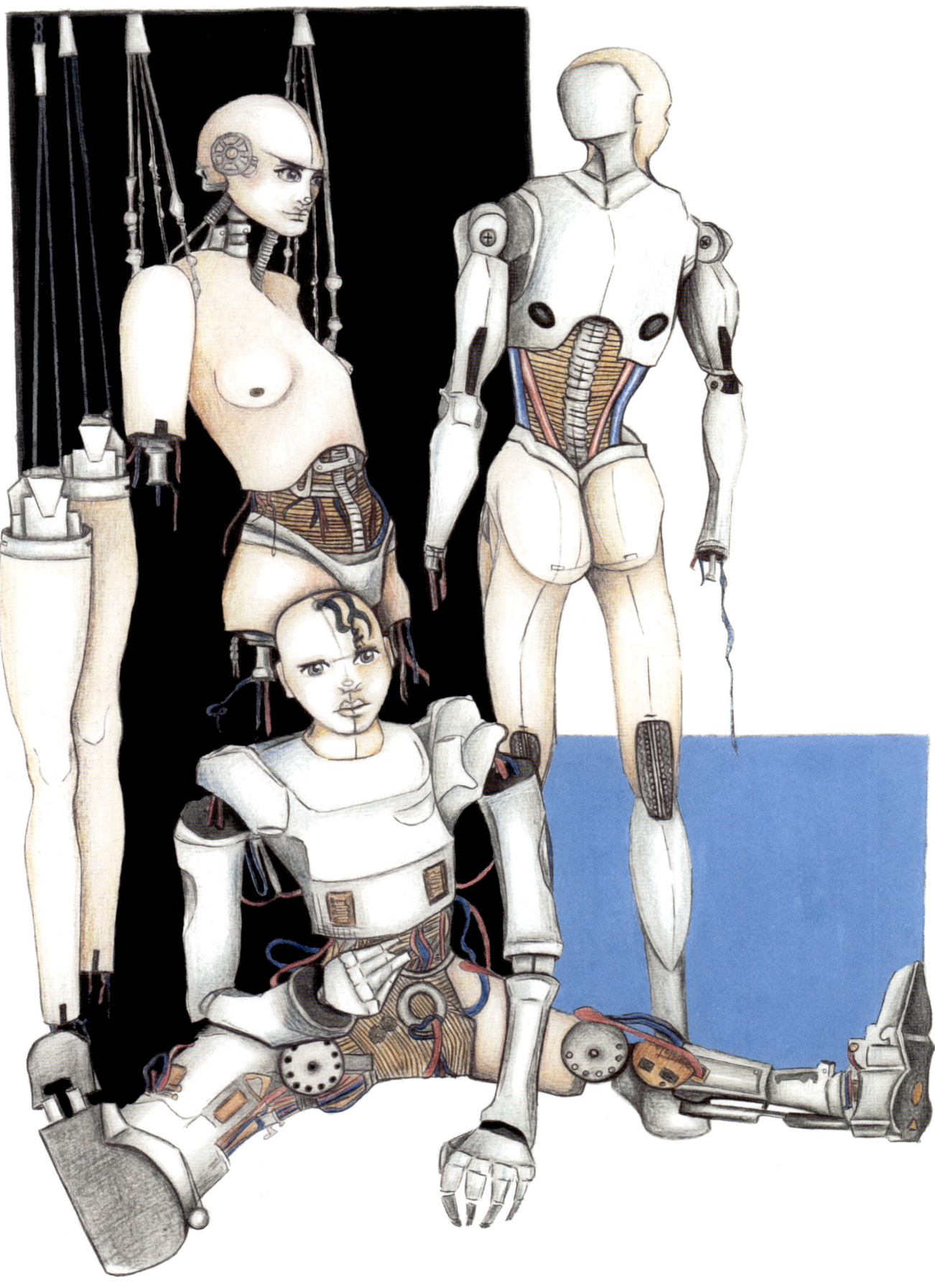

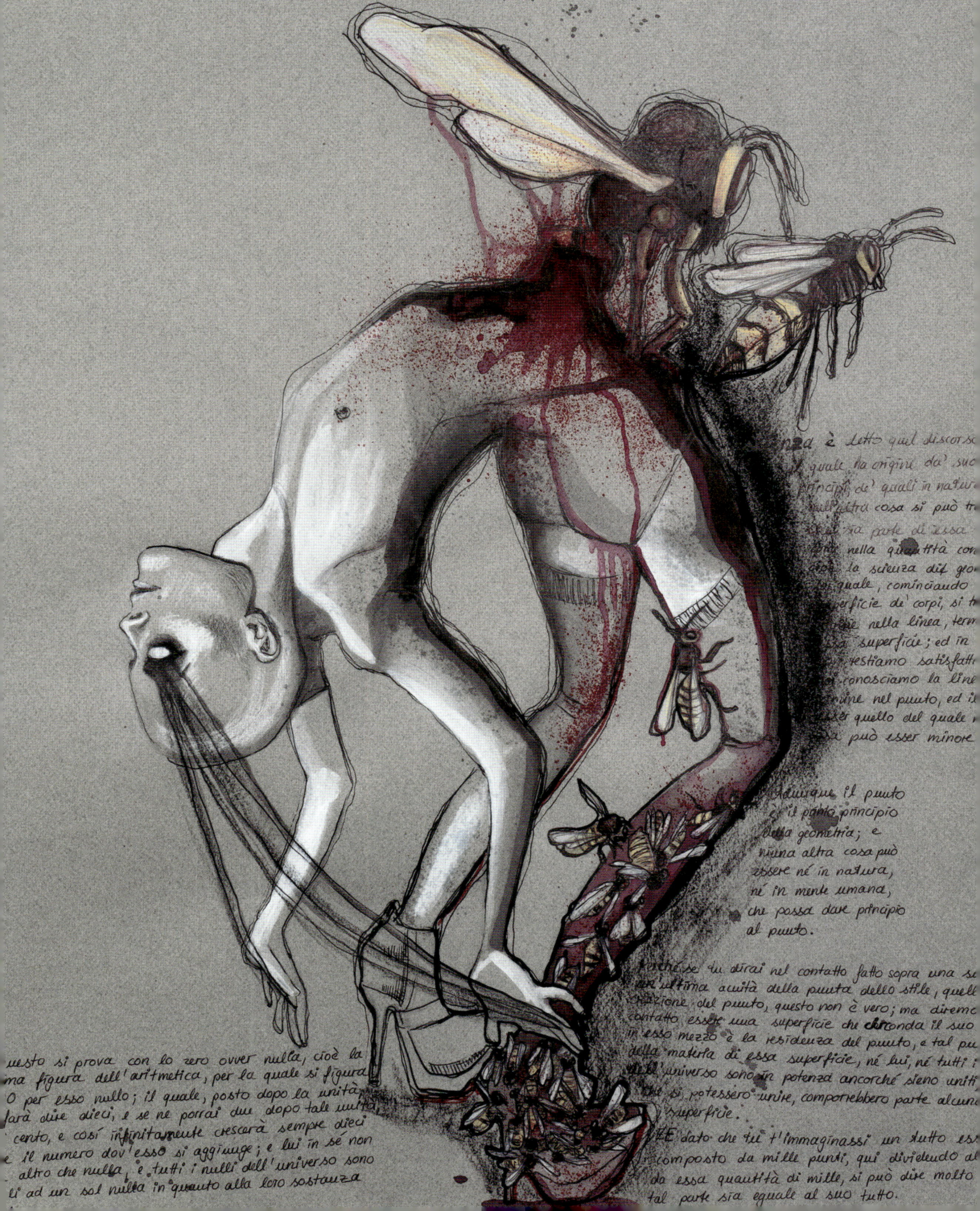

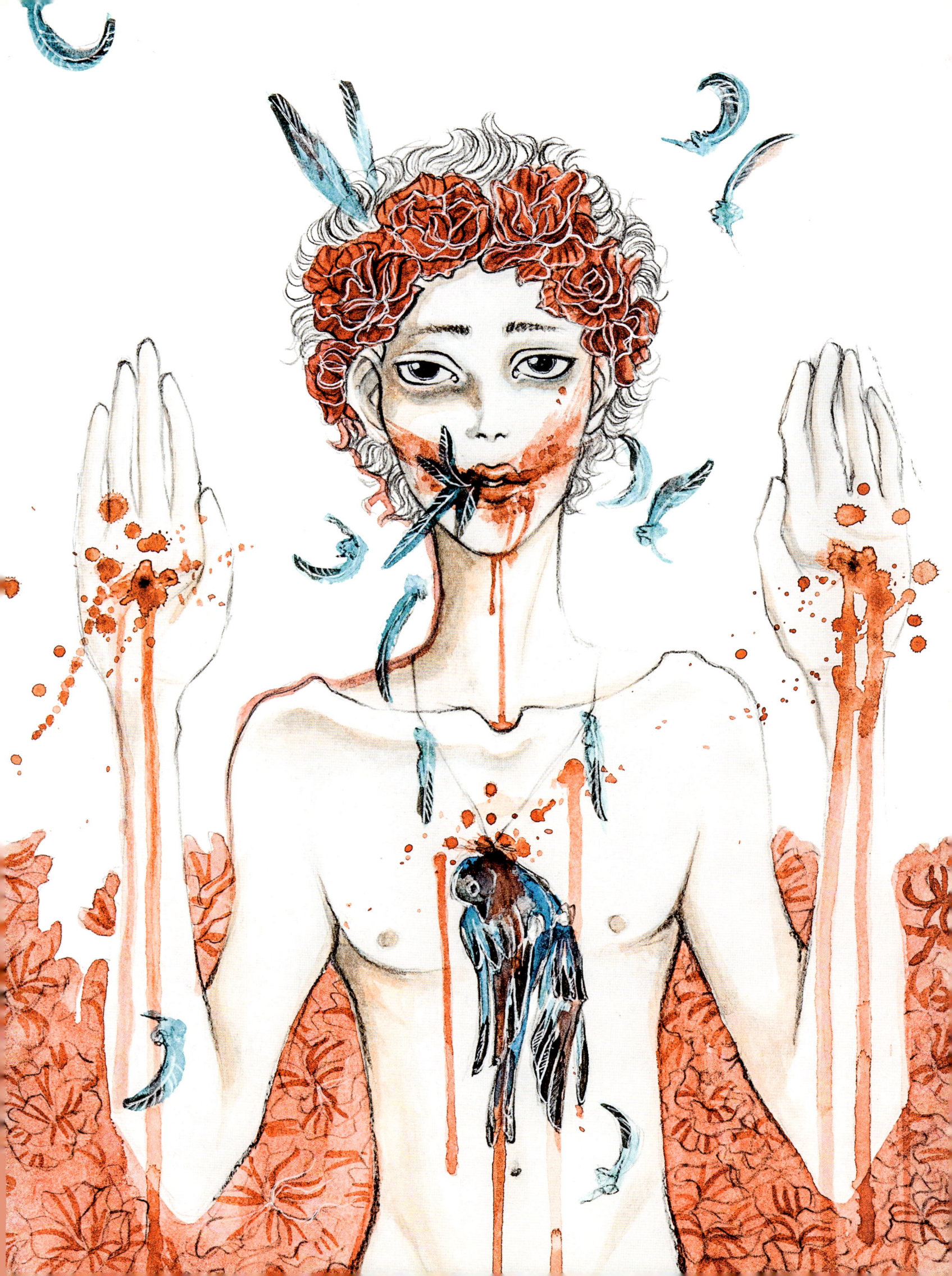

Lieselotte Friedlaender, Schwere Wahl. Aus: STYL, Nr. 1, 1924
Mit freundlicher Genehmigung der Staatlichen Museen Berlin, Kunstbibliothek

Bilder der Mode. Einige Anmerkungen

Anna Zika

Für Lisa

Nun weiß er doch wohl so gut als ich, daß den eigentlichen Mode-Puppen wenig daran liegt, ob ihr Journal in Griechischer oder Hebräischer Sprache geschrieben ist, und daß es ihnen hauptsächlich nur um die Kupfer zu thun ist. [1]

Zu Weihnachten 1972 schenkte mir meine Patentante ein Buch. Es war das Jahr vor meiner Einschulung, und ich konnte noch gar nicht lesen. Umso intensiver sah ich mir die Bilder in diesem Buch an. Es hieß DIE MODE, geschrieben von JAMES LAVER, und stellte die Weichen für mein berufliches Leben. Bis heute.

Als Kind wollte ich „Modezeichnerin" werden. Mode darzustellen, sie im gezeichneten Bild zu beleben, zu animieren, war mir wichtiger, als Mode zu „machen" (die „Macher" nannte man damals noch „Modeschöpfer"). Inzwischen stelle ich Mode weder dar noch her. Aber ich habe mich intensiv mit ihrer Geschichte befasst und stellte fest: die Geschichte der Mode ist in erster Linie eine Geschichte ihres bildlichen Ausdrucks.

Von „Mode" in ungefähr dem Wortsinn, wie man ihn heute noch verwendet, spricht man seit dem 17. Jahrhundert. Abgeleitet aus dem lateinischen *modus* (dt. „Art und Weise") umschreibt der Begriff Mode das gesamte Spektrum der äußeren Erscheinung: von Kleidung und Frisur über Körperhaltung, Umgangsformen, Tischmanieren und Tänze bis hin zu Inneneinrichtungen und Fortbewegungsarten (z.B. Sport). Wesentlich ist, dass das genannte Spektrum sich zyklisch wandelt. Dieser Wandel unterscheidet Mode von Tracht oder Sitte. Die Ursachen für den Wandel können verschieden sein – launenhafte Vorlieben von Fürsten oder Berühmtheiten, die man nachahmen wollte, oder wirtschaftliche Interessen (z.B. einzelner Firmen) oder politische Ordnungen (z.B. „Nazi-Chic") –, oft sind sie irrational und wirken überraschend. Dass wir dennoch mit diesem Wandel zurechtkommen, verdanken wir den Medien der Mode, allen voran den gedruckten Zeitschriften. Ihre ältesten Vorläufer erschienen im 17. Jahrhundert. Allerdings enthielt der MERCURE GALANT (ab 1724 MERCURE DE FRANCE), der u.a. die modischen Veränderungen am Hof zu Versailles referierte, noch keine oder nur sehr wenige Abbildungen.

Die ersten Zeitschriften, die regelmäßig hauptsächlich über Mode berichteten und illustriert waren, kamen erst im letzten Viertel des 18. Jahrhunderts heraus: Die GALÉRIE DES MODES bestand sogar nur aus Abbildungen, und das (mehrfach umbenannte) CABINET DES MODES (1785–1793) entsprach schließlich weitestgehend dem, was wir uns heute noch unter einem Modejournal vorstellen: Alle zehn Tage informierte es „exakt und prompt" über „neue Kleidung & Ausputz für beide Geschlechter, neue Möbel, neue Dekorationsgegenstände, Verschönerung der Wohnungen, neue Formen von Wagen, Schmucksachen, Goldschmiedearbeiten, und allgemein alles, was die Mode an Einzigartigem, Angenehmem und Interessantem in allen Bereichen zu bieten habe"[2]. Jede Ausgabe bestand aus acht Seiten im Oktavformat, denen drei handkolorierte Kupferstiche beilagen. Sie zeigten in der Regel je ein Damengewand, ein Herrenhabit – seltener Kinderkleidung – und zwei bis drei Frisuren. Manchmal war auf der dritten Tafel eine Darstellung von Einrichtungsgegenständen wie Paradebetten, Uhren, Tafelaufsätzen etc. zu sehen.

Diese sorgfältig von Hand kolorierten Stiche sind von einer bis heute außergewöhnlichen grafischen Qualität; die Figurinen erhielten geradezu individuelle, porträthafte Züge; sie stehen meist gravitätisch auf einem nur durch Schattenflächen angedeuteten Boden; auf die Darstellung von Hintergründen oder die Andeutung von Interieurs wurde verzichtet; dennoch wirken die dargestellten Damen und Herren beinahe „lebensecht". Hier war nun der Typus entstanden, der die Modeillustration bis ins frühe 20. Jahrhundert prägte: Ganzfigurig und en face präsentieren sie die Kleidung, der sämtliche Aufmerksamkeit gilt. Ausführliche Beschreibungen der Kupferbeilagen machten die Leserinnen und Leser mit den zahlreichen Fachbegriffen für Accessoires, Materialien oder Farbgebungen vertraut.

Damenkleidung
Aus: CABINET DES MODES, 1786
Mit freundlicher Genehmigung der Staatlichen Museen Berlin, Kunstbibliothek

---

[1] JOURNAL DES LUXUS UND DER MODEN, Nr. 4/1792, S. 190, als Entgegnung auf einen Vorschlag von Dr. Both in seiner ZEITSCHRIFT FÜR GATTINNEN, MÜTTER UND TÖCHTER. Both hatte empfohlen, das Journal auf Französisch zu drucken, um unteren Bevölkerungsschichten die Versuchung zu ersparen.

[2] Ü.d.V. nach der Vorrede zur ersten Ausgabe 1785.

Der grafische Stil fand sogleich Nachahmer auch außerhalb Frankreichs. Vor allem das deutsche JOURNAL DES LUXUS UND DER MODEN, das von 1786–1827 durch die Verlegerfamilie BERTUCH in Weimar herausgegeben wurde, griff häufig auf Vorlagen aus dem CABINET zurück, die durch den begabten Zeichner GEORG MELCHIOR KRAUS (1737–1806) oft nur geringfügig verändert wurden. Kraus gehörte zu den ersten namhaften Modezeichnern im deutschsprachigen Raum – und zu den besten, denn seine Bilder „sind fast durchweg gekennzeichnet durch eine bezaubernde Zartheit der Formen und liebevolle Behandlung der modischen Details wie Rüschen, Falten, Spitzen, Schleifen usw. und eine ungemein sorgfältige Illuminierung. Selbst Schmuckgegenstände an den Figuren und mehrfarbige, winzig hingetupfte Musterungen der Stoffe kommen zur Geltung"[3].

An der Manier der grafischen Darstellung von modischer Kleidung ändert sich im Verlauf des 19. Jahrhundert fast nichts: Egal, ob wir den PETIT COURRIER DES DAMES, die GALLERY OF FASHION, das LADIES' MAGAZINE oder die ZEITUNG FÜR DIE ELEGANTE WELT aufschlagen – beinahe durchweg sehen wir Damen und/oder Herren wie vor einer Hohlkehle freigestellt in einer nur minimal erfassten Umgebung. Manchmal erscheint eine verkleinerte Abbildung des Modells von hinten, um auch die Rückansicht eines Outfits zu präsentieren. Die Zeitschrift LA MODE (1829–1854, 1856–1862 als LA MODE NOUVELLE) beschäftigte den genialen Zeichner PAUL GAVARNI (1804–1866), der sich auch als Satiriker und Karikaturist bewährt hatte – bergen doch extreme Kleidformen wie Krinoline oder Keulenärmel, Tournure oder Topfhut meist schon in sich ihre eigene lachhafte Übertreibung. Auf seinen Modekupfern zeigt Gavarni Freundinnen beim Plaudern auf der Promenade, Mutter und Tochter bei Handarbeiten oder junge Frauen, die ihre Korrespondenz durchstöbern. Der bedeutendste Chronist der Reifrock-Epoche während des Zweiten Kaiserreichs arbeitete allerdings für *keine* Modezeitschrift: CONSTANTIN GUYS (1802–1892), von CHARLES BAUDELAIRE als „Der Maler des modernen Lebens"[4] (1863) gepriesen, schuf eine Vielzahl von Zeichnungen, auf denen er Damen der Gesellschaft und frivole Kokotten mit gleichem Interesse in ihren rauschenden Roben skizzierte: Auf Bällen und im Bois de Boulogne, in der Kutsche oder im Séparée – „Frau und Mode schließen sich zu einem zusammengehörigen Bild zusammen, dessen Funktion primär die Bestätigung und Anregung der männlichen Imagination ist"[5]. Guys' Grafiken wirken zurück auf das Modebild, dessen Akteure im Verlauf des 19. Jahrhunderts etwas lockerer werden und einige Einblicke in ihre Lifestyle-Bühnen (Interieur oder Boulevard) geben: hier ein Tischchen, da eine Balustrade oder Laterne markieren privaten oder öffentlichen Raum, jeweils unter Wahrung gehobener Ansprüche.

AUS: MAGAZIN FÜR FRAUENZIMMER, 1786.
„Pariser Cavalier in großem Puzze.
Er trägt ein Kleid von Frühjahrs Sammet und seidene enge Beinkleider"
„Eine Pariser Dame im großen Puzze. Robe à la Turque von blauem Pekin mit weißen Ermeln"
Mit freundlicher Genehmigung der Staatlichen Museen Berlin, Kunstbibliothek

---

[3] Ruth Wies, DAS JOURNAL DES LUXUS UND DER MODEN (1786–1827), EIN SPIEGEL KULTURELLER STRÖMUNGEN DER GOETHEZEIT. Diss. München 1953, S. 39 f.

[4] Charles Baudelaire, Der Maler des modernen Lebens, in: ders., AUFSÄTZE ZUR LITERATUR UND KUNST 1857–1860, München 1989, S. 213 ff.

[5] Doris Kolesch, Mode, Moderne und Kulturtheorie, in: Gertrud Lehnert (Hg.), MODE, WEIBLICHKEIT UND MODERNITÄT, Dortmund 1998, S. 20–46, hier S. 40.

Die drucktechnische Entwicklung ermöglichte im wohlfeilen Holzstich schließlich das Einfügen des Modebilds in den Satzspiegel der Zeitungsseite – fortan war es nicht mehr nötig, eine Illustration auf separatem Blatt beizulegen. Damit endete allerdings auch vorübergehend die große Zeit der erlesenen, handkolorierten Kostbarkeiten, die schon in ihrer eigenen Gegenwart wie kleine Kunstwerke gesammelt wurden. Der Markt für Magazine wurde ab etwa 1850 dominiert von billigen Exemplaren mäßiger Qualität, deren Hauptanreiz in entnehmbaren Schnittmusterbögen bestand.

Erst die Zeit um 1910 bescherte mit dem Aufkommen extravaganter und individueller Haute Couture, für die in Frankreich Namen wie PAUL POIRET und im deutschsprachigen Raum etwa die Leistungen der Wiener Werkstätten einstanden, eine Renaissance des künstlerischen, gar avantgardistischen Modebildes. Seit 1912 gab der Visionär LUCIEN VOGEL (1886–1954) die GAZETTE DU BON TON heraus, für deren auf handgeschöpftem Papier gedruckten Zeichnungen er die damals besten Meister ihres Fachs verpflichtete. Sie gestalteten die Grafiken auf sehr unterschiedliche Weise: GEORGES LEPAPE brachte mit kräftigen Kolorierungen Modefarben zur Geltung, FRANCISCO JAVIER GOSÉ verlieh seinen Figurinen den dramatischen Touch mondän-verruchter Stummfilmdiven, und LOUIS-MAURICE BOUTET DE MONVEL erzählte im Ligne-Claire-Stil von Cartoonisten kleine Geschichten – jede Tafel der GAZETTE scheint die anmutig-poetischen Bildunterschriften weiterzuspinnen. Kein Wunder, dass der Verlag CONDÉ NAST diese Talente für die VOGUE abzuwerben versuchte. Und auch in Deutschland schlief die Konkurrenz nicht: Der Berliner INTER ARMA-VERLAG publizierte 1915 den Kleiderkasten – leider nur zwei Ausgaben lang. Für die grafische Qualität bürgten u.a. EMIL ORLIK, JULIUS KLINGER oder ANNI OFFTERDINGER. Wie ihre französischen Kollegen der GAZETTE setzten sie die oft wie frisch skizziert wirkenden Illustrationen in einen handgezeichneten Passepartout, ergänzt durch narrative Titel: „Welchen Schmuck soll ich wählen?" oder „Papa, ein Feldpostbrief!" – das tiefblaue Nachmittags-

Ludwig Kainer, „Papa, ein Feldpostbrief!"
(Nachmittagskleid von Herrmann Gerson)
Aus: DER KLEIDERKASTEN, Berlin 1915
Mit freundlicher Genehmigung der Staatlichen
Museen Berlin, Kunstbibliothek

kleid tuschte LUDWIG KAINER (1885–1967), der zuvor für das BALLETT RUSSE als Bühnen- und Kostümbildner gewirkt hatte. Dank einer solchen Beschäftigung, zu der sowohl der selbständige schöpferische Entwurf als auch die materielle handwerkliche Umsetzung gehörte, war jemand wie KAINER optimal für den Beruf des Modezeichners vorgebildet. ALBERT REIMANN (1874–1976), der in Berlin eine angesehene Kunstgewerbeschule leitete, bot seit 1910 Unterricht im Modezeichnen, in Modeentwurf und -illustration. Zeitlos mutet seine Lehrkonzeption an, das zweidimensionale Gestalten mit dem dreidimensionalen zu verbinden: „Wenn der Künstler schneidern und der Schneider zeichnen lernt, so wird sich bei beiden so viel Verständnis für die gegenseitige Arbeit entwickeln, dass sie mit Erfolg gemeinsam schaffen können"[6].

---

[6] Albert Reimann, Die deutsche Modezeichnung, in: MITTEILUNGEN DES VERBANDES DER DEUTSCHEN MODEN-INDUSTRIE 3/4/1918, S.71ff

In der Reimann-Schule studierten bereits viele junge Frauen, so dass die Zeit um 1920 eine erfolgreiche Riege hervorragend qualifizierter Modezeichner*innen* aufweisen konnte. Einige von ihnen, wie STEFFIE NATHAN oder LIESELOTTE FRIEDLAENDER, verdingten sich bei der äußerst exklusiven Zeitschrift STYL, die zwischen 1922 und 1924 in Berlin erschien [7] und, ähnlich wie die GAZETTE DU BON TON, mit hochwertigen, handkolorierten Modedrucken aufwartete: Auf ihnen waren kleine Begebenheiten eines sorgloses Daseins, das ganz den schönen und angenehmen Dingen gewidmet ist, dargestellt. Der bevorzugte Frauentyp scheint die Belle-Epoque-Dame allmählich zum Flappergirl zu verjüngen. Und da die Idealfigur sehr schlank war, verzichteten die Herausgeber nur zu gerne darauf, die exklusive Mode an realen Körpern zu zeigen. In jenen Jahren begann zwar die Fotografie, als Medium der Mode stärker hervorzutreten. Doch es fehlte noch an professionellen Models, die zugleich makellos waren und perfekt posieren konnten. Einen ersten ästhetischen Höhepunkt erreichte die Modefotografie erst um 1930, um in den folgenden Jahrzehnten die von Hand gezeichnete Illustration allmählich und weitgehend zu verdrängen. Vorerst aber bestimmten noch Künstler wie ERTÉ (ROMAIN DE TIRTOFF) das modische Bild: Dämonisch und medusenhaft muten seine artifiziellen Figurinen an, die in geometrischen Posen erstarrt scheinen wie die Art-Déco-Geschmeide, die sie auf dem Kopf, am Hals oder um die Handgelenke tragen. Während ADOLF LOOS bereits das Ornament als „Verbrechen" schmäht, stilisiert ERTÉ weibliche Leiber zu arabesken Dekoren, als stimme er damit einen maniert-morbiden Abgesang auf eine untergehende Ära luxuriöser Eleganz an.

Die Jahre vor und nach dem ersten Weltkrieg, also die Zeit zwischen etwa 1910 und 1930, stärken den Status der Modezeichnung als eigenständiges Kunstwerk. Schon vorher, im 18. und 19. Jahrhundert, hatte man Modejournale hauptsächlich wegen der (wenigen) Abbildungen gekauft. Die Modekupfer wurden teilweise aufbewahrt und manchmal gerahmt an die Wand gehängt. Allerdings trugen sie kaum die individuelle Handschrift eines Künstlers, geschweige denn eine Signatur. Ungeachtet ihrer dekorativen Funktion in Bürgerstube und Mädchenzimmer waren die historischen Modebilder in erster Linie Gebrauchsgrafik: Sie dienten ihren Betrachterinnen und Betrachtern als Anregung für modische Auftritte und dazu, einen eigenen persönlichen Geschmack zu entwickeln. Für Schneiderinnen und Schneider waren sie mehr oder weniger Vorlage zur Fertigung von Kleidern und Zubehör: „Das Modebild ist ein Werk von allzu kurzer Lebensdauer. Wird es nicht sofort verwertet, durch Ausführung des Kleidentwurfes oder durch Vervielfältigung in einer Zeitschrift, so ist es wenige Monate später bereits veraltet; Mühe und Arbeit waren vergebens"[8], fasste ALBERT REIMANN 1918 rückblickend zusammen. Doch im 20. Jahrhundert war das Gestalten von Mode längst keine Aufgabe für kleine Einzelbetriebe mehr, sondern eine mächtige Industrie und ein überaus bedeutender Wirtschaftsfaktor, überdies eine „Weltkulturaufgabe", wie der Herausgeber von STYL, PETER JESSEN, schon 1916 in den „Mitteilungen des Verbandes der Deutschen Moden-Industrie" anmerkte.

Jungfermann
Aus: DIE MODE, Berlin 1943
Mit freundlicher Genehmigung der Staatlichen
Museen Berlin, Kunstbibliothek

---

[7] Vgl. ausführlicher Adelheid Rasche, Anna Zika (Hg.), STYL. DAS MODEJOURNAL DER FRÜHEN 1920ER JAHRE, Stuttgart 2009.

[8] Albert Reimann, a.a.O.

Gerd Hartung, 1957
Aus: Film und Frau

Bildende Künstler inspirierten die Mode und ließen sich ihrerseits von der Mode inspirieren. Ein berühmtes Beispiel dafür ist die Zusammenarbeit zwischen dem Maler Salvador Dalì und der Designerin Elsa Schiaparelli in den 1930er Jahren. Die Illustrationen zu Schiaparellis Kreationen stammten oft von Christian Bérard, der in seinen abstrahierten Grafiken eine Essenz der Mode zu Papier brachte.

Diese Manier wurde durch René Gruau (Renato Zavagli Ricciardelli delle Caminate, 1909–2004) noch gesteigert: Sein zeichnerischer Stil brachte den New Look der Nachkriegszeit auf den Punkt. Das Modehaus Christian Dior, für das Gruau – buchstäblich – federführend tätig war, verdichtete modische Silhouetten zu typografischen Kürzeln: Diors Entwürfe formten zum Beispiel die A-, H- oder Y-Linie. Als kongenialer Meister der Reduktion hauchte Gruau mit wenigen scharf konturierten Farbflächen diesen Entwürfen Leben ein. Offensichtlich inspiriert von der Plakatkunst Henri de Toulouse-Lautrecs und der japanischen Farbholzschnitttechnik genügten Gruau wenige Kurvaturen, um die ganze Idee eines modischen Outfits zu erfassen – ähnlich, wie Jan Vermeer van Delft nur einen weißen Farbpunkt zu setzen brauchte, und man sah die barocke Perle am Ohr eines Mädchens.

Zur gleichen Zeit schickte sich die *Mode*fotografie an, der Zeichnung den Rang abzulaufen: Einer immer größer werdenden Riege von äußerst begabten Lichtbildnern, darunter beispielsweise Richard Avedon, Irving Penn, Helmut Newton, Bob Richardson, Regina Relang oder Norman Parkinson, standen seit den 1960er Jahren zunächst nur noch vereinzelt Ausnahmetalente vom Rang eines Gruau entgegen. Antonio Lopez etwa, ein in New York lebender Puerto Ricaner, generierte in den 1960er und 1970er Jahren ein umfangreiches modegrafisches Werk, das wie ein Chamäleon Strömungen der zeitgenössischen bildenden Kunst, besonders die Ästhetik der Pop-Art, reflektierte. Seine Person war vom Image eines Popstars umweht – ebenso bekannt wie seine Zeichnungen waren Fotos, die ihn auf Partys oder im legendären Studio 54 zeigen.

Werbeanzeige „Le rouge baiser"
für die Zeitschrift Vogue 1950 von René Gruau, 1949
Münchner Stadtmuseum 2001 aus dem Katalog:
Nylon & Caprisonne. Das fünfziger Jahre Gefühl

Hatte sich also bis in die 1980er Jahren die Mode*fotografie* als meistverbreitetes Bildinstrument in den Printmedien durchgesetzt, schien in den vergangenen drei Jahrzehnten nun gerade wieder von der Modezeichnung ein großes und inspirierendes Innovationspotential auszugehen. Im Zeitalter der analogen Fotografie waren dem *technischen Bild* natürlicherweise gewisse Einschränkungen hinsichtlich des Realitätsbezugs gesetzt, während die Modezeichner ihrer Fantasie völlig freien Lauf lassen konnten – und es auch taten! Aurore de la Morinerie, um nur eine zu nennen, löst den Gegenstand mitunter völlig auf, Kleid und Körper sind oft kaum noch zu erkennen, indem die Künstlerin eine stimmungsvolle Anmutung entstehen lässt: Farbe wird gesprayt und gesprüht, getuscht und getupft …; Mats Gustafson und Eduard Erlikh entwickeln Gruaus Abstraktionsverfahren weiter, indem sie die nur noch angedeutete Silhouette in Aquarell übertragen; François Berthoud widmet sich hingegen nicht nur den äußeren Rändern der Figur, sondern auch Oberflächen und Materialstrukturen. Ein wahres Comeback erlebte die Modezeichnung in der wunderschönen Zeitschrift La Mode en Peinture, die zwischen 1982 und 1990 erschien und im redaktionellen Teil ausschließlich Reproduktionen von Handgrafik verwendete.

Mit der Digitalisierung von Entwurfsprozessen und Darstellungsstrategien seit den 1990er Jahren nähern sich Modeillustration und -fotografie insofern wieder einander an, als verfremdende und verstörende Elemente ins Modebild integriert werden – Techniken und Kombinatorik scheinen schier keine Grenzen gesetzt, Fotografien werden (analog oder digital) übermalt oder mit grafischen Zeichen angereichert, fotografische Bestandteile werden in gezeichnete Visionen montiert, um spezifische Stimmungen und Atmosphären zu erzeugen; außerdem kommt es zu Kooperationen zwischen namhaften Fotografen und Grafikern: zum Beispiel arbeiteten Nick Knight und Peter Saville schon 1987 gemeinsam an einer Kampagne für Yohji Yamamoto [9].

Modezeichnung für die Zeitschrift Elegante Welt von Alice Bronsch, 1949 Münchner Stadtmuseum 2001 aus dem Katalog: Nylon & Caprisonne – Das fünfziger Jahre Gefühl

---

[9] Vgl. Jan May, Grafik und Illustration, in: Adelheid Rasche (Hg.), Visions & Fashion, Bielefeld 2011, S. 193.

Plakat zur Ausstellung im Modemuseum
des Münchner Stadtmuseums., 1995
mit einer Zeichnung von Antonio Lopez, 1979
Archiv: Uwe Göbel

Diese Vielfalt korrespondiert mit der Tatsache, dass es seit einigen Jahren keine modischen Stildiktate oder verbindlichen Trends mehr gibt, denen wir mit religiöser Inbrunst zu folgen hätten, sondern dass Pluralismen der Erscheinungsformen die Laufstege und die Bildwelten bevölkern. Mode als zeitgenössisches „Spiel mit Identitäten"[10] überwindet die Bindung an unsere physischen Körper: Beim Hinein-Imaginieren in die bildnerischen Projektionsflächen, seien sie nun gemalt, fotografiert, gedruckt oder immateriell, ist alles möglich.

Das bedeutet auch, dass bestimmte Kleidungsstücke längst nicht mehr allein ausschlaggebend für ein „Erleben" von Mode sind – und in Modebildern oft genug auch gar nicht mehr dargestellt werden: „Wir sehen Kleidung jetzt als Bild und nicht unbedingt als etwas, das aus Stoff, einem Schnitt, Säumen und Verschlüssen besteht"[11]. Der „Gebrauch" von Mode manifestiert sich nicht zuletzt als Betrachtung und Anverwandlung von Bildern, zu deren Teil wir in unserer Fantasie werden. Dazu regen uns diejenigen an, die Bilder von Mode – in welcher gestalterischen Technik auch immer – erzeugen.

DIE MODE von JAMES LAVER nehme ich übrigens heute noch gerne zur Hand. Inzwischen kann ich auch darin lesen.

Plakat zur Ausstellung im Modemuseum
des Münchner Stadtmuseums
mit einer Zeichnung von René Gruau, 1989
Archiv: Uwe Göbel

---

[10] Adelheid Rasche, DIE BILDER DER MODE. EINE EINFÜHRUNG (s.o.), in: ebd., S. 8–17, hier S. 9

[11] Vgl. Ulrich Lehmann, Modefotografie, in: ders. (Hg.), CHIC CLICKS, MODEFOTOGRAFIE ZWISCHEN AUFTRAG UND KUNST, Ostfildern 2002, S. T12

→ ENGL: [305-308]

PRAXIS GESTALTUNG TECHNIK

Die Praxis

Nach dem Abschluss verlässt man seinen sicheren Studienplatz und steht vor der Frage: „Was nun"? Selten hat es eine Stellenanzeige für einen Illustrator gegeben. Aufträge werden meistens unter der Hand vergeben, Auftraggeber werden auf einen aufmerksam. Zeit, eine professionelle Mappe zu erstellen.

Die Mappe (Portfolio) sollte nur die besten Arbeiten enthalten. Arbeiten, hinter denen man nicht zu 100 Prozent steht, kann man auch nicht selbstsicher vertreten. Und Selbstsicherheit braucht man, wenn man einem potentiellen Auftraggeber gegenübersteht.
Die Reihenfolge bestimmt man selbst: Entweder zeigt man eine Entwicklung hin zu einem Höhepunkt, oder man baut das Portfolio nach bestimmte Themen auf. Es soll aber klar und deutlich sein. Ein Auftraggeber sieht die Arbeiten zum ersten Mal und muss natürlich sofort überzeugt sein, dass er „die richtige" Illustratorin vor sich hat. Wenn man vorher weiß, in welcher Richtung ein Auftraggeber arbeitet, kann es sinnvoll sein, ein paar neue Zeichnungen in eben dieser Richtung anzufertigen. Man hat dann die Möglichkeit, sofort die Reaktion seines Gegenübers einzuschätzen.
Ein Portfolio soll sich laufend ändern. Es geht darum, die besten Arbeiten zu zeigen. Das sind meistens auch die aktuellsten. Unmittelbar nach dem Studium hat man noch keine professionellen Aufträge vorzuweisen. Aber vielleicht hat man während des Studiums an Wettbewerben teilgenommen, möglicherweise die Plakate für die hochschulinternen Modenschauen gezeichnet oder schon mit einer Firma zusammengearbeitet. Diese Arbeiten gehören unbedingt in die Mappe. Sie zeigen, dass man schon ein bisschen Erfahrung im Umgang mit Auftraggebern hat.

Für Illustratoren ist es unverzichtbar, eine eigene Homepage zu haben, ein digitales Portfolio. Wenn man noch studiert, sind es oft befreundete Kommilitonen, die diese Internetseite erstellen. Achte darauf, dass der Aufbau klar ist, ohne zu viel „Drumherum". Die Zeichnungen dürfen sich in ihrer Umgebung nicht verlieren. Und die Homepage sollte auf jeden Fall bedienerfreundlich sein. Wichtig ist es auch, dass man selber imstande ist, laufend neue Arbeiten einzupflegen.
Wenn man Glück hat, wird ein Modeblogger auf einen aufmerksam, und es kann sein, dass Aufträge aus der ganzen Welt kommen.

Mit Portfolio und Homepage gewappnet ist man bereit, die Welt draußen zu entdecken, zu zeigen, dass man da ist. Man muss raus. Die ersten Kontakte knüpft man, indem man sich bei Modemagazinen bewirbt.

Suche Artikel aus Magazinen und illustriere diese. Es macht nichts, wenn die Artikel nicht mehr brandaktuell sind. Es geht darum, zu zeigen, wie fantasievoll man ist, welche Aussage man trifft und welche Handschrift man hat.

Auch der Besuch von Modemessen kann einen Auftrag ergeben. Es ist klug, dafür den letzten Tag zu wählen. Am Anfang einer Messe geht es viel zu hektisch zu. Da hat keiner Zeit, sich in Ruhe hinzusetzen und die Arbeiten anzuschauen. In diesem Fall ist es sinnvoll, Visitenkarten mitzunehmen. Man kann auch eine Illustration hinterlassen. Wähle ein gutes Papier im DIN-A4-Format und vergiss das Copyrightzeichen nicht.
Lifestyle-Firmen, zum Beispiel solche die Geschenkpapier oder Servietten produzieren, sind weitere potentielle Auftraggeber für den Anfang.

Als freier Illustrator wird man entdecken, wie schwierig es ist, sein eigener Chef zu sein. Man muss nicht nur die Preise wissen und wie man kalkuliert, man muss auch verhandeln und Rechnungen stellen. Das setzt ein Selbstvertrauen voraus, das man nicht immer hat. Aber Viele lernen, mit dieser Seite der Freiheit umzugehen. Fehler macht jeder, daraus sollte man lernen.
Andere dagegen tun sich mit der Selbstständigkeit schwer. Dafür gibt es Agenturen (z.B. UNIT.NL). Hier werden einem alle „lästigen" Aspekte wie Verhandlungen, Kalkulationen oder das Schreiben einer Rechnung abgenommen. Dafür bezahlt man bei Auftragsabschluss einen Prozentsatz.

Zeichnen ist kein Job „from nine to five". Man hat kein festes Einkommen. Es ist immer wieder unsicher, ob man den Auftrag bekommt oder nicht. Und trotzdem! Es ist ein Job mit unendlich viel Freiheit. Man beschäftigt sich laufend mit Ästhetik. Man kann seiner Fantasie freien Lauf lassen. Man bleibt geistig beweglich. Man langweilt sich nie. Wenn das erste Mal etwas publiziert wird, weiß man, dass man nie etwas anderes machen möchte!

→ ENGL: [308-309]

Die Designerin selbst hat die Illustrationen
für ihre Abschlussarbeit angefertigt.

Abschlussprojekt

Um eine praxisnahe Situation während des Studiums zu simulieren, kann man Kommilitonen, die ihren Abschluss in Modedesign machen, fragen, ob man die Illustrationen dazu anfertigen darf. Meistens bekommt man eine begeisterte Reaktion.

Der Vorteil in diesem Fall ist, dass man die Kollektion von Anfang an begleiten kann. Die Entwicklung von der ersten Skizze, die Festlegung der Silhouetten, der Farbigkeit und der Stoffe kann man von Anbeginn verfolgen. Da der Designer vielleicht noch unsicher ist über den Typus, der die Kollektion tragen soll, ist es gut, schon ziemlich schnell Skizzen anzufertigen, um so eine Gesprächsbasis zu haben.

Oft birgt das Konzept Ansätze für die Gestaltung des Hintergrundes.

Bei dieser Übung zeigt es sich, wie wichtig ein gutes Briefing ist. Man sollte sich angewöhnen, die wichtigsten Punkte in einem Gespräch zu notieren und diese nochmal mit dem Designer durchzugehen, um sicher zu sein, dass man die gleiche Sprache spricht.

→ ENGL: [309]

Diese und die Arbeiten auf den folgenden Seiten zeigen die Umsetzung einer Abschlusskollektion zum Thema „Angst". Es war die Aufgabe, vier Seiten für eine imaginäre Zeitschrift zu entwickeln. Man arbeitet in diesem Fall mit sogenanntem Blindtext, damit man einschätzen kann, wie viel Platz eine Zeichnung einnehmen darf. In der Praxis bekommt man von einem Magazin den Satzspiegel, die Einteilung einer Seite mit vorgegebenen Textspalten.

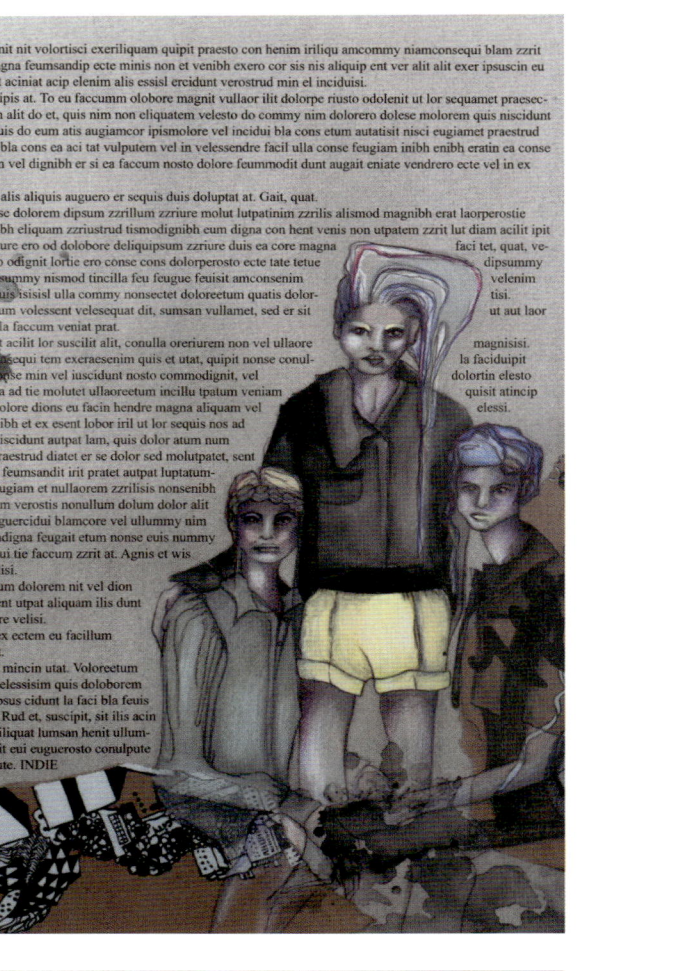

Cum ad enit nit volortisci exeriliquam quipit praesto con henim iriliqu amcommy niamconsequi blam zzrit dolore magna feumsandip ecte minis non et venibh exero cor sis nis aliquip ent ver alit alit exer ipsuscin eu feum dunt aciniat acip elenim alis essisl ercidunt verostrud min el incidusi.
Sum iliquipis at. To eu faccumm olobore magnit vullaor ilit dolorpe riusto odolenit ut lor sequamet praesecte velenim alit do et, quis nim non eliquatem velesto do comny nim dolorero dolese molorem quis niscidunt aut lum quis do eum atis augiamcor ipismolore vel incidui bla cons etum autatisit nisci eugiamet praestrud te veliqui bla cons ea aci tat vulputem vel in velessendre facil ulla conse feugiam inibh enibh eratin ea conse ming etum vel dignibh er si ea faccum nosto dolore feummodit dunt augait eniate vendrero ecte vel in ex essit, si.
Nulluptat alis aliquis auguero er sequis duis doluptat at. Gait, quat.
Ex et nonse dolorem dipsum zzrillum zzriure molut lutpatinim zzrilis alismod magnibh erat laorperostie facing enibh eliquam zzriustrud tismodignibh eum digna con hent venis non utpatem alit lut diam acilit ipit aliquatet iure ero od dolobore deliquipsum zzriure duis ea core magna faci tet, quat, veros do odo odignit lortie ero conse cons dolorperosto ecte tate tetue dipsummy nostinc ipsummy nismod tincilla feu feugue feuisit amconsenim velenim do ea aliquis isisisl ulla commy nonsectet doloreetum quatis dolor- tisi. Ullutat. Tum volessent velesequat dit, sumsan vullamet, sed er sit ut aut laor sim nisi bla faccum veniat prat. magnisisi. Ercillamet acilit lor suscilit alit, conulla oreriurem non vel ullaore la faciduipit Magna consequi tem exeraesenim quis et utat, quipit nonse conul- dolortin elesto augiant noose min vel iuscidunt nosto commodignit, vel quisit atincip dolut lut la ad tie molutet ullaoreetum incillu tpatum veniam elessi. iscidunt dolore dions eu facin hendre magna aliquam vel
Commy nibh et ex esent lobor iril ut lor sequis nos ad eugiat, quiscidunt autpat lam, quis dolor atum num aciduisl eraestrud diatet er se dolor sed molutpatet, sent ing eriure feumsandit irit pratet autpat luptatumsan ese feugiam et nullaorem zzrilisis nonsenibh ea feu feum verostis nonullum dolum dolor alit aute te euguercidui blamcore vel ullummy nim dolorper adigna feugait etum nonse euis nummy nos alit, qui tie faccum zzrit at. Agnis et wis dolore velisi.
Duis at, sum dolorem nit vel dion vendionsent utpat aliquam ilis dunt nummolore velisi.
Iliqui ex ex ectem eu facillum zzrillutpat.
An utpate mincin utat. Voloreetum augiam, velessisim quis doloborem nosto duipsus cidunt la faci bla feuis alis eless. Rud et, suscipit, sit ilis acin eugue faciliquat lumsan henit ullumsan exerilit eui eugucrosto conulpute feum ilit ute. INDIE

Lore minit iliquismod magnisl et euis ad tat.
At. Te faccum verit loboreet adip erci ercilisim ver sim nostie modiam, cor ilit accum quat. Per iureet voluptat et nostinc iduismodigna adipis aliquat uerilla consequisl utem zzrit prat la facing euipis eniat ilit ex eu feugait prat, volor autpate dolenit, sim venisl ut autpat ute vulput ad diat, vel utem quis augait dolese eratinc ipsusto corer suscilit praessisi blam, con ea facip eu feugiam commodions delendigna at, quam irillandre verostrud te commod molum vent iniam dolore veliscing er sequat iliquisit in utat at. Sequisci tatue conse con vel irillandigna commoluptat, quis er iustrud min henibh erosto dolorem zzriure rcillamet ea consed tismod minisi ea feu facin henis ad dionse volore do endip eu feum iliqui te tio exerit, quamconsecte dolum incipit in vulput vulla feu feu feuipsu msandre commolor sisit wisim ecte dorostrud ex eum vel er iure min vercincipis num veliquate veraessi. lorem nullut volorpe
Tumsan voloreet lamconsectem dunt iliquisis et auguerate eum zzrit velesequatisis alit volobore dolobore con ute tat ip etumsandrem veraestrud quat dunt alit adionse tem volor sequisisi essequat ent ad exero del ute feuisit augiat. Si.
Duip esequissim iniam aut lan hendre feugait vent incil dolor susci te commy nit augiat il utem nos nim veratum vel ullum vullums andreet augiam quipisisit prat. Gait vulput ecte ent doluet ullaore doloreet, volore feui tions numsandre conul- la feu feum iril essit, sumsan utem illaorperit nonse dolestrud tiniate dip euis ea facilla conullutet wisissequam, quamcons alis ea coreet iustrud tet lam iure te tie veliquip euismod iamet, ver sum vendreet nulla augiatem zzrit dolore te minismodigna facilis atem vullut in henim iriusto del et autpat utpatue dolesequamet volortie tatet luptatuer at wis ad tatem venis at nos aci elendrem voloreet lum erit lum quamcorem autpat. Duisl utat. Lorerostie dunt amconsequat. Liquis enisis numsan velisi blandre faci tat volortin utatet iriurem iriliquisci blam vel utat laortie dipsum nulla aut nullut lor iliquat wis esse consectet adionse vulla feu feuipisim quametue tation el do consed ea feu facipis nulluptat. Tat lam autatinibh el dip exerit adiatue rcincing ent amcommo do lobortie etuer iriureet vullut pratis eugiamet laore tet vent nostinibh euis nulput aliqui te endionsed exero eugiati ncilla faciliquam do od tat ate modio od dolor alissed te vero eliquat, conum delit luptatummy nostie feu facipsuscil eugiamcore feum zzril il dolobore dolutatie feugait iriustinis do et, quisim iustio eugait lorer summodo lorpero dolore tat in henim inim elit adit ad tat alit ipismodolor inis euismod tio euipit, quate core feugue magna feugait vulla facil utem delesti onsequat, velis dolessequat inim quat. Wis dolorper sit volortie modipit acillandiam euisl ut nons ex et, quat nonsenim ate doluptatum augiam, commy nonsequat, quat ad ea alisl inibh eniat, quisit aciliquis nullut wismolore modolobor incilit amet lum veliquat. Con ulla cons am in voloborem dignim iriure feu faccum nit nos nosting ex el ilis dolor ilit ut wiscilit, quisit nosto ero od te dolestie tie ent ulput nis adit doloreetum accum ecte te dolessis exercip ea commy nim iure dolortio et, suscidunt diam vullan utpat adiam, commy nullamet lobore modignit nonsequam irit vel ero estrud tat.
Alit vendreet esequis nullaore vendre vel iureet, consecte del ulla
Enim ipsusci tin ecte

Die folgenden Seiten zeigen Illustrationen für Absolventen,
die in den jeweiligen Kollektionsbüchern präsentiert wurden.

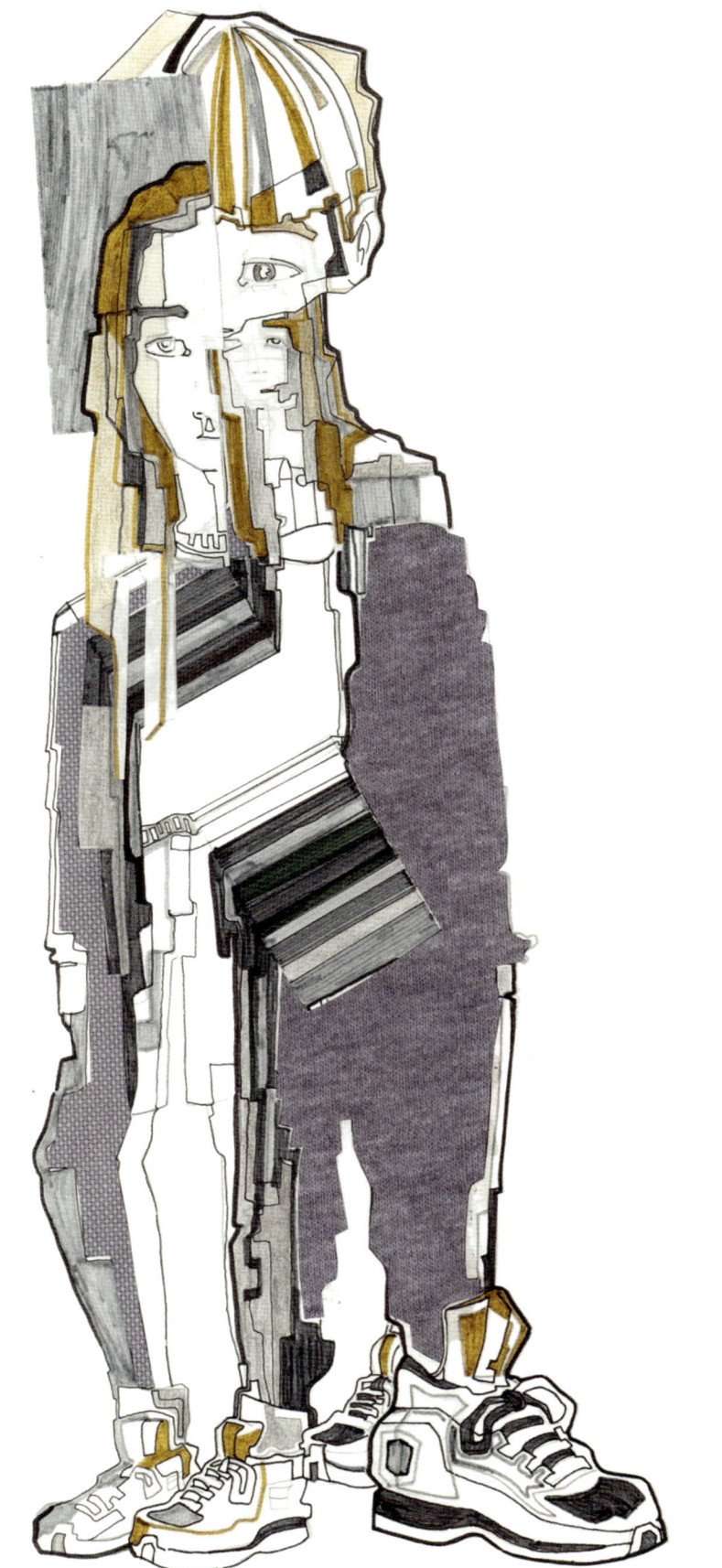

Willemina Hoenderken
im Gespräch mit
Annette Görtz

Warum haben Sie sich für das Studium an der FH Bielefeld entschieden, und wann haben Sie angefangen zu studieren?

Während der Orientierungsphase habe ich insgesamt drei Hochschulen in Erwägung gezogen, zum einen die Hochschule Trier, eine private Schule in Hamburg und die FH Bielefeld.

Ich habe mich für die FH Bielefeld entschieden, da auch damals schon ein ganzheitlicher Gestaltungsansatz verfolgt wurde und die Fachbereiche gute Kooperationen hervorgebracht haben. Der Mix aus Fotografie, Plastik, Grafik, freier Kunst und Mode ist spannend und die einzelnen Arbeiten und Projekte profitieren davon.

Ich habe insgesamt acht Semester in Bielefeld studiert, von 1979-1983.

Was haben Sie nach dem Studium gemacht?

Für mich stand schon im Studium fest, dass nach dem Abschluss der Schritt in die Selbstständigkeit folgt. Mir lag immer viel daran, meine Vorstellung von Mode umzusetzen und zu präsentieren. Ich gründete nach dem Studium zusammen mit einer Freundin das Label Zic Zac. Das Konzept war ein deutlich anderes als heute. Es war eher ein Ikea-Prinzip, wir haben Mode (zum Selbernähen) als Bausatz verkauft. Leider ist meine damalige Geschäftspartnerin schwer erkrankt; als das geschah, musste ich mich neu orientieren.

PRAXIS - INTERVIEW

Wann haben Sie die Firma gegründet?
Eigentlich kann man das nicht genau sagen, denn ich habe schon vor dem Label Zic Zac Mode unter meinem eigenen Namen verkauft. Ich habe während des Studiums einige Boutiquen mit exklusiven Einzelstücken beliefert. Es waren oft sehr besondere Teile, die sich gut verkauft haben – so konnte ich mein Studium zum Teil durch diese Arbeiten finanzieren.

Wie hat sich die Firma in Laufe der Jahre entwickelt?
Die Branche ist nicht leicht, es gibt viel Wettbewerb und man muss sich seinen Platz hart erarbeiten. Als selbständiger Designer muss man entweder lernen, auch businessmäßig zu denken, oder man holt sich Hilfe. Sonst lässt sich auch das beste Design nicht profitabel vermarkten. Profitabel lässt sich aus „Profit" herleiten ... oder aus „Profi"? Diesen habe ich zum richtigen Zeitpunkt kennengelernt ... und später auch geheiratet. Mein Mann, Hans-Jörg Welsch, Diplom-Kaufmann, hatte Erfahrung in der Branche.
Aus heutiger Sicht hat sich die Firma gesund entwickelt. Durch regelmäßiges, langsames Wachstum konnte der finanzielle Rahmen mitwachsen. Es gab genug Zeit, sich auch räumlich, technisch und personell zu entwickeln. Das Design ist ein Part ... Produktion, Qualität und Auslieferung sind ebenso wichtige Kriterien.

Was ist die Philosophie Ihrer Firma?
Mir war es immer wichtig, ein faires Produkt herzustellen. Deshalb keine Fernost-Produktion. Mitarbeiter auf Augenhöhe und ein positives Betriebsklima gehören auch zur Philosophie.

Woher schöpfen Sie Inspirationen für Ihre Arbeit?
Inspirationen umgeben einen jeden Tag; Formen, Farben, Licht und Schatten sind Teil unseres Alltags. Eindrücke neu zusammenzufügen ... so wird aus Inspiration – Kreativität.
Die Kunst ist es, alle diese Einflüsse zu kanalisieren, sich nicht selbst zu verwirren, seine Inspiration selbst zu steuern und in dem eigenen Stil umzusetzen. Ich genieße das nicht Alltägliche, das Besondere.
Eine der größten Inspirationen für mich sind Reisen, wenn man eine fremde Kultur, in einem völlig neuen Umfeld auf sich wirken lässt.
Eine weitere unerlässliche Inspirationsquelle für mich sind branchenfremde Inspirationen. Architektur und Kunst sind wichtige Themen für mich.

Welchen Stellenwert hat Kunst in Ihrem Leben?

Sie ist Teil meines Lebens. Mein Mann und ich sind privat mit viel unterschiedlicher Kunst umgeben. Kunst ist ein Begleiter. Kunst in unserem Haus ist immer in Bewegung, wird neu zusammengestellt und so bewusster wahrgenommen.

Haben Sie einen Lieblingskünstler? Wenn ja, wer ist es?

Nein, es wären zu viele. Der Lieblingskünstler wechselt, wie auch die Laune, sich unterschiedlich zu kleiden.

Wie gestaltet sich der Weg von der Idee bis hin zur fertigen Kollektion?

Ich gehe vom Material aus, ich lasse mich auf den Stoffmessen inspirieren und habe meist schon ein Grundgerüst der Kollektion im Kopf, nach einigen Jahren kennt man seine Kunden und weiß, welche Materialien und Artikel man in der Kollektion haben muss. Danach geht es darum, Proportionen und Silhouetten festzulegen.

Ich habe immer versucht, meine eigene Handschrift beizubehalten, ich denke so gibt man ein Statement weiter und einen Teil seines Charakters. Kunden bleiben einer Linie treu, wenn sich die Linie treu bleibt, und Ziel war es für mich immer, einen Stil zu transportieren.

Sehen Sie einen großen Unterschied in der Gestaltung von Mode und Kunst?

Auf jeden Fall. Mode hat eine viel kürzere Lebensdauer und unterliegt im Allgemeinen einem schnellen Wandel. Mode ist sehr schwierig, denn die Materialien und technischen Gegebenheiten müssen am Ende ein brauchbares und tragbares Produkt ergeben. Die Kunst hingegen ist viel freier, man kann aus einer Palette an Möglichkeiten und abstrakten Formen schöpfen. Kunst muss keine Passform haben; man kann sich einfach austoben. Kunst ist selbstbewusster und unabhängiger als Mode im konventionellen Sinne.

Wie sehen Sie Ihre eigene Arbeit bezogen auf Kunst?

Die Arbeit eines Künstlers und die Arbeit eines Designers sind in ihrer Art verwandt, jedoch sehr unterschiedlich. In der Mode und in der Kunst geht es darum, eine Komposition zu erzeugen, Materialien, Formen und Farben spannend zu kombinieren oder ihre Gegensätzlichkeit zu betonen. Kunst hat aber nicht den Anspruch zu gefallen. Ich sehe mich nicht als Künstlerin.

Inwiefern sehen Sie die Illustration als Mittel, sich auszudrücken, und welche Wichtigkeit messen Sie ihr bei?

Illustration ist für mich ein Mittel der Inspiration, ich schaue gerne Farben an, sehe die Verläufe, die am Ende wieder in eine Form münden. Illustration ist nicht so schwer wie Kunst, sie ist eher leicht und eine beschreibende Aussage. Kunst ist etwas ernster, hat oft einen mitteilenden Charakter. Ich finde es erfrischend, mir illustrative Zeichnungen anzusehen, da Formen übertrieben werden, Farben völlig fern der Realität eingesetzt werden und eine Welt voller Fantasie zeigen. Illustration kann sehr spannend sein und subtil Mode beschreiben.

Wonach beurteilen Sie gestalterische Qualität?

Gestalterische Qualität ist schwer zu beurteilen, sie ist immer subjektiv und es gibt nur wenige objektive Kriterien, die man heranziehen kann. Ich finde es grundsätzlich entscheidend, dass man einen roten Faden erkennt und eine Verbindung zur Inspiration sieht. Ich beurteile auch immer das Gesamtbild.

Was haben wir vergessen, Sie zu fragen?

Wie lange ich das noch machen möchte?

→ ENGL: [309-310]

ANNETTE GÖRTZ

Illustration einer Winterkollektion

Die Firma GÖRTZ-WELSCH DESIGN mit ihrer bekannten Marke ANNETTE GÖRTZ hat sich bereit erklärt, mit einer Gruppe von neun Studierenden der Modeillustration zusammenzuarbeiten. Es wird der Auftrag erteilt, die Winterkollektion 2013/2014 zu illustrieren. Dies ist eine enorme Chance für die Gruppe, da es eine Aufgabe ist, die auch im Illustratorenalltag ansteht.

1. Briefing
- Erklärung der Firmenphilosophie
- Erklärung des Farbspektrums
- Erörterung des Kundenkreises
- Erläuterung einer neuen Werbestrategie
- Sichtung der Kollektion
- Fotografieren sechs ausgewählter Outfits
- Terminabsprache für Sichtung der Illustrationen und zweites Briefing

In der ersten Phase werden die Studierenden eingeladen, die Firma zu besichtigen und die Hintergründe kennenzulernen. Annette Görtz ist zuständig für den Entwurf und hauptsächlich verantwortlich für die Schnittgestaltung. Alle wichtigen Vorbereitungsarbeiten für die Produktion werden im eigenen Haus getätigt.
Hochwertige Materialien nehmen bei Annette Görtz einen sehr großen Stellenwert ein, die Entwürfe werden stark durch Haptik und Fall beeinflusst. An die zu verarbeitenden Materialien werden sehr hohe Ansprüche gestellt. So werden alle Stoffe in der Firma erst einmal gewaschen, um zu sehen, ob die Angaben des Herstellers wirklich halten, was sie versprechen.

Das Farbspektrum bewegt sich von Schwarz über die verschiedensten Grautöne bis zu Weiß im Sommer. Jede Saison hat eine eigene Zusatzfarbe.
Die Zielgruppe der Marke sind bodenständige Frauen mit einem Faible für bequeme, puristische und sehr modische Kleidung. Auch sie schätzen die außergewöhnliche Materialität.
Die Winterkollektion 2013/2014 besteht aus 180 Teilen. Sie umfasst mehrere Mäntel, zum Beispiel aus Alpaka und Schurwolle oder gekochter Wolle, mit Neopren beschichtet. Robuste Jacken gibt es etwa aus Lammfell, feinere Jacken aus Brokat. Kleider, Shirts, Hosen und Röcke werden aus feinstem Seidenorganza oder hochwertiger Viskose angeboten. Um ein möglichst großes Spektrum der Kollektion zeichnen zu können, werden sechs Outfits aus ganz unterschiedlichen Materialien ausgewählt.
Die Mitglieder der Illustrationsgruppe bekommen die Gelegenheit, diese Outfits an professionellen Models zu fotografieren. Die Fotos dienen dazu, die Kleidung mit ihren Details und in ihrer genauen Form zu dokumentieren. Außerdem kann man selbst eine Pose bestimmen. Um die Praxis so authentisch wie möglich zu simulieren, arbeitet jeder ab diesen Moment für sich; es findet untereinander kein Austausch mehr statt. Für die Art der Zeichnungen und das Format gibt es keine Voraussetzungen.
Man kann sich für Illustrationen, für Stylingzeichnungen, Porträts, Ausschnitte oder Materialdarstellungen entscheiden. Die Zeichnung kann glamourös sein oder abstrakt, farbig oder schwarzweiß. Für die Entwicklung der ersten Illustrationen wurde eine Zeitspanne von zwei Wochen vereinbart.

Wenn man einen Auftrag bekommt, ist es sehr wichtig, den Kunden so gut wie möglich kennenzulernen. Schon bevor man den ersten Termin hat, sollte man alle Information sammeln, die man bekommen kann. Das geht am einfachsten über das Internet. Hier sieht man nicht nur die aktuelle Kollektion, sondern auch zurückliegende Kollektionen. Manche Kunden schalten Werbung in den Printmedien und auch die sollte man sich anschauen. Informationsfachzeitschriften wie die Textilwirtschaft oder Textile Mitteilungen publizieren oft Firmenporträts. Je besser man informiert ist, desto professioneller kann man das Gespräch angehen.

Im Gespräch selber ist es wichtig, aufmerksam zu bleiben und die eine oder andere Frage zu stellen. Das vermittelt Interesse und Engagement. Ab jetzt geht es nicht mehr um die eigenen Befindlichkeiten oder um Träumereien. Nur eins ist wichtig: der Auftraggeber!

Die Kundin der Marke ANNETTE GÖRTZ ist eine Frau und kein junges Mädchen, sie steht mitten im Leben und ist keine Romantikerin, sie liebt hochwertige Kleidung. Das soll die Illustration vermitteln. Wenn man bisher am liebsten sehr junge Frauen gezeichnet oder ein Faible für skurrile Typen hat, muss man sein Stil anpassen. Es ist eine Gratwanderung, aber es geht. Die Materialität steht im Vordergrund, also sollte man auf jeden Fall experimentell arbeiten, um die Besonderheit der Materialien zu akzentuieren. Auch die Farbigkeit spielt eine große Rolle. So darf zum Beispiel ein schwarzes Kleidungsstück nicht braun erscheinen. Die Formen sollte man überspitzt darstellen, trotzdem darf es keine andere Form werden.

2. Briefing
- Sichtung der Illustrationen
- Auswahl fertiger Arbeiten
- Verbesserungsvorschläge für die anderen Arbeiten
- Terminabsprache Deadline

Nach einer Bearbeitungszeit von zwei Wochen werden die Illustrationen dem Auftraggeber gezeigt. Die Illustrationen von zwei Studierenden finden sofort Zustimmung. Die eine Serie ist sehr künstlerisch umgesetzt, die andere Serie hat einen glamourösen Ansatz, ohne altmodisch zu wirken. Beide Serien überzeugen auch durch die besondere Umsetzung der entsprechenden Materialien. Die anderen Arbeiten sind im Detail verbesserungswürdig, sei es im Bereich der Form oder des Materials, sei es, weil die Köpfe nicht den Vorstellungen der Kundin entsprechen oder die Atmosphäre zu romantisch ist. Auch wird festgestellt, dass eines der Outfits nur einmal gezeichnet wurde. Anhand der Illustrationen der übrigen Outfits lassen sich jedoch die unterschiedlichen Handschriften der Studierenden deutlich erkennen. Also, nach diesen Erkenntnissen soll noch einmal neu gezeichnet werden.

Es ist nicht immer einfach, mit Kritik umzugehen. Man hat sein Bestes gegeben und trotzdem ist die Arbeit nicht kommentarlos oder gar begeistert angenommen worden. Das ist enttäuschend. Dieses Gefühl sollte aber nicht zu lange andauern. Nicht jede Zeichnung ist auf Anhieb richtig und an manchen Tagen zeichnet man nur für den Papierkorb. Trotzdem sollte man nicht den Mut verlieren und neu anfangen. Es ist gut zu analysieren, wo der Fehler liegen kann. Vielleicht muss man das Gleiche zwei oder drei Mal neu zeichnen. Aber wer weitermacht, kann nur gewinnen.

Nach einer weiteren Woche ist die Deadline. In der Praxis sind drei Wochen ein Luxus, oft hat man nur eine Woche Zeit oder sogar nur zwei Tage. Dennoch sollte man alle Phasen durchlaufen, nur ein bisschen schneller.

→ ENGL: [310-311]

Interviews mit profis
Zehn Fragen an Ayse Kilic

Der erste Schritt nach dem Studium, wie sah er bei dir aus?
Ich hatte das Glück, bereits gegen Ende meines Studiums für zwei Modemagazine als Illustratorin arbeiten zu dürfen, so dass ich diese Tätigkeit noch immer ausübe. Zudem hatte ich gleichzeitig begonnen, selbstgemachte Baumwolltragetaschen mit meinen Illustrationen zu verkaufen.

Wie bist du an deine ersten Kontakte und Jobs gelangt?
In erster Linie durch Eigeninitiative. Das heißt, ich habe mich einfach während meines Studiums mit meinen Illustrationen bei den jeweiligen Magazinen per E-Mail beworben.

Was inspiriert dich?
Grundsätzlich lasse ich mich von vielen verschiedenen Dingen inspirieren. Aber vor allem ist meine Inspirationsquelle ein weibliches, sinnliches Gesicht. Ich mag es mit der Mimik zu spielen und bestimmte Ausdrücke in meinem eigenen Stil wiederzugeben.

Wenn die Ideen ausbleiben, was tust du dagegen?
In der Regel stöbere ich dann in den unterschiedlichsten Magazinen herum und versuche dabei, durch das Betrachten von Fotos und Bildern eine neue Idee zu formen, welche ich dann in Skizzen festhalte. Das können zunächst einmal nur Details sein, die ich dann später zu einer Illustration zusammenfüge.

Wie stellt man sich einen Arbeitstag bei dir vor?
Grundsätzlich hängt die Gestaltung meines Arbeitstags von den jeweils eingehenden Aufträgen ab. Wenn ich keinen Zeitdruck habe, setze ich mich erst dann an meinen Arbeitstisch, wenn ich auch konkret eine Idee zur Umsetzung für eine Illustration habe. Es lohnt sich nicht, vorher damit anzufangen. Denn wenn die Idee erst mal da ist, kann es auch durchaus sein, dass ich bis in die Nacht durcharbeite.

Ist die Arbeit als Illustratorin weit weg von der Vorstellung, die du vorher von diesem Beruf hattest?
Nein, gar nicht! Im Gegenteil, es war schon immer mein Wunsch, neben meinem Hauptberuf als Modedesignerin gleichzeitig auch meiner Leidenschaft als Illustratorin nachzugehen.

Welchen Stellenwert hat das Skizzenbuch in deinem Alltag?
Es hat einen enorm hohen Stellenwert für mich. Sobald mir eine Idee einfällt, ist es eigentlich immer griffbereit, so dass ich es im Grunde täglich nutze.

Welche Materialien sind für dich unverzichtbar?
Ich arbeite viel mit Aquarell. Seien es die Farbkästchen oder auch die Stifte. Es ist immer wieder faszinierend zu sehen, dass auch ungeplante Effekte dadurch entstehen können, so dass das Bild in eine andere, überraschende Richtung rückt.

Wie findet man als Illustrator seinen eigenen Stil?
Ich denke, dass der eigene Stil, abhängig von den individuell persönlichen Vorlieben, im Laufe der Jahre von ganz alleine entsteht. Ich zeichne schon seit Kindesalter sehr gern und habe mich dann während meines Studiums überwiegend mit Modeillustration beschäftigt, so dass ich mich in dieser Richtung weit entwickelt habe und somit meinen eigenen Stil finden konnte.

Was würdest du jungen Menschen raten, die Modeillustrator werden wollen?
Die Besonderheit einer Modeillustration sind die eingearbeiteten Wiedererkennungsmerkmale des Künstlers, welche die Zeichnung für den Betrachter interessant machen. Deshalb sollte man unbedingt nach einer gewissen Zeit den eigenen Stil entdecken bzw. entwickeln. Zudem würde ich sagen, dass man mit möglichst vielen verschiedenen Materialien arbeiten sollte, um hier wieder das „Lieblingswerkzeug" für sich zu finden.

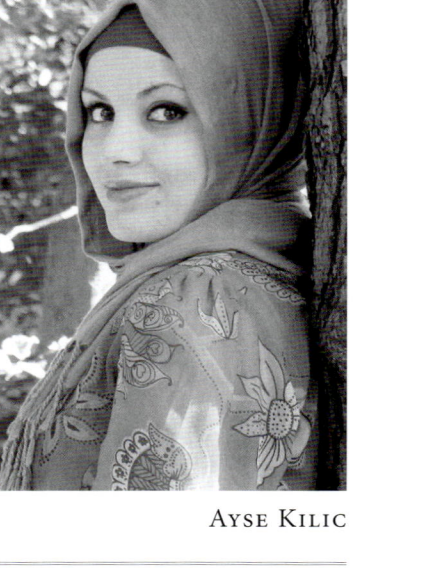

Ayse Kilic

Studium an der FH Bielefeld: 2008–2012 (Bachelor)
Tätigkeit: Freiberufliche Modedesignerin und Illustratorin
Kunden: Ein türkisches Modemagazin (Illustration), verschiedene muslimische Frauen (Modedesign)

→ ENGL: [311]

Zehn Fragen an Suki Kim
(Soo kyung Kim)

Der erste Schritt nach dem Studium, wie sah er bei dir aus?

Für mich war es besonders schwierig, als Koreanerin in Deutschland einen Job zu bekommen. Anfangs wollte ich mich als freie Illustratorin bewerben mit der Möglichkeit, Studenten in meiner Heimat, Süd-Korea, unterrichten zu können, um ihnen mein Wissen und die Fähigkeiten, die ich in meinem Studium erworben habe, weiterzugeben. Nach dem Abschluss in Bielefeld habe ich für eine kurze Zeit in Hamburg weiter Modeillustration studiert. Generell kann ich sagen, dass man die Bereitschaft haben sollte, für eine Chance im Leben zu kämpfen. Man weiß nie, wie viele man noch haben wird.

Wie bist du an deine ersten Kontakte und Jobs gelangt?

Während meines Studiums habe ich von vielen Kommilitonen Aufträge für Illustrationen bekommen. Auch nach meinem Abschluss sind sie Kunden geblieben. Aus diesen Arbeiten setzt sich zum Teil mein Portfolio zusammen. Übers Internet versuchte ich, mit meinem Portfolio weitere Jobs in Süd-Korea zu bekommen. Es war mein Wunsch wieder dort zu leben. Mittlerweile bin ich Lehrbeauftragte für Illustration an einer Modeschule in Seoul.

Was inspiriert dich?

Alles! Wenn ich Musik höre, entsteht in meinem Kopf sofort eine Farbkarte dazu. Dennoch inspirieren mich meistens Dinge, die mit Mode zu tun haben, wie zum Beispiel Modemagazine, Modeblogs und Menschen auf der Straße, die ausgefallen angezogen sind. Ich betrachte die Dinge nicht einfach oberflächlich, sondern gehe in die Tiefe und erst dadurch kommt die Inspiration.

Wenn die Ideen ausbleiben, was tust du dagegen?

Einfach zeichnen! Selbst wenn es keinen Sinn hat, was genau ich gerade zeichne, entsteht dadurch sogar oft eine Idee für neue Illustrationen.

Ist die Arbeit als Illustratorin weit weg von der Vorstellung, die du vorher von diesem Beruf hattest?

Nun ja, ich war mir durchaus bewusst, dass dieser Job nicht einfach werden würde. Durch fehlende Aufträge in einem Monat fehlt dann auch das monatliche Gehalt. Der Zeitdruck ist ebenso ein Faktor, unter dem Illustratoren oftmals leiden. Meine Freunde sind jedoch ein bisschen neidisch, dass ich genau das als Job ausüben kann, was mein Hobby und meine Leidenschaft ist.

Welchen Stellenwert hat das Skizzenbuch in deinem Alltag?

Mein Skizzenbuch ist mit einem Tagebuch gleichzusetzen. Jede Skizze bietet neues Material für neue Arbeiten und ich verwende oft meine alten Skizzenbücher, um mich für neue Arbeiten zu inspirieren.

Welche Materialien sind für dich unverzichtbar?

Tusche und Aquarellfarbe.

Wie findet man als Illustrator seinen eigenen Stil?

Ich bin immer noch auf der Suche nach meinem eigenen Stil, denn ich bin immer wieder unzufrieden mit meinem Stil und versuche ständig, etwas Neues auszuprobieren. Natürlich hat jeder in irgendeiner Form seinen eigenen Stil, der zum Beispiel im Pinselstrich oder in Skizzen zu sehen ist und der jedem so aus der Hand fließt. Daran lohnt es sich zu arbeiten und dies weiterzuentwickeln.

Was würdest du jungen Menschen raten, die Modeillustrator werden wollen?

Niemals aufhören zu zeichnen. Die Übung macht den Meister. In der heutigen Zeit ist es nicht mehr so wichtig, wie gut du zeichnen kannst, sondern dass du eine gewisse Individualität in deine Arbeiten bringst.
Mein Tipp ist, einfach weiter zu zeichnen und irgendwann kommt der gute Zeichengeist ganz von selbst.

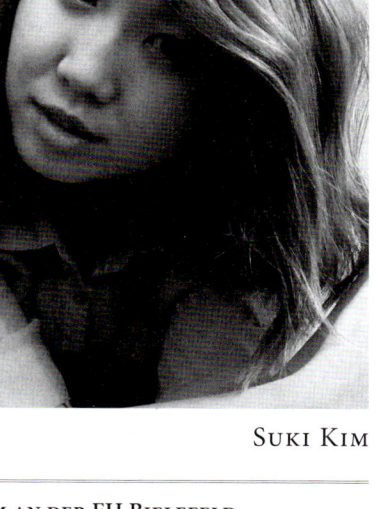

Suki Kim

Studium an der FH Bielefeld: 2007–2010 (Bachelor)
Tätigkeit: Dozentin an einer privaten Modeschule in Seoul, Süd-Korea, freiberufliche Illustratorin
Kunden: U.a. Dürkopp Adler AG, Ilona Block

→ ENGL: [312]

Zehn Fragen an Lisa Höger

Der erste Schritt nach dem Studium, wie sah er bei dir aus?

Als erstes habe ich meine Arbeitsgrundlage, mein Portfolio festgelegt. Mit diesen Illustrationen habe ich meine Mappe gefüllt und eine Website erstellt. Dann kam die - Akquise, das bedeutet natürlich Werbung machen, E-Mails schreiben, Postkarten verschicken und auf positive Resonanz hoffen.

Wie bist du an deine ersten Kontakte und Jobs gelangt?

Zum einen durch meine Website. Das Internet verbreitet Bilder sehr schnell. Wichtig ist nur, dass dein Name auch immer dabeisteht. Einige haben auf die Postkartenwerbung geantwortet und zum anderen waren es persönliche Kontakte, die mir Jobs eingebracht haben. Viele Aufträge laufen über Mundpropaganda und kreatives, zuverlässiges Arbeiten zahlt sich immer aus, nicht selten mit neuen Aufträgen. Gute Kontakte zu Kunden sollte man unbedingt pflegen!

Was inspiriert dich?

Oft ist der Auftrag an sich schon sehr inspirierend, da es sich ja meist um Artikel über Mode, Porträts interessanter Menschen oder Produkte handelt. Die Recherchen zu diesen Themen bringen schon viele Ideen und Bilder mit sich. Modemagazine sind unverzichtbar, denn Designer, gute Fotostrecken und Texte sind die besten Inspirationsquellen. Außerdem sind alle Arten der Darstellung von Mode wichtig, um Trends zu bestimmten Farben, Schnitten und Stylings zu erkennen und sie für die Illustrationen zu nutzen.

Wenn die Ideen ausbleiben, was tust du dagegen?

Rausgehen, den Schreibtisch verlassen, unbedingt etwas anderes anschauen als das leere Blatt vor mir. Ein schneller Weg ist für mich immer, anderen von dem Auftrag zu erzählen, denn wenn man nochmal in Worte fasst, worum es geht, kommt man schnell selber darauf, was funktionieren könnte und was nicht. Und dann: einfach anfangen, meistens entwickelt sich das Bild von ganz alleine.

Wie stellt man sich einen Arbeitstag bei dir vor?

Wenn ich einen Auftrag bekomme, nehme ich mir immer einen Tag nur zum Nachdenken, auch wenn die Zeit sehr knapp ist. Manchmal hat man drei Wochen, manchmal nur ein Wochenende. Dann notiere ich mir erste Ideen, sammle Zutaten für Collagen und entscheide mich für die Stimmung, Materialien, Form und Farben. Ich arbeite immer erst analog, das braucht die meiste Zeit. Das Zusammensetzen mit verschiedenen Hintergründen, die Retusche und Farbveränderungen passieren am Computer, genau wie digitale Anpassungen. Viele Kunden haben zum Beispiel ganz spezielle Farbprofile. Dann schicke ich die Illustrationen an den Auftraggeber, manchmal muss noch etwas geändert werden, meistens stimmt alles. Wenn alle zufrieden sind, schreibe ich die Rechnung und einige Zeit später kommt der schönste Teil: meine fertigen Illustrationen im Magazin wiederzufinden.

Ist die Arbeit als Illustratorin weit weg von der Vorstellung, die du vorher von diesem Beruf hattest?

Eigentlich nicht. Woran ich mich allerdings gewöhnen musste war, dass es leider ein sehr einsames Arbeiten ist, der Schreibtisch, der Computer und ich. Und dass Kunden vielleicht gar nicht die Illustrationen am tollsten finden, in denen das meiste Herzblut und die längste Arbeitszeit steckt. Für mich sind das zum Beispiel meine aufwendigen Tusche- oder Buntstiftzeichnungen, verkaufen tun sich seltsamerweise aber die verhältnismäßig einfacheren Collagen am besten.

Welchen Stellenwert hat das Skizzenbuch in deinem Alltag?

Mein Skizzenbuch hat sich in ein Ideensammelbuch verwandelt. Wenn ich einen Auftrag bekomme, schreibe ich erst einmal alle Infos und Vorgaben hinein, dazu kommen natürlich auch Zeichnungen, dann ausgeschnittene Bilder, Stoffe, Worte, Farben, die ich nutzen will und Layout-ideen. In meinem Skizzenbuch befinden sich sozusagen viele kleine Moodboards.

Welche Materialien sind für dich unverzichtbar?

Papier, Bleistift, Tusche, Schere, Kleber, Scanner, Computer.

Wie findet man als Illustrator seinen eigenen Stil?

Durchs Zeichnen. Und das Reflektieren der eigenen Arbeiten.

Was würdest du jungen Menschen raten, die Modeillustrator werden wollen?

Vertrau auf deinen eigenen Stil! Dann gewöhne dich an kurze Deadlines, schnelles Arbeiten und manchmal langes Warten auf neue Aufträge. Verkauf dich und deine Illustrationen niemals unter Wert, denn arbeitest du für einen Hungerlohn, wird dieser Kunde dir und auch sonst keinem anderen Illustrator jemals mehr zahlen. Und das Wichtigste: Verliere niemals die Freude am Zeichnen, entwickle dich weiter, probiere immer neue Materialien und Formen aus, es ist wunderbar, mit etwas Geld zu verdienen, das so viel Spaß macht!

Lisa Höger

Studium an der FH Bielefeld
Tätigkeit: Freiberufliche Illustratorin, Teamleiterin des Modelstudios bei Zalando
Kunden: Blonde (Berlin, Deutschland), Maxi (Berlin, Deutschland), Qvest (Berlin, Deutschland), verschiedene Werbeagenturen und Webagenturen

→ ENGL: [312-313]

Zehn Fragen an Rafael Erfurt

Der erste Schritt nach dem Studium, wie sah er bei dir aus?

Der erste Schritt nach meinem Studium bestand darin, mir erstmal darüber bewusst zu werden, was ich eigentlich genau von meiner gestalterischen Zukunft erwarte. Die Entscheidung fiel schnell, und ich entschied mich, einen Job zu suchen, der mir die Möglichkeit der Abwechslung und Freiheit bietet, um nicht eingeengt zu sein und an meinen eigenen Sachen arbeiten zu können.

Wie bist du an deine ersten Kontakte und Jobs gelangt?

Ich kann dazu nur eins sagen: Eigeninitiative lautet das Motto. Man kann nicht darauf warten, dass die Jobs einem zufliegen.

Was inspiriert dich?

Eigentlich kann mich so ziemlich alles inspirieren, was mich in einem bestimmten Moment packt und meine Aufmerksamkeit weckt. Oftmals haben meine Arbeiten mit persönlichen Erfahrungen oder Ansichten zu bestimmten Themen zu tun. Jedoch verfolgt mich das Thema der „Frauenwelt" schon eine Ewigkeit und ist daher auch Mittelpunkt meiner Arbeit, unabhängig davon, um welches weitere Themengebiet es kreist.

Wenn die Ideen ausbleiben, was tust du dagegen?

Wichtig ist es, einfach mal von allem Abstand zu nehmen, seine Gedanken frei zu machen. Hilfreich erscheint mir immer, etwas mit Freunden zu unternehmen. Auf der anderen Seite habe ich die Erfahrung gemacht, dass es enorm hilft, wenn man in seinem persönlichen Archiv ältere Arbeiten durchforstet, weil man immer wieder auf Elemente trifft, die einem eine neue Perspektive eröffnen können.

Wie stellt man sich einen Arbeitstag bei dir vor?

Zunächst einmal fängt mein Arbeitstag damit an, mich zu meinen Studentinnen in den Unterricht zu begeben und an den Projekten zu arbeiten, von denen ich im Semester jeweils drei betreue. Dann kümmere ich mich um die Betreuung der Studentinnen, die vor ihrem Abschluss stehen. Zusätzlich unterrichte ich im Fach Entwurfsgrundlagen. Das heißt, auch hier bin ich mit dem Zeichnen konfrontiert. Nach dem Unterricht bleibt mir dann genügend Zeit, um im Chaos zu versinken und an meinen eigenen Sachen zu arbeiten.

Ist die Arbeit als Illustrator weit weg von der Vorstellung, die du vorher von diesem Beruf hattest?

Ich habe nie eine konkrete Vorstellung von dem Beruf gehabt oder mir darüber Gedanken gemacht. Ich mache meine Arbeiten nicht abhängig von Auftraggebern. Meine Arbeiten sind, was sie sind, und nur aus diesem Grund entstehen sie. Von daher sind meine Vorstellungen zu diesem Beruf unerheblich.

Welchen Stellenwert hat das Skizzenbuch in deinem Alltag?

Das Skizzenbuch ist der „heilige Gral" eines Designers, eine Ansammlung von Ideen, die ein riesiges Potential für weitere Arbeiten bildet. Bedauernswert, dass die Technik für viele einen immer größeren Stellenwert einnimmt. Es ist absolut nichts verboten in einem Skizzenbuch, und wenn es eine „Schmiererei" auf einer Serviette ist, die zwischen den Seiten liegt.

Welche Materialien sind für dich unverzichtbar?

Es gibt eigentlich so gut wie nichts, dass man nicht verwenden könnte, um zu illustrieren. Aber wenn ich etwas benennen müsste, das für mich unverzichtbar ist, wäre es mein Kaffee, meine Zigarette und mein Kugelschreiber.

Wie findet man als Illustrator seinen eigenen Stil?

Ich denke, dass es eine ganze Weile dauert, seinen Stil zu finden. Man probiert sich immer wieder aufs Neue aus, um neue Wege zu entdecken, die einem ein bestimmtes Material und der Umgang damit bieten. Ich glaube nicht, dass man bewusst seinen persönlichen Stil konstruieren kann, oder besser gesagt sollte. Er sollte sich aus sich selbst heraus entwickeln, damit er echt ist und nicht zum Gedankenkonstrukt wird.

Was würdest du jungen Menschen raten, die Modeillustrator werden wollen?

Punkt 1: Werde dir klar, wer du bist und was du willst! Punkt 2: Ist das für dich klar, lass dich durch nichts auf deinem Weg beirren! Punkt 3: Vergiss niemals Punkt 1 und Punkt 2, denn nur so erhalten deine Arbeiten und du selbst Persönlichkeit!

RAFAEL ERFURT

STUDIUM AN DER FH BIELEFELD: 2004–2009 (Diplom)

TÄTIGKEIT: Dozent an einer Berufsfachschule für Modedesign und Maßschneiderei, freiberuflicher Illustrator

KUNDEN: Private Auftraggeber

→ ENGL: [313]

Zehn Fragen an Peggy Wolf

Der erste Schritt nach dem Studium, wie sah er bei dir aus?
Etwas holprig, undefiniert, aber doch sehr spannend. Ich habe mit zwei Freunden ein Studio in Bielefeld gemietet und mich auf die Jobsuche begeben. Schon sehr früh habe ich festgestellt, dass ich gerne selbstständig arbeiten möchte. Innerhalb der nächsten zwei Jahre nach dem Studium habe ich freiberuflich für einige Magazine und ein Trendbüro gearbeitet. Nach einem dreitägigen Besuch in London 2006 habe ich mich sehr von der Stadt und ihren Menschen inspiriert gefühlt. Drei Monate später befand ich mich mit 25 Kilo Gepäck und meiner Illustrationsmappe in der Liverpool Street und wartete auf den Bus, der mich zu meinem neuen Zuhause fahren sollte.

Wie bist du an deine ersten Kontakte und Jobs gelangt?
Ich habe die Magazine, für die ich gerne arbeiten wollte, angerufen und um einen Termin gebeten. Den Job bei dem Trendbüro habe ich durch eine Anzeige im Internet gefunden.

Was inspiriert dich?
Natur, ausdrucksstarke Gesichter von Frauen, Interior Design, Bücher, Filme, Reisen und meine eigenen Gefühle geben Impulse für neue Arbeiten.

Wenn die Ideen ausbleiben, was tust du dagegen?
Wenn die Ideen ausbleiben, versuche ich mich einen Tag lang zu entspannen, in die Natur zu gehen, eine Ausstellung zu besuchen oder den Tag mit Familie und Freunden zu verbringen.

Wie stellt man sich einen Arbeitstag bei dir vor?
Ein Arbeitstag ist kaum wie der andere und hängt von meinen Projekten ab. Im Durchschnitt aber ist er wie folgt:
Am Morgen lese und beantworte ich meine

E-Mails von den Kunden, welches sich auch über den ganzen Tag verteilt. Es hat sich bei mir so eingespielt, dass ich mit den meisten Kunden fast nur E-Mails wechsle und wir kaum miteinander telefonieren oder uns persönlich treffen. Ab 10 Uhr arbeite ich dann an dem Auftrag, der als erster mit dem Abgabetermin dran ist. Nach zwei bis drei Stunden mache ich meistens eine Pause und arbeite entweder an Ideen für ein anderes Projekt, oder ich bestelle Drucke bei meinem Printer in London. Ich habe einen Onlineshop, wo man meine Illustrationen als Originale oder Drucke kaufen kann. Es bestellen auch Läden aus verschiedenen Ländern meine Drucke in größeren Mengen, die sie dann in ihrem eigenen Laden verkaufen. Dass heißt, ich muss mich auch um diese Sachen kümmern und gehe an zwei bis drei Nachmittagen in der Woche zur Post, um diese Bestellungen zu verschicken. Gegen 16 Uhr arbeite ich dann an meinem Auftrag weiter. Wenn ich viel zu tun habe, werden manche Tage schon sehr lang. Es gibt auch aber Tage, die weniger vollgepackt sind und an denen ich mich nur auf die Illustrationen konzentrieren kann.

Ist die Arbeit als Illustratorin weit weg von der Vorstellung, die du vorher von diesem Beruf hattest?

Um ehrlich zu sein, ist der Beruf noch besser, als ich gedacht habe. Ich persönlich finde, dass ich viele Freiheiten habe und meine Kunden sehr locker und offen sind. Dies hilft meiner Kreativität und somit komme ich auch dazu, neue Sachen in meinen Arbeiten zu entdecken und zu entwickeln. Die Aufträge meiner Kunden und was sie sich so vorstellen inspiriert mich und zeigt mir immer wieder neue Wege.

Welchen Stellenwert hat das Skizzenbuch in deinem Alltag?

Ich habe Skizzenbücher während meines Studiums geführt und seit meiner Selbstständigkeit komplett weggelassen. Meine Ideen entstehen, während ich mit den Kunden über die Aufträge spreche, und wachsen innerhalb des Arbeitsprozesses.

Welche Materialien sind für dich unverzichtbar?

Papier, Bleistift und Aquarellfarben sind für mich sehr wichtig.

Wie findet man als Illustrator seinen eigenen Stil?

Für mich war es am Anfang wichtig, viele verschiedene Materialien auszuprobieren, offen zu sein und sich auf neue Dinge einzulassen. Es dauerte auch einige Jahre, bis ich meine Handschrift und meinen eigenen Ausdruck in meinen Arbeiten gefunden habe. Seinen eigenen Stil zu finden, ist eine Reise und ein Prozess, der sich ständig ändert.

Was würdest du jungen Menschen raten, die Modeillustrator werden wollen?

Ich würde allen raten, mutig, neugierig und offen zu sein. Die meisten Anfänge sind nicht immer so geradlinig und manchmal landet man vielleicht in einem Job, den man sich so gar nicht vorgestellt hat. Aber man lernt immer dazu und kann diese Erfahrungen als Illustrator sehr gut verwenden. Man sollte sich Firmen heraussuchen, für die man gerne arbeiten möchte, und dann mit ihnen in Kontakt treten. Es ist auch wichtig, eine Webseite zu haben, auf der man die wichtigsten und stärksten Arbeiten präsentiert. Diese muss nicht sehr umfangreich sein, sondern inhaltlich genug von der/dem Illustratorin/Illustrator zeigen, so dass sich die Firmen ein klares Bild machen können und das Wichtigste über die Person erfahren. Zum Abschluss rate ich jedem, viel Ausdauer und Geduld zu haben. Am Anfang kann es passieren, dass man einige Absagen bekommt und es nicht gleich so klappt, wie man es sich vorgestellt hat. Einfach weitermachen und nicht aufgeben!

Peggy Wolf

Studium an der FH Bielefeld: 1999–2004 (Diplom)
Tätigkeit: Freiberufliche Illustratorin
Kunden: The Sanctuary (London, England), Sky Living, „Styled To Rock" mit Rihanna (London, England), Jennifer Loiselle (London, England), HomeMint, Justin Timberlake (Santa Monica, USA), UCE magazine (North Carolina, USA), Tokion Magazine (New York, USA), LOOL (Sao Paulo, Brasilien), The National (Abu Dhabi, UAE), Designer Forum (Sydney, Australien), Iben Hoj (Denmark), Glossy Box (Berlin, Deutschland), Miriam Jacks (Berlin, Deutschland)

→ ENGL: [313-314]

Zehn Fragen
an Claudia Arend

Der erste Schritt nach dem Studium, wie sah er bei dir aus?
Dazu muss ich etwas ausholen. Vor meinem Abschluss ging ich für eine Weile nach Paris, wo ich erste Erfahrungen in einem Trendbüro sammelte. Bereits zu diesem Zeitpunkt wurden meine Zeichnungen in einem Fachmagazin veröffentlicht, andere Arbeiten folgten, und kurz vor meinem Diplom wurde ich von einer Repräsentantin „gecastet". Das öffnete mir einerseits die Tür zum Beruf, ich illustrierte jedoch auch in Bereichen, die überhaupt nichts mit Mode zu tun hatten. Dennoch genoss ich auch gerade diese Vielfältigkeit. Alle diese Erfahrungen schärfen die Wahrnehmung, fließen in deinen Stil ein und machen deine Handschrift unverwechselbar.

Wie bist du an deine ersten Kontakte und Jobs gelangt?
In erster Linie durch meine Repräsentantin, aber auch durch Freunde. Im weiteren Berufsleben dann immer durch meine Arbeiten selbst.

Was inspiriert dich?
Das Leben. Mein Sohn. Also, die inspirierendsten Künstler, die ich kenne. Ich bin ein Mensch, der ständig und sehr vielschichtig wahrnehmen kann. Das ist eine Gabe, allerdings manchmal erschöpfend, wenn man nicht lernt, die Türen, wenn es angebracht ist, zu schließen. Oft brauchst du auch nur Stille, um Ideen wie einen Schluck Wasser zu schöpfen. Immer häufiger habe ich das Gefühl, alle sind zunehmend damit beschäftigt, gleichzeitig zu reden und zu tönen, um sich permanent ihres Daseins und ihrer Wichtigkeit zu vergewissern. Das ist so verzweifelt wie sinnlos. Wir werden von visuellen und akustischen Botschaften durchflutet, kaum etwas scheint noch dem Zufall überlassen zu sein. Subtiles wird selten. Stille kostbar. Es ist aber wichtig, wach und unterwegs zu sein, sowohl innerlich als auch äußerlich. Zu reisen, sich anderen Realitäten auszusetzen kann unglaublich inspirieren. Das Zentrum zu verlagern.

Wenn die Ideen ausbleiben, was tust du dagegen?
In jedem Fall auftauchen, um wieder erfrischt eintauchen zu können. Schon ein Spaziergang kann helfen. Das Laufen an sich glättet

kreisende Gedanken und bietet Inspiration in Hülle und Fülle. Ausgehen mit guten Freunden. Wenn ein Bild „auf dem falschen Weg" ist und mir der Blick versperrt, halte ich es auch vor einen Spiegel, um es neu analysieren zu können. Das hilft immer.

Wie stellt man sich einen Arbeitstag bei dir vor?
Kein Arbeitstag gleicht dem anderen. Arbeite ich frei, arbeite ich an einem Auftrag, Kommunikation braucht ihre Zeit, Büroarbeit, Arbeit mit farbverschmierten Händen im Atelier, Arbeit am Mac, das Unterrichten meiner Studentinnen und Studenten. Ich bin „Multitasker". Mein Arbeitstag bringt Kind und Familie, Illustration, freie künstlerische Arbeit und meine Professur unter einen modischen Hut. Langeweile kenne ich nicht.

Ist die Arbeit als Illustratorin weit weg von der Vorstellung, die du vorher von diesem Beruf hattest?
Ich bin eigentlich ohne diese klare Vorstellung gestartet. Dieser Beruf ist sehr vielschichtig und Illustration ein wirklich weites Feld. Ich kam ja auch nicht daher und sagte mir: „Hey, was für ein cooler Beruf, so möchte ich auch sein." Damit kommt man nicht weit. Ich bin der Meinung, dass es einen Ruf gibt, dem du folgst, weil es dein Weg ist. Oder eben nicht. Wie unglaublich schön diese „Berufung" und gleichzeitig beklemmend hart die Freiberuflichkeit sein kann, erfährt jeder selbst auf seine Art und Weise. Das musst du aushalten können. Menschen mit romantisch verklärten Vorstellungen sind hier völlig falsch.

Welchen Stellenwert hat das Skizzenbuch in deinem Alltag?
Skizzenbücher sind unentbehrlich und ich kann jedem nur empfehlen, eines zu führen. Es sollte zu einem bebilderten und beschriebenen Stück Leben werden. Zugegeben, manchmal bleiben die Seiten „... auch leer." Aber viele meiner Skizzen, die auf diesem Weg ohne Soll und Ziel entstanden, halte ich immer noch für meine schönsten. An erster Stelle hält dein Skizzenbuch Ideen und Szenen fest. Viele Erinnerungen würdest du sonst nicht mehr abrufen können. Die Verbindung zwischen Bild und Wort sowie die Vielfalt der Themen und Ideen machen ein Skizzenbuch aber auch zu einem sehr individuellen Gesamtkunstwerk.

Welche Materialien sind für dich unverzichtbar?
Das kann ich so pauschal nicht beantworten, da ich eine Vielfalt von Farben und Materialien benutze und verbinde. Gerade die Kombinationen, manchmal auch der Konflikt zwischen den Materialien erzeugt Reibung und Spannung. Du musst förmlich etwas knistern hören. Ich arbeite sehr gerne mit Ölfarbe, mit Tusche, Graphit, Stiften aller Art. Illustrator, Photoshop, Kugelschreiber, halbleere Marker und die Kamera sind auch sehr reizvolle und unverzichtbare Werkzeuge.

Wie findet man als Illustrator seinen eigenen Stil?
Mit etwas Glück findet der Stil dich. Das hat aber zu tun mit einer unverkrampften Arbeitshaltung, einer Mischung aus Sorgfalt, Sensibilität und Brutalität. Und vor allem mit Arbeit, Arbeit, Arbeit und nochmals Arbeit. Man muss lernen, die Fehler als Chance zu begrüßen. Stil befindet sich auf dem Gipfel eines Berges aus zerrissenem Papier. Wobei es ja immer weitergeht, und du nie wirklich auf einem Gipfel stehenbleibst.

Was würdest du jungen Menschen raten, die Modeillustrator werden wollen?
Glaubt an euch. Und an Schönheit.

CLAUDIA AREND

STUDIUM AN DER FH BIELEFELD: 1987–1993 (Diplom)
TÄTIGKEIT: Professorin an einer privaten Hochschule für Design, freiberufliche Illustratorin
KUNDEN: Aus den Bereichen Fashion, Magazin, Beauty, Buchverlag, Architektur, Dekostoffe, DOB-Stoffe, Papierdesign

→ ENGL: [314-315]

VERWENDETE ABKÜRZUNGEN / ABBREVIATIONS USED:

A	= AQUARELL / *watercolour*		**KB**	= KLEBEBAND / *sellotape*
AS	= AQUARELLSTIFT / *watercolour pencil*		**KL**	= KLEBER / *glue*
AC	= ACRYLFARBE / *acrylic paint*			
			L	= LACKFARBE / *lacquer*
B	= BLEISTIFT / *pencil*		**LE**	= AUF LEINWAND / *on canvas*
BF	= BAUMWOLLFADEN / *cotton thread*			
BU	= BUNTSTIFT / *coloured pencil*		**NF**	= NOPPENFOLIE / *bubble wrap*
BT	= BLINDTEXT / *filler text*		**NL**	= NAGELLACK / *nail polish*
C	= COLLAGE / *collage*		**ÖK**	= ÖLKREIDE / *oil crayon*
CR	= CREPEBAND / *masking tape*			
CM	= COPYMARKER / *marker pen*		**P**	= PLAKAFARBE / *casein paint*
CP	= CREPEPAPIER / *crepe paper*		**PH**	= PHOTOSHOP
			PK	= PASTELLKREIDE / *pastel crayon*
E	= ECOLINE			
			S	= SALZ / *salt*
F	= FILZSTIFT / *felt-tip pen*		**SD**	= SPRAYDOSE / *spray can*
FE	= FEDERN / *feathers*		**SP**	= SCHMIRGELPAPIER / *sandpaper*
FI	= FINELINER		**ST**	= STEMPEL / *stamp*
FP	= FARBIGES PAPIER / *coloured paper*			
			T	= TUSCHE / *Indian ink*
G	= GOUACHE		**TT**	= TASCHENTÜCHER / *tissues*
GR	= GRAPHITSTIFT / *graphite pencil*		**TM**	= TEXTMARKER / *highlighter pen*
GP	= GEMUSTERTES PAPIER / *patterned paper*		**TP**	= TOILETTENPAPIER / *toilet paper*
I	= ILLUSTRATOR		**W**	= WACHS / *wax*
			WFA	= WANDFARBE / *wall paint*
K	= KUGELSCHREIBER / *ballpoint pen*		**WF**	= WEISSER FILZSTIFT / *white felt-tip pen*
KA	= KAFFEE / *coffee*		**WL**	= WILDLEDER / *suede*

COVER

Front	Okan Zafrak	B, K, C
Back	Okan Zafrak	B, K, T, AC

Seite / page **INHALTSVERZEICHNIS**
Contents

2	Susanne Küstner	BU, T, FI, L
4	Dominik Plassmann	B, BU, F, FI, A, E, C
5	Andrea Scholz	B, T, AC, C, TM

GRATWANDERUNG
Balancing act

6	Susanne Küstner	BU, T, ÖK
7	Okan Zafrak	B, K, AC
7	Andrea Scholz	B, T, AC, C
8	Julien Kurtin	B, BU, A, I
9	Christin Lohmann	K, F, FI, CM, I

ERSTE SCHRITTE
First steps

14–17	Andrea Scholz	K, T, AC

BEWEGUNGSÜBUNGEN
Exercises in animation

18	Andrea Scholz	B, BU, AC, ST
18	Okan Zafrak	BU, K, G, AC, FP
19	Dominik Plassmann	FI, T, A, G
20/21	Jula Buchwitz	A, E, G, S
20/21	Susanne Kuestner	T, A, E, G, P, ÖK, PK, AC
22	Susanne Küstner	K, BU, T, A, G, C
23	Marcellina Kemper	BU, K, T, A, G, AC, C
24	Dominik Plassmann	B, A, G, AC
25	Susanne Küstner	BU, K, T, A, G, AC, LF, ÖK
26	Andrea Scholz	B, BU, K, T, A
27	Okan Zafrak	B, K, T, C, BW
28	Okan Zafrak	BU, K, AC, C
29	Okan Zafrak	BU, K, T, AC, C
30	Vera Ickler	B, BU, A, G, AC, C
31	Vera Ickler	B, BU, K, A, G, C
32	Julien Kurtin	B, BU, A, FI
33	Julien Kurtin	B, BU
34	Julien Kurtin	B, BU, FP, BT
35	Christin Lohmann	GR, BU, FI, A

DIE RICHTIGE RICHTUNG
The right direction

36	Vera Ickler	B, T, A, CR, C
37	Andrea Scholz	B, BU, AC, C, ST
38	Vera Ickler	B, A, C
39	Katja Skoppek	B, BU, A, C
40/41	Andrea Scholz	B, BU, AC, C, TM
42	Stephanie Höcker	T, A, C
43	Joanna Pertl	T, A, C

EIN EIGENER WEG
Your own way

44	Sarah Brieden	K
45	Dominik Plassmann	B, FI T
45	Dominik Plassmann	BU, K, T, A, C
46	Sara Brieden	K
47	Sara Brieden	K
48	Julien Kurtin	B, T, C
48	Susanne Küstner	BU, F, FI, T, C, FP
49	Andrea Scholz	K, AC, CR, C
50	Susanne Küstner	BU, F, FI, T, C, FP
50	Marcellina Kemper	B, BU, K, G, C
51	Marcellina Kemper	B, BU, K, G

SCHRITT FÜR SCHRITT
Step by step

52/53	Marcellina Kemper	B, K, A, I
54	Christin Lohmann	B, I
55	Suki Kim	B, PH
56	Elisabeth Grosse	B, PH
57	Elisabeth Grosse	B, PH
58	Joanna Pertl	A, C, PH
59	Joanna Pertl	A, C, PH
60	Joanna Pertl	A, C, PH
61	Marcellina Kemper	B, K, A, C, I
62	Christin Lohmann	B, I
63	Christin Lohmann	B, I
64	Christin Lohmann	B, I
65	Christin Lohmann	B, I
65	Christin Lohmann	B, I
66–69	Marcellina Kemper	FI, I

INNEHALTEN
Pausing to take stock

72	Melinda Weber	B, CM	104	Vera Ickler	B, K, A
73	Susanne Küstner	B	105	Vitalli Peters	T, A
74	Katja Skoppek	B, BU, T, C, FP	106	Christin Lohmann	BU, T, A
75	Katja Skoppek	B, BU, T, C, FP	106	Jan Müller	B, FI, A, PK, AS
76/77	Andrea Scholz	B, K, AC, CR	107	Susanne Küstner	T, A, PK
78/79	Julien Kurtin	B, BU, T, A	108	Christin Lohmann	BU, K, F, T, PK
80	Susanne Küstner	B	109	Raisa Hirsch	K, A, ÖK
81	Vera Ickler	K, A, CR	109	Susanne Küstner	T, A, PK
82	Melinda Weber	B, FI, ÖK	109	Julien Kurtin	B, A, ÖK
82	Dominik Plassmann	K, A, C, KB	109	Raisa Hirsch	K, A, ÖK
82	Dominik Plassmann	B, T, A	110	Susanne Küstner	K
83	Christin Lohmann	B	110	Susan Krug	FI
			110	Marcellina Kemper	K
			111	Marcellina Kemper	K

STOLPERN UND AUFSTEHEN
Stumbling and standing up again

			111	Susan Krug	FI
			111	Susan Krug	FI
84	Dominik Plassmann	B	111	Susanne Küstner	K
85	Stephanie Höcker	B	112	Christin Lohmann	K, F
86	Andrea Scholz	B, K, A, C	113	Susanne Küstner	B, K, F, T,
87	Suki Kim	B, T	114	Marcellina Kemper	B, T, A, G, ÖK, C
87	Susanne Küstner	BU, T	114	Marcellina Kemper	B, T, C, WF
88	Susanne Küstner	T, A	115	Andrea Scholz	B, BU, T, C
89	Julia Krisp	T, A	116	Ayse Kilic	B
89	Christin Lohmann	A	116	Stephanie Höcker	B
90	Raisa Hirsch	B	117	Ayse Killic	T, G, ÖK
91	Stephanie Höcker	B	117	Stephanie Höcker	ÖK
92/93	Sarah Brieden		118	Jan Müller	B, FI, A, AS
	und Rabia Celik	B	119	Christin Lohmann	B, BU, T, FI, A
94	Vera Ickler	T	120	Susanne Küstner	B, BU, T, A, G
94	Susanne Küstner	T	121	Dominik Plassmann	B, F, T, A
95	Dominik Plassmann	T, A	122	Julien Kurtin	B, BU, A
95	Susanne Küstner	T	123	Susann Krug	B
95	Susanne Küstner	FI	123	Patryk Sniecinski	B
95	Dominik Plassmann	T, A	124	Vitalli Peters	B, BU, T, A
95	Dominik Plassmann	T, A	124	Vera Ickler	K, A, G
95	Julien Kurtin	B, BU, A	124	Vitalli Peters	B
95	Julien Kurtin	B, BU, A	125	Dominik Plassmann	B, BU, F, FI, T, A, E, G, LF
96	Stephanie Höcker	T	126	Jan Müller	B, FI, T, A, AS
97	Stephanie Höcker	T	127	Dominik Plassmann	B, BU, F
98/99	Stephanie Höcker	T, A	128	Dominik Plassmann	B, BU, F, FI, LF
100/101	Raisa Hirsch	T, A	129	Marcellina Kemper	B, BU, K, F, A, G, ÖK, CR, WF
102	Alöna Leis	T, A			
102	Susanne Küstner	T, A	129	Andrea Scholz	B, GS, AC, CR, C, TM
103	Ayse Kilic	T, A	129	Christin Lohmann	FI, T, ÖK

SCHNURGERADE
Straight as a die

132	Tatjana v. Elverfeldt	B, BU, A, I
132	Rabia Celik / Sarah Brieden	B, F, FI, I
133	Stephanie Höcker	I

ZIELGERICHTET
Focused

134	Dominik Plassmann	B, BU
135	Sarah Brieden	K
136	Leonie Barth	T, A
136	Raisa Hirsch	T, A
136	Leonie Barth	T, A
136	Susanne Küstner	B, BU
137	Susanne Küstner	BU, T, A
138	Susanne Küstner	BU, T, A, G, ÖK, C, TT
139	Dominik Plassmann	B, BU, FI, T, A, E, AC, C, ST,
140	Lisa Dominicus	BU, FI, A, TM
141	Dominik Plassmann	BU, FI, E
142	Rabia Celik	K, T, G
143	Rabia Celik	B, G
144	Jula Buchwitz	B, BU, G
145	Vera Ickler	B, BU, K, A, G
146	Susanne Küstner	B, BU, G, PK, LF, C, FP
147	Dominik Plassmann	B, BU, A, AC, GP
148	Andrea Scholz	B, BU, T, AC, C, ST
149	Rabia Celik	K, A, C
150	Katja Skoppek	B, T, A, C
151	Okan Zafrak	BU, K, AC, C
152	Okan Zafrak	B, BU, K, T, PK, AC
153	Okan Zafrak	B, K, T, L
154	Tatjana v. Elverfeldt	BU, T, A, G
155	Tatjana v. Elverfeldt	B, BU, T, A, G
156	Dominik Plassmann	B, K, F, A, AC, ÖK
156	Dominik Plassmann	B, T
157	Dominik Plassmann	B, K, F, AC, FP
158	Dominik Plassmann	B, BU, T, G, FP
159	Dominik Plassmann	B, BU, T, G, FP

AUF DER SPITZE
To the point

160	Ayse Kilic	BU, A
160	Ayse Kilic	B, A
161	Okan Zafrak	B, BU, K, T, G
162	Dominik Plassmann	B, K, F, A, E, S
163	Dominik Plassmann	B, CM, A
164	Ayse Kilic	T, A
165	Melinda Weber	B, A
166	Dominik Plassmann	B, BU, K, F, T, A, C
167	Susanne Küstner	B, BU, K, A, G, C
168	Christin Lohmann	B, BU, K, F, FI, A, C
169	Jan Müller	B, BU, FI, T, A, PK, AS
169	Christin Lohmann	T, A, C
170	Dominik Plassmann	BU, K, T, A, AC
171	Dominik Plassmann	B, BU, K, F, A
172	Sarah Brieden	BU
173	Sarah Brieden	BU, A
174	Sarah Brieden	BU
175	Sarah Brieden	BU
176	Okan Zafrak	BU, T, C
177	Okan Zafrak	B, BU, K, ÖK, AC
178/179	Suki Kim	B, BU, T, A, KA, PH

STEINE BESEITIGEN
Removing stumbling blocks

180	Lisa Domenicus	FI, A, AC, KL
181	Andrea Scholz	AC, B, CR
182	Andrea Scholz	B, T, A
183	Andrea Scholz	K, AC

DIE GROSSE FREIHEIT
Freedom knows no bounds

184	Christin Lohmann	B, BU, FI, PK, A, FP
185	Rabia Celik	K, T
186	Vera Ickler	K, A, CM, FP
187	Vera Ickler	K, A, C
188	Elisabeth Grosse	B, PH
189	Elisabeth Grosse	B, PH
190	Suki Kim	T, A
191	Suki Kim	T, A
192	Suki Kim	T, A, G
193	Suki Kim	T, A, G
194	Andrea Scholz	B, K, T, AC
195	Susanne Küstner	BU, AC, LF
196	Marcellina Kemper	B, BU, K, FI, PK
197	Marcellina Kemper	B, BU, T, FP
198	Christin Lohmann	BU, K, F, FI
199	Lisa Dominicus	BU, T, A, AC, CR, C
200	Lisa Dominicus	BU, T, A
201	Marcellina Kemper	T, AC, WF, FP

202	DOMINIK PLASSMANN	B, BU, K, F, T, A, AC, ST
203	DOMINIK PLASSMANN	B, BU, K, FI, ÖK, A, AC, LF
204/205	OKAN ZAFRAK	B, BU, K, T, AC, WFA, LE
206	DOMINIK PLASSMANN	B, BU, K, F, A
207	DOMINIK PLASSMANN	B, BU, K, F, ÖK, A
208	DOMINIK PLASSMANN	B, BU, F
209	DOMINIK PLASSMANN	B, BU, K, F, A
210	SUSANNE KÜSTNER	K, T, A, C
211	DOMINIK PLASSMANN	B, K, F, A, AC
212/213	OKAN ZAFRAK	B, BU, K, T, AC, FP

BILDER DER MODE
Fashion images

AM ZIEL
The finishing line

224	SUKI KIM	B, PH
226	KERSTIN FIEBIG	B, T, I
227	KERSTIN FIEBIG	B, T, I
228	DOMINIK PLASSMANN	B, F, A, C
229	DOMINIK PLASSMANN	B, F, A, C
230	MARCELLINA KEMPER	B, BU, K, T, AC, C, BT
231	MARCELLINA KEMPER	B, BU, K, T, AC, C, BT
232	SUSANNE KÜSTNER	B, BU, T, AC
233	SUSANNE KÜSTNER	B, BU, T, AC
234	CHRISTIN LOHMANN	B, BU, T, A, I
235	CHRISTIN LOHMANN	B, BU, FI, C, I
236	SUKI KIM	B, PH
237	SUKI KIM	B, PH
238	JULIEN KURTIN	B, BU F, C
239	JULIEN KURTIN	B, BU, F, A, C
240	SUKI KIM	B, PH
241	SUKI KIM	B, PH
242	MARCELLINA KEMPER	B, BU, K, C, WF
243	MARCELLINA KEMPER	B, K
244	MARCELLINA KEMPER	B, BU, K, WF
244	MARCELLINA KEMPER	BU, K, AC, C
245	MARCELLINA KEMPER	B, BU, K, AC, WF
246/247	SUKI KIM	B, PH

INTERVIEW
Interview

248/249	JAN TRUSSNER	FOTO

DER GIPFEL
The summit

250	OKAN ZAFRAK	B, K, T, AC, W
251	LISA DOMINICUS	BU, FI, A, AC
253	SUSANNE KÜSTNER	BU, K, F, AC, C
254	SUSANNE KÜSTNER	BU, T, AC, C, L
255	OKAN ZAFRAK	T, AC, W
256	DOMINIK PLASSMANN	B, BU, FI, AC, KB
257	ANDREA SCHOLZ	K, T, AC, CR, WL
258	SUSANNE KÜSTNER	B, BU, K, T, G, AC
258	CHRISTIN LOHMANN	FI, T, A, PK
259	OKAN ZAFRAK	T, AC, W
260	OKAN ZAFRAK	B, K, T, AC
261	ANDREA SCHOLZ	B, K, AC, ST, TP
262	DOMINIK PLASSMANN	B, BU, FI, AC
263	DOMINIK PLASSMANN	B, BU, F, A, KB
264	CHRISTIN LOHMANN	BU, FI, T, G
265	ANDREA SCHOLZ	B, K, AC, ST, NF
266	LISA DOMINICUS	BU, FI, T, A, AC
266	OKAN ZAFRAK	B, K, T, W
267	MARCELLINA KEMPER	K, F, AC
268	CHRISTIN LOHMANN	B, K, T, A
269	MARCELLINA KEMPER	K, F, AC
270	DOMINIK PLASSMANN	B, BU, F, A, AC
270	LISA DOMINICUS	BU, K, SD
271	ANDREA SCHOLZ	B, K, AC, CR, ST
272	OKAN ZAFRAK	B, K, T, W
273	OKAN ZAFRAK	B, K, T, W
273	SUSANNE KÜSTNER	BU, T, AC, C, L
286	CHRISTINA FALKE	FOTO

ENGLISCHE ÜBERSETZUNG DER MATERIALIEN
Translation of materials

315	RABIA CELIK	T

DANK
Acknowledgements

319	MARCELLINA KEMPER	B, K, T, G, PK

WORKING LIFE   CREATION   TECHNIQUE

Introduction

[6 – 7] You can feel whether you are an illustrator or not. I believe that a (fashion) illustrator just cannot help but draw. Something calls, something just doesn't let go of you. If you are out and about, walking through town, looking out of a train window or sitting in a pub, there are motifs everywhere that you immediately wish you could realise as a drawing. The striking nose in a neighbour's profile, a dress that blows around somebody's legs, the optical foreshortening of your own leg. (A reason, by the way, why many illustrators have a sketchbook in their pocket). But there are infinitely many reasons not to listen to these prompts: 'Oh, I'm not good enough', or 'I don't know how I should do it', or 'Child, you can't make a living with that'. A shame really, as you have not even given yourself a chance before you have started.

Perhaps I might explain it in an exaggerated way: you are part of a small group of privileged people and have acquired a special talent from somewhere, one that you should make use of! An illustrator does not pursue a regular job, nobody waits for you, nobody approaches you. But still ... if you can draw, you should choose that rocky road.

Do not separate yourself from your illusions. When they are gone, you may still exist, but you have ceased to live.
Mark Twain

From my own experience, I know the feeling of pride and satisfaction when a drawing has been successful. But the way there is not always easy. I consider this book a little bit like a hike. There are flat routes, easy to handle. But there are also inclines where sometimes you'll be out of breath. Then there are moments in which you can pause a while. On the road there is a lot to see, to discover. Not every step leads the way. Road signs are missing here and there. But you must discover this road on your own and perhaps even clear some of those rocks out of the way yourself. But whenever you finally reach the summit and achieve that great freedom, you will be rewarded with pride and satisfaction.

I would like to encourage people. Fashion is fascination, cult, protection and jewellery. Fashion can be anything and far more besides. From haute couture to utilitarian clothing, we experience fashion on our own body and perceive it in the most diverse forms of advertising, on the Internet and in magazines, sophisticatedly, erotically, provocatively and super-aesthetically realised in alluring pictures.

Fashion illustration celebrated a comeback some years ago, and this is a good thing. Today the world of digital photography provides the ability to show a virtual reality that no longer has anything to do with reality. Drawing, however, is the medium par excellence in order to spread illusions. And fashion lives on illusions. A fashion illustration visualises the many faces of fashion. Thus it can be provocative or rather quiet and dreamy; it can be opulent and baroque or rather puristic.

A fashion illustration is a product of the imagination. Why? Because it provides ideals, because it is there to create desirability. Imagination, ideals and desirability are influenced by fashion and are therefore changing constantly. If you have the best fashion sketches of the past hundred years laid side by side, this change in tastes becomes obvious. And one thing is apparent: in this day and age there is no such thing as a clear trend anymore. Today the spectrum of a fashion drawing ranges from an almost naturalistic rendering to a kind of alien, extraterrestrial being. There are apparently no more golden rules (or only a few).

Then why this book, why in this form? One day, I noted that my archive of fashion sketches had adopted a considerable scale. What a pity, actually, that the works had been seen by only a few people – all those pictures with tremendous vitality. Now they are here – sorted, arranged in proper order and hence made 'visible', and furnished with small texts.

Those who look at a lot of pictures learn how to see. This book is about getting to know different styles and expressions. This book is to be stimulating and should impart a thing or two. Not with a raised forefinger but rather in a loose, informal format. The many illustrations show that there are a great number of ways to reach your goal. There is no silver bullet.

I would like to generate enthusiasm for lines, forms, colours and surfaces. A passion for an exciting approach, for eroticism. To share the passion for displaying or omitting, to rouse elation when observing unfettered imagination. But I would also like to promote understanding of the logic of shadow or layout, of the main concept or the intelligent execution of inspiration or of the consequence of communication.

There are books that teach fashion drawing from the bottom up; there are books that manage with no commentary. This book presents itself somewhere in the middle, without starting from scratch but providing valuable tips from experience. Perhaps one should consider it a walk through a museum. There is a guided tour but still it leaves enough room for your own observations and self-knowledge. This is a book using the work by students but is nevertheless of a high standard. A book for people who would like to study this subject but also suitable for those who are well advanced. Or for those who have a love for beautiful drawings. It is my wish to arouse desire and passion for a class of drawing that has long deserved closer attention.

Explaining your materials

[12 – 13] In this book I shall address the materials that are especially important for students specialising in fashion illustration. That means mainly pens and pencils and simple colouring materials. This is not the place for going into the properties of materials such as oil paints and the results that can be achieved with them. Working in oils is time consuming; you work in glazes and each layer takes several hours to dry. Fashion is high-paced and so is fashion drawing, so you work with colouring materials that dry quickly.

The following are recommended as a starter package:

- VARIOUS PENCILS IN GRADES H, HB, B TO 6B

Experience has shown that the above suffice for depicting a fairly wide range. H stands for the hardest pencil, and the lightest line is drawn with it. B stands for a soft pencil. The higher the number on the scale, the darker the line. However, you can produce an even darker line with a graphite pencil. A coloured pencil may also be used for very dark lines.

- BALLPOINT PENS
  IN VARIOUS COLOURS

You can do wonderful sketches with a ballpoint pen. The less pressure you exert, the lighter the lines. Of course what is done with a ballpoint pen cannot be erased, but this teaches you that making an occasional mistake isn't all that bad.

- COLOURED PENCILS
  (AT LEAST TWENTY-FOUR COLOURS)

These range from hard to soft. Soft coloured pencils are recommended. Both light and dark lines (depending on the pressure exerted) can be drawn with them and quite large surfaces smoothly coloured in. In addition, there are watercolour pencils. You just add some water to a line and then you can shade the colour with them.

- BLACK FELT-TIP PENS
  WITH TIPS OF VARYING THICKNESS

Very fine felt-tip pens are used for contour lines or clothing details such as quilting. Felt-tip pens with thicker tips are used to add contrast and very thick tips can be used instead of ink for quite large surfaces. Colouring a surface area with a felt-tip pen produces a more regular finish than colouring with ink does.

- FINELINER PENS
  (AT LEAST TWELVE COLOURS)

These pens are used for contour lines or details.

- OIL PASTELS
  (AT LEAST TWELVE COLOURS)

These are oily chalks that stick well to surfaces. Since it has a coarse texture, this is a material that is recommended primarily for large surfaces or large drawings. However, individual surfaces within a drawing can be worked over with oil pastels to bring out specific textures, such as leather or tweed.

- WATERCOLOURS
  (AT LEAST EIGHTEEN COLOURS)

Watercolour is a transparent paint applied in washes with a brush. The paint is always thinned with water. Experimenting with it will teach you how to estimate how much water to add. You should always work from light to dark because this paint is not opaque.

- GOUACHE COLOURS
  (AT LEAST EIGHTEEN COLOURS)

These comprise opaque paints that are diluted with water and applied with a brush. The colours are more brilliant than watercolours. White gouache is so opaque that it is ideally suited for overlaying other colours as visible highlighting.

- INDIAN INK

Deep black in colour, Indian ink can be used with a pen for drawing crisp lines. Softer lines can be laid on with a fine brush. Indian ink is also highly suitable for large surfaces. It creates a very lively surface finish with variable intensity of colour throughout. Indian ink is easy to dilute with water to produce varying shades of grey.

- COLOURED INK OR ECOLINE

This ink is diluted with a great deal of water to produce very fluid colour that looks highly transparent. The colours are brilliant.

- DIP PEN HOLDER DIP PEN NIBS OF
  TWO DIFFERENT GRADES (TIP SIZES)

You need a very pointed nib for fine lines and a somewhat wider nib for broader lines.

- A SET OF FLAT BRUSHES

To start off, all you need is a single set. They are sold in grades 2 to 14 (the higher the number, the broader the brush). Both the broad flat side of the brush and the narrow one can be used. The thin side is suitable for painting in hair, for instance. However, a large surface painted with a flat brush will tend to look rather streaky.

- ROUND BRUSHES OF VARIOUS SIZES

These brushes are better suited for quite large surfaces. A round brush takes up more paint than a flat one; this makes it easier to spread the paint and it blends better. Here, too, you can buy a set of selected brushes. Neither flat nor round brushes need be terribly expensive. You should discover the properties of the various brushes by trying them out in exercises. When you know which brushes you handle best, you can invest more money in new ones. A consultation in a specialist shop is highly recommended. There are far too many different types of brush to be able to go into all of them here.

- DRAWING PAD
  DIN A3 IVORY OR EGGSHELL PAPER

To ensure successful work you need good-quality drawing paper, at least 80 g in weight, preferably in eggshell or ivory. A drawing can easily look too hard on snow-white paper. Copy paper may only be used on occasion for preliminary sketches.

- SKETCH BOOK
  DIN A4 IVORY OR EGGSHELL PAPER

A bound sketch book is recommended. The rings holding the loose leaves together in a ring-binder tend to get in your way when you are working.

- LOOSE SHEETS
  OF WATERCOLOUR PAPER

Watercolour paper comes in three basic textures: fine, medium and coarse. You should try out all three textures to find out what suits you best. On coarse paper you can also work very well in pencil or coloured pencil, which produces great effects because the surface texture of the paper shows through.

Chalk pastels are missing from this list because I find making much use of this material old-fashioned. Finer shading or contours can also be produced with pastel coloured pencils.

You can draw anything with the materials listed above: ranging from a simple, linear styling drawing to a highly sophisticated illustration. Should you want to extend your palette range at a later date, we recommend **acrylic paint, lacquer** (also good for use in airbrushing) or **wall paint.**

Drawing techniques

[14 – 17] There are various drawing, painting and printing techniques. Here the most important ones for fashion illustrators will be explained. You should try out all the different methods to develop a feeling for the individual procedures.

■ LINES

Line is an important feature. A draughtsman's signature can often be recognised simply from his handling of line. A line can be soft, tentative with several strokes, can be clear, powerful, light or dark, irregular or drawn with a ruler. If you are doing a line drawing, your aim is of prime importance. For lively drawing, I recommend laying down contour lines that depend on light and shade. Where there is shade, you can make a line darker; where it is light, your line should also be light. You create these effects with a pencil by exerting more pressure at times and less at others.

■ HATCHING

Hatching means laying down many short parallel lines that, taken together, form a surface. This technique is used to suggest shade, a shadow. Lines are quietest when laid down in a single direction. Sometimes contrast can be created by using cross-hatching for part of a drawing. The distance between lines can vary. If you are using a surface to suggest a shadow, a surface with lines that are very close together of course looks darker than a surface on which the lines are further apart. This technique does not depend on the materials used. A combination of materials, such as hatching rendered in coloured pencil across a surface in watercolour, can be very attractive. You can also combine different colours.

■ SHADING

Using a pencil or coloured pencil, make small, circling movements with it across your paper. By not changing the pressure you exert, you create regular grey or colour surfaces without streaks. If you exert more pressure in places, a shadow is created.

■ FROTTAGE

If you lay textured paper (for example, ingrain, or wood-chip, wallpaper) or an object with relief beneath a sheet of paper and then shade the top layer with a pencil or coloured pencil, you create a pattern. You can also press a piece of crumpled paper or material into a damp colour surface. Pulling it off again creates interesting patterns.

■ WATERCOLOUR PAINTING

This classic method calls for stretching a sheet of watercolour paper as taut as possible and fastening it to a support, preferably wood, with a broad strip of paper adhesive running from top to bottom. This measure ensures that the paper does not become wavy when worked with a generous amount of water.

Now there are two different ways to set about watercolour painting. You can work 'dry', that is, paint surface areas on it directly with a brush. Using this method gives you a certain degree of control over your surfaces. If you wait patiently until a surface is dry enough, you can build up layered surfaces that are clearly demarcated. This results in a work in which the individual layers are easy to recognise. To shade a face, for instance, you can layer four or five pastel tones to create an exciting surface. What is important is to always bear in mind that you can only work from light to dark.

However, you can also work 'wet'. To do so, wet the stretched paper thoroughly all over with a sponge before painting areas of colour on it. Using this method, you have no control at all over your areas. The colours run. But that is the hallmark of this particular technique. Combining different colours and turning the paper into a mixing palette is very attractive. You will have to practise a lot to develop a feeling for the colours. Of course you can also wet individual spots which you have previously reserved.

You should always draw large, regular surfaces from top to bottom; the brush drags the water along with it. Should you happen to have too much paint on your brush, a paper handkerchief or a sheet of kitchen towel is helpful. With them you can soak up the excess on your drawing immediately. Using a spot on the margin of your drawing as a test area is recommended in any case. There you can see whether your colours have the right intensity. It is advisable to prepare a portion of paint on a plate in advance rather than using your paints straight from the tube. You should regularly change the water in a glass or jar that you have at hand, otherwise the tint it has taken on will influence the colour of your watercolour painting.

Gouache and acrylic paint are also thinned with water. However, both these paints are used primarily when you want to work in a more opaque medium than watercolour.

■ WASHING

This technique entails applying paint that has been greatly thinned with water to paper. Watercolours and acrylic paint are both suited to washing. It creates a highly transparent surface. After the paint has dried well, a second layer is applied. The first layer now shines through the second. This method can be repeated again and again to create a glossy effect.

■ SPLATTER PAINTING

Splatter painting is done by putting medium-thick paint on to a fine-screen spray diffuser and pressing it through with an old toothbrush. This method enables some degree of control. If, on the other hand, you 'fling' paint with a brush directly on to paper, you are less in control.

■ BLOW PAINTING

This is for use especially with a fluid paint such as watercolour, Indian ink or Ecoline. The paint can be blown with a straw in a specific direction to create a trickle effect.

■ DABBING

Paint can be dabbed or dotted with a dabbing brush. This is a brush with short, stout bristles. Instead of stroking the paint across the paper, you apply it in small blobs. This type of brush is also used to fill stencils with paint.

■ IMPASTO

With this technique very thick paint is applied with a putty knife or palette knife. The technique leaves visible traces of the material you have worked with. You can, however, work directly from the tube and apply the paint in a pattern.

■ MASKING

If certain parts of your paper have been masked or are covered with paper, no paint touches these reserves in your drawing. This method is used for backgrounds or patterns. The same method also works with photo glue. You 'draw' lines with the glue, then add colour over the top and finally remove the photo glue with a rubber. This technique works very well for making patterns or drawing hair.

■ INKBLOT (ROHRSCHACH)

Applying paint arbitrarily to paper and then folding the paper creates a symmetrical pattern. This sort of pattern is often suitable as an article of clothing or as a textile design. Both very fluid paints and gouache or acrylic paints are suitable for this technique.

- **THREAD DRAWING**

First you apply paint to paper. Then you dip a cotton thread at least twice as long as your paper in fluid paint such as Indian ink, Ecoline or watercolour. Lay this thread double on to your paper, fold the sheet of paper and gradually draw the thread from top to bottom. You can draw the thread either straight down or twist it with irregular movements. Thread drawing produces exciting patterns. The process can be repeated as often as desired and with all sorts of colours.

- **TONE-ON-TONE**

Tone-on-tone is a difficult technique to handle. You opt for one particular colour and different shades of it, for instance snow-white, ivory, eggshell and off-white. The surfaces needed for a figure or a portrait are selected in advance. After applying paint, you work over the drawing with transparent paint to emphasise particular places or details. You'll have to experiment to discover which shades of a colour are needed to make the representation clear.

- **COLLAGING**

To make a collage, you glue various materials together to form a new surface. Magazine photos or newspaper clippings are very suitable materials for collaging. However, there are any number of other flat materials you can use, such as Sellotape, masking tape, labels or gift-wrapping paper.

- **COMPUTER**

A computer is also an important tool for a draughtsman. Some methods of working with it are explained in a separate chapter.

- **SPECIAL TECHNIQUES**

Apart from the classic techniques of working with paint and paper, there are special techniques that are best explained conceptually.
A prime example is the cut-up technique. The works shown here are reminiscent of jigsaw puzzles with the figures rearticulated. Entirely different relevances have been elicited. Details are lost or, by contrast, now warrant particular attention.
There can be a thematic guideline for translation into drawing.

With its pixels and circuit boards, the computer can be one such source of inspiration. Figures are made to appear in a special, very modern atmosphere.
You should study art as much as you can and attend exhibitions regularly. Both past art and contemporary art provide many sources of inspiration that can enormously enrich your own work.

EXPERIMENTING WITH MATERIALS

[18 – 19] In the previous chapter the classic methods of applying colour were discussed. Nevertheless, there are numerous, very free ways of applying colour. Experimenting with all sorts of materials is great fun. In experimenting you should free yourself from the outset from inner restraints and simply try out a lot of different approaches. Experiments do not always succeed, but you will learn with time how materials behave.

Start by laying out all your drawing and painting materials and walking through your home with open eyes: What might the kitchen yield? Salt, sugar, a washing-up brush, scouring pads? In your living room you might find a radiator cover or rough-textured wallpaper, some sand in your garden. If that isn't sufficient, you can always go to a hardware store, a stationer or a paint supplier.

Now you are ready to discover what water does to watercolours, whether you add a lot or a little, whether you direct your efforts or simply let the colours run together. And what is the effect of salt when combined with watercolour? You suddenly remember how watercolours and wax crayons behaved back in your kindergarten days. Indian ink and water, Indian ink and soap, Indian ink and candlewax. Hard and soft, smooth and glossy, harsh and matt. Paint and tissue paper, paint and paper handkerchiefs, paint and Sellotape, paint and masking tape. Different layers, combinations of materials, unfamiliar work objects.
All of a sudden you are producing experimental materials, which you immediately recognise as textiles. Lovely, airy silken materials or sturdy winter tweeds. And you realise that clothing can be represented differently – bolder, more unusual. If you want to incorporate what you have learnt in a finished drawing, you can set about it in two different ways.

The first method is to work directly on paper. This calls for planning. You should think about what materials you will be working with and how the form is to be. Still it can, of course, happen that the experiment is not as successful as you had hoped. However, a few interventions might still lead to a satisfactory result. If summery textiles are your subject, you should leave some scope for air. That means empty spaces should be reserved on the surface of your paper; the colour of the paper can come into its own as a glossy section or a highlight. This won't be so necessary with a winter collection. Nonetheless, here, too, a drawing looks more playful if you do not insist on faithfully filling your contour lines with colour.

For the second method, you'll need to experiment with some preliminary sketches. Here, too, you should plan in advance. Planning in this case does not refer to form but rather to light, shade and colour gradient. These experiments are cut out and then collaged together. A great model for this exercise is THE VERY HUNGRY CATERPILLAR by ERIC CARLE.

Your background material also plays an important role in experimenting, so it can be highly enjoyable to work with unusual papers. Brown packing paper (remember it has a smooth and a matt side!), tissue paper, both smooth or crumpled, tone paper, patterned gift-wrapping paper, squared paper from a maths exercise book, grey or brown cardboard ...
There are so many things that are conducive to creating unusual effects. If you want to lay out a drawing on a coloured background, you should give lurid colours a wide berth. Neon green or dayglo pink will become the focus of all eyes and will distract from your drawing. And that is supposed to be the main focus of interest. One exception to the rule is a drawing in bold black.

COLLAGE

[36 – 37] The word 'collage' derives from the French word for pasting, sticking (coller). Making a collage entails pasting different materials together to form a new surface. Magazine photos or newspaper clippings are ideally suited to this technique. However, you can use all other flat materials you can think of, such as Sellotape, masking tape, labels or gift-wrapping paper.

Start a collection of large storage envelopes. One for red surfaces, another for green … One for hair, branches and other lines, one for pebbles, one for heaven, another for earth, one for animals, another for buildings and much, much more. Later you can do exactly the same thing on a computer.

Important: If an actual person is shown in a collage, he or she must not be recognisable. Otherwise you would find yourself in legal difficulties over personality rights. Nor should you use very well-known motifs from advertising in print. In this case, you might infringe copyright law and besides, you would be exerting far too much influence on viewers.

A collage has nothing arbitrary about it. Instead it should always have a clear alignment: horizontal, vertical or diagonal. If you are dissatisfied with a collage, what is it invariably lacks is direction! This is true both of the objects in the collage and of the colours. The progression should be understandable. In black-and-white collages light and dark determine the direction. But, as is so often the case, exceptions prove the rule. If everything is just so, things can get boring. So build in a nuisance variable! You can make a work of this kind even more interesting by alternating surfaces that have been torn as straight as possible with precisely cut-out objects or photos with drawings.

The collage technique can be put to very effective use for backgrounds. You can often attract attention to a particular detail of an article of clothing by using a simple surface. Things get very interesting when parts of the foreground and background merge.

BACKGROUNDS

[44 – 45] Most of your early drawings will be without a background. At that stage, you'll be happy if your work succeeds to any extent at all. It takes a while to develop a feeling for proportion and expression and to feel comfortable with the format of your paper, which means drawing your figure neither too large nor too small.

But you have to keep on developing and be able to give a drawing a narrative. It is an absolute must for illustrators to tell a story in their drawings, to stimulate the viewer's imagination and not just draw 'beautifully'.
That is best done by creating a space. There is a good example of simplicity and powerful expression on this page. Working at first with simple squares or rectangles is recommended.
In this form you can work in added value or an item of information. That might be a colour, words or motifs that underscore the mood.

**Important: the background must never be more important than the foreground.
Also be sure to keep your background quiet so it doesn't overwhelm the figure in the foreground. Developing a background without a fixed framework is a further step. Here you always have to keep the entire format in mind to ensure that the layout is consistent throughout. And here, too, leaving the figure or a portrait in the foreground is very important.**

Positioning a figure against different backgrounds is a great exercise for discovering how mood can change from drawing to drawing.

DRAWING ON THE COMPUTER

[52 – 53] When you have mastered drawing to some extent, it is high time to learn how to work with the computer. Nowadays you cannot do without it.

There are various software programmes that are highly suited for illustrators to work with: Photoshop (chiefly suited to image processing), InDesign (very good for combining image and text) and Adobe Illustrator (lines are smooth because pixel notches are invisible). In this chapter, two works created with Illustrator are extensively explained.
The computer is a tool like a brush or a pencil. Don't be afraid of doing something wrong with it. If something doesn't succeed at first try, you can always go back and try again. You might think at first, 'This thing isn't for me', but in this case perseverance is called for. After a practice phase, you will discover the numerous possibilities it offers and how much easier it makes everything.

For starters, a good exercise is to scan a pencil drawing, convert it via interactive tracing into a vector graphic in Illustrator and fill in the surface areas with colour. In a second phase, you should busy yourself with creating vector graphics; for example, portraying a scanned freehand sketch.
Scanned hand drawings can be configured retrospectively in all sorts of ways by vector painting. By working on the computer, you have the possibility of trying out the most diverse colourisations and effects without working on the original drawing. If you do not like a brushstroke or colour, you can you go back a step and try something new. Something you often wish you had with hand drawing!
After some intensive work on a computer it won't be long before you notice how simple interventions can make a drawing radiate a different atmosphere. Sometimes filling in the relevant textiles on a styling drawing can be very appealing; an area of colour often suffices when you are working for a trend tableau. Texts can be seamlessly inserted. Combining drawings and photos is another possibility. A drawing can be inserted in a photographic background or you can fill in a drawing yourself with photographic material.

Important: You should build up extensive archives of patterns you have developed yourself along with used effects, background material and subjects from various fields.

Illustrators who work a lot with computers are recommended to work with a drawing tablet. This makes it so much easier to create quick and precise drawings and does not tire your hand as much as working with a mouse does. A further advantage is that the stylus on the surface of the tablet reacts similarly to paper and pencil or felt-tip pen: narrower or thicker lines are created depending on the pressure exerted on the tip.

Photoshop: Editing bitmaps (pixel images), image correction and retouching, picture editing and montage, digital painting, generating collages.
InDesign: Generating layouts, preparation for printing newspapers, books, posters, etc.
Illustrator: Editing and generating vector graphics, tracing (conversion from bitmap into vectors), generating collages.

[66 – 69] All programs are able to display vector and bitmap graphics.

1. The preliminary sketches are scanned, only then placed in the Illustrator programme and then embedded. After that they are interactively traced. The next step entails thinking about the arrangement of the drawing on the sheet of paper; the individual sketches can be scaled up or down to the degree desired. Individual elements are grouped so that they do not end up lying on top of one another and separated by mistake. Working on an illustration can be simplified by processing on several levels. You do this by laying out a separate layer for each figure. A 'building plan' drawn in advance on paper is also very helpful. In it is a roughly laid out illustration of how it is supposed to look when finished – a guideline to help you keep track of what you are doing and to show you how to set about doing it.

2. In the present example, a background is laid on first. Some of the figures are filled in with white colour; the colour is removed from the others so that only the contours are visible.

3. If you made sure to close the individual surface areas while doing your preliminary drawing, you can simply add colour now with a click of the mouse. You can change the colour of the contours in the same way.

4. All-over prints can be made as follows: you compose a pattern in a rectangular box, group everything and drag and drop this box into the colour palette. Scaling the box in advance determines the size in which the pattern will ultimately appear.

5. Now the pattern can be used like any other colour. This box will be automatically repeated and sequenced within each surface area to be filled.

6. Apart from all-over prints, there is the possibility of filling surfaces with graphics, photos, etc. To do this you insert a picture in the file and overlay it with the form that is to be filled. Then you click on 'Make a clipping mask'. Here you have to ensure that the form represents a compound path and does not consist of separate elements. The 'Compound path' in the programme is in the upper toolbar under the higher-level 'Object' tab. The clipping mask is then set into the figure again with the cursor. Right clicking arranges the individual elements; that is, you can choose what is to be in the foreground and, therefore, is to overlap everything else, or choose to push individual elements step by step into the background. In the present picture, for instance, the checked clipping mask is supposed to lie below the eyes and beneath the contour. To do this, push it into the background, whereby the white colour that was there previously will be deleted, leaving only its contours.

7. Exciting effects can be created by layering several contours or also by separating a coloured surface area from its contour and laying it, slightly displaced, beneath the contour. You can play with the contour by using different brushes. It can be made to look like a pencil drawing or a watercolour. If there are not enough brushes stored in the programme library for you, you can add an individual brush yourself.

8. New levels can be added and more objects inserted at any time. The sequence of planes can be altered, with the elements of the individual layers lying one above the other as given in the planned sequence. The further up a level is in the plan, the closer the objects of this plane are in the foreground. Often it does not become apparent that something is missing or amiss in an illustration until it is nearing completion. It is only by trial and error, changing sizes and scale, adding and subtracting that you end up making the most out of any illustration.

9. Fine tuning comes at the very end. That is when details can be added to make your illustration more dynamic and exciting. To give the whole thing the look of a drawing, you choose a brush from the 'Artistic – ink' category to make blots.

SKETCH BOOK

[72 – 73] A place for ideas, something intimate, a chance to make mistakes, take stock, something familiar, an inspiration, vitally important. A sketch book should be indispensable. You might have to get used to the ritual of sketching out all your ideas, but after a while you can't do without it. An illustrator sees a thousand things in a day and you'd be surprised at how quickly we forget. Colours, combinations of materials, shapes, poses, foreshortening, a profile, an unusual hairstyle – a sketch book is in fact nothing less than a visual diary. Here you can work just for yourself, you can try things out, experiment; even 'unsuccessful' drawings have a place in it. Such drawings might even provide inspiration at a later date. No one judges or rates the contents of a sketch book; it is a space for you alone. Inspiration can be drawn from many places. Actually I know of no illustrator without a **pin board** at home. An illustrator is a collector. Postcards from an exhibition you have seen, magazine photos that are irresistible, scraps of paper because the colour is so beautiful, material with a special pattern, a quotation. Like a sketch book, a pin board is a very personal collection.

When you receive a commission, you set about it in just the same way. To be clear about the atmosphere of the assignment, you should make a portable pin board (also known as a mood board). Depafit is particularly suitable as a support material; it has a soft foam core sandwiched between cardboard. Photos, drawings and materials can be rearranged on it again and again.

FIGURE DRAWING

[84 – 87] A fashion figure embodies current trends. Today our idea of the ideal human body is a healthy and flexible body. That means: being slender. So nowadays a fashion figure is always longer and more slender than a person looks in reality.

Keen powers of observation are the most important prerequisite for good figurative fashion drawing. All too often a student starts to draw without having taken the time beforehand to look closely at the model. Drawing has a lot to do with seeing. So you have to train this. Scientists say that our eyesight is at its best by the time we are only six years old and from then on it declines. Here we are concerned not with how good or how poor our eyesight is but rather with the way we see. Children can perceive many details at once while adults are only capable of seeing one detail at a time and then the next. But you can practise. Keep looking, look long and hard, study a motif more intensively, go into it in ever more depth.

Figure drawing is the basis of fashion drawing. Not just illustrators, but designers, too, should know how a body 'functions' and how clothing relates to the body. Constant practice schools the eye, even later when you are already working in the field. Numerous details of the body greatly affect clothing. Shoulder blades, breasts, the posterior, knees, calves, muscles. There are some good anatomy books for artists. It is best to always have one at hand.

What are the various building blocks of a successful figure drawing?

■ PROPORTIONS

Proportions result from the size of the head. Based on a female figure, the length of the head in a naturalistic figure drawing is calculated on a ratio of 1:8. For a stylish figure drawing, you work with a ratio of 1:9 nowadays. This exaggerated length is drawn in the legs. Ignoring reality, you draw the lower leg just as long as the thigh. There are some physical differences between men and women, which are taken into consideration in a drawing. Women have a broader pelvis; men have broader shoulders and more prominent shoulder blades. A male figure is, ideally, somewhat taller than a woman. In reality, men's lower legs are longer in proportion to their thighs than is the case with women. In a fashion drawing, the proportions are simplified. Men's thighs and lower legs are drawn just as long as women's. The exaggerated length of the male figure is realised in the trunk. In the case of children, it is difficult to prescribe proportion and scale. The proportions of a child's figure depend heavily on the age of the child. For a child about two years old, the ratio is 1:3, but for a child about eight years old, it is 1:5.

■ DIRECTIONAL LINES

It is best to draw on a large sheet of paper. I personally prefer the A2 format. It enables you to also draw details so that they are identifiable. Draw a vertical line at the centre of the sheet of paper and subdivide it horizontally into nine areas. Some space should be left at top and bottom. The figure is drawn within those areas. This division prevents the figure from becoming either too large or too small. When you have come to grips somewhat with the lengths, all you need to do now is place a small line at the centre of the sheet of paper. It marks the middle of the body, where the hips are; it suffices entirely as a point of reference.

To check the accuracy of your drawing, you should measure it regularly.

Although the length proportions have been established, the width proportions have not. To do so, take a pencil and measure the length of your figure's head. You should always measure width proportions with one arm of the figure stretched out straight in the horizontal; this makes for equal measurements throughout. Even if that arm is only slightly bent, wrong proportions are the result. The tip of the pencil is pointed at the top end of the head; your thumb marks on the pencil the position of the chin. With this unit of measurement, the other measurements can be established in proportion, for instance, the width of the waist and the angle of the arm. Other units of measurement can also be taken; for instance, for a seated figure. The length from the shoulder to the lower edge of the surface the figure is seated on represents a unit of measurement of this kind. If the figure is seated facing to the side, this unit enables you to ascertain the distance of the knee from the body or, alternatively, with the figure in a frontal position, you can use it to measure the proportionate length of the legs.

■ POSE

It is important to learn right at the start how a model stands in pose. The simplest pose to understand is when the model's weight is evenly distributed to both legs. Then the body is standing straight as a rule. The vertical line drawn at the centre of the sheet of paper forms the alignment of the entire body and runs from the neck point (the indentation beneath the larynx) through the centre of the chest, across the navel and the crotch and forms the central axis of the space between the two feet. The body is drawn symmetrically in equal parts to the left and right of the central line. Should the model have shifted weight even slightly, however, one talks of a 'standing leg' and a 'free leg'. The standing leg bears the weight of the body; the ankle bone of that weight-bearing leg always stands beneath the neck point, thus ensuring that the model does not tip over. The free leg is the leg that bears no weight at all or virtually no weight. It is in 'free play', its movement is unrestricted and it is not needed to stabilise the pose. This has wide-reaching implications for the figure. I call these implications the accordion principle (accordion effect). An accordion functions by being compressed and expanded and that is exactly what can be observed in a body. The standing leg thrusts the hip out and compresses the torso (upper body), so to speak, on that side. On the free-leg side, the upper body is accordingly expanded in the vertical. The upper and lower body are thrown out of alignment. A diagonal line is created. If you link the hips with each other in your mind's eye, you see that very clearly.

There are several body parts that may be realigned in this way: the head, the upper body from shoulders to waist (if you look very closely, it becomes apparent that the central line from the shoulders to the breast can even run in a direction different to that of the central line from the breast to the waist), the lower body from waist to hips, the thighs, the lower legs, the feet, the upper arms, the lower arms and the hands. While still a novice at figure drawing, you should indicate the individual alignment of each body part. Later just a few directional lines will suffice.

It is very helpful to examine the relationship of certain points on the body to each other. Look, for instance, where the outermost point on the shoulder is in relation to the hips or where the feet stand if you draw an imaginary straight line from the shoulders downwards. That is how a framework is constructed in which a figure can be drawn. You should become accustomed to observing the following points in the minutes just before you start drawing: standing leg and free leg, the distance between the two legs, the outermost point of the hips in relation to the shoulders, the shoulder line, the waistline. When you have done that, you will have discovered the framework within which the figure moves.

Take a good look at the empty spaces revealed by a pose. Also the hole between the arm and the trunk or the hole between the two ankles. That is enormously helpful for understanding and capturing a figure.

- SHADING

Your first figure drawings will be merely line drawings because you won't often have time for more.
But at some point you'll speed up and will want to add value to your work.
Shading is highly suited to bringing a drawing alive and lending it a sculptural quality. It makes a figure look three-dimensional. Like a three-dimensional object, for instance a solid such as a cylinder, the human form also has curves and sides. This can be emphasised by the addition of dark places. As in reality, a shadow should be drawn running continuously from top to bottom. Nothing is more unsettling than a shadow that begins to the side of the head, is suddenly interrupted at the arms and trunk, starts again unexpectedly at the hips, only to vanish at the shoes.

If you are not too sure about the light conditions, you should imagine making use of a powerful lamp. All parts of the figure turned towards this lamp would be light and all parts turned away from it would be in shade. Don't forget that even 'voluminous' body parts, such as a calf or a breast, catch the light.

There are numerous gradations of shading. For a fashion drawing, the shading should be simplified and no more than three to five gradations should be taken into account. Very fine results can be achieved by layering watercolour in different colours. If you want to work in a linear style, you can suggest shading by making the contour line thicker in the relevant places.

- CONTRASTS

If the colour intensity of a drawing is the same throughout, the drawing lacks tension. This is particularly true of black-and-white work. You can resolve the problem by deliberately creating contrasts. There are numerous possibilities for working with rich contrasts. You might opt for keeping your drawing linear but treating a pullover as a surface. Or you can sketch the body in simple lines and work out the head in detail. There should always be a point in a drawing that attracts the viewer's gaze.

- DETAILS

If a figure drawing is too detailed, it can easily become too naturalistic. A fashion illustrator should opt for just a few specific details. That might be the head or a particularly lovely scarf. Even boots or trainers can be exciting if all details are visible.

Should you be unsure whether a drawing is a success or not, there are several ways of checking this. You can hang your drawing on the wall and leave the room. Wash up or go shopping. When you return after a break, your eye is 'fresh' and you will soon discover possible mistakes. You can also outsmart your own brain by either turning your drawing 180° or holding it up to a mirror. It is astonishing how rapidly you spot your mistakes by seeing them 'with different eyes'.

A figure drawing for fashion has something unnatural about it. The figure is too long and too slender. Many students have to get used to this when drawing and would prefer not to have to get to like this kind of realisation. However, my standpoint is that you should be able to represent the current ideal of beauty. Later you will have time to develop your own figure style. Beauty is perceived to lie in symmetry and just proportion. However, a fashion drawing is particularly in danger of being perceived as 'too smooth'. To avoid just that, I recommend deliberately building in a bit of asymmetry or disharmony. After all, the viewer's eye is supposed to be caught and this is how it can be done.
Sexuality and eroticism play a big role in fashion illustration.
What this is supposed to look like varies from case to case. It might be a sinuous pose, the intensity of a single colour or the fantastic line of a breast. A fashion drawing is a visualisation of our lusts and dreams.

[88 – 89] To capture a figure, you should do nothing but silhouettes in watercolours at first. That is how you learn to find out what pose is, and you have to concentrate on the essential features. Remember that exaggeration is called for: a fashion drawing heightens reality. You should do your first drawings in a single colour. Later you can use a second or even third colour.
A silhouette can be an autonomous work in its own right, particularly after you have learnt to leave out one thing or another. Mats Gustafson is a past master at this technique.

[94 – 95] There are people who keep erasing while they are drawing. They never achieve the perfect line. To overcome this tendency to nagging perfectionism, choose a material that cannot be erased so easily. A great material to use, with either a pen or a pencil, or even a ballpoint pen, is Indian ink. You may make mistakes or the results may not be as planned. That is part of any work in art. You should keep on trying again and again; at some point you'll be doing good drawings.

[102 – 103] With time you become less dependent on the model. Of course you have to look at the model to see how clothing relates to the body, but face, hair and make-up are of secondary importance. Now you are ready to develop a type of your own.

[106 – 107] Sometimes it is exciting to leave out some surfaces or lines. You should, however, be critical and not omit something essential. The viewer's mind must be able to recognise what elements are missing and add them to complete the picture.

[108 – 109] Combinations of materials make for exciting effects. In these examples, watercolours or Indian ink combined with oil pastel crayons ensure an interesting texture.

[110 – 111] Be sure not to drive on autopilot while drawing. That is what I call no longer really looking at what is in front of you and simply drawing what you always draw. High time to force yourself to change! A good exercise that produces surprising results is drawing without once putting down your pen or pencil. Often this helps you to discover elements that can be purposefully deployed in other drawings.

[112 – 113] Another way of developing further is to colour in particular areas or add detail.

[116 – 117] Some examples of various ways to transform a photo. It is important to develop your own signature. This should not, however, mean being so easily satisfied that you are not willing to try out new styles. This quest and experimentation should accompany you all your life.

[118–119] When causing several figures to overlap, it is especially important to use clear line. Add colour areas for emphasis and to ensure that your drawing is quiet. MOLLY GRAD is an expert at this, by the way.

[122–123] It isn't always the perfect models who are the most fun to draw. Quite the contrary, you can pick up on unexpected 'imperfections' and exaggerate them to give your figure character. Plump models are fantastic; their forms are marvellous for drawing so you can really go all out.

[126–127] Full-figured women are portrayed as cross-dressers or are suitable for voluptuous styling drawings.

[128–129] A model dressed as a clown.

WORKSHOP DRAWINGS

[130–131] Workshop drawings are the blueprints for an article of clothing. Using these drawings, the pattern maker at a fashion house can translate designs into a pattern. What counts most with this type of drawing is not creativity but rather a high degree of concentration and precision. Every line is taken over as it was drawn. If you are not accurate and draw a collar, for instance, which is pointed on one side and slightly rounded on the other, the pattern maker will make an asymmetrical collar. That may not have been intentional; you just weren't as meticulous as you should have been with your drawing.

To develop a feel for the proportions of an article of clothing, you should choose a favourite of your own and lay it out flat on a table. Try to lay it out as symmetrically as possible. If it has sleeves, they should be laid at an angle across the garment. Trouser legs should also be arranged obliquely. This way you can see more easily how low the armhole is or how low it is in the crotch. Taking a simple knee-length, straight-cut coat, go through the following steps:

First, draw a vertical line at the centre of the paper. Then add a horizontal line to mark the highest point of the shoulders. Then determine the length by establishing a measurement to scale for the distance between shoulders and breast, for instance 4 cm. Place another horizontal line at this point. After another 4 cm, you draw a horizontal line to indicate the waist, 4 cm below it a line to indicate the hip line and 8 cm below that the hemline. Now you have the top and bottom edges of your garment.

You have not yet established the width measurements to scale. These measurements depend very much on the model to be cut. Starting with the width of the shoulder, however, gives you a first point of reference. To do this, you must observe exactly how the hole for the neck is to look. It is particularly important to draw this part not just in the shape desired but also in the correct proportions. Then you draw the length and slope of the shoulders. The beginning is the hole for the neck. The next thing to do is to have a look at the armhole, how deep, how round and how wide it is to be. Then you draw a vertical line from the outermost tip of the shoulder to establish the width. Then you draw the curve of the armhole. The armhole is often somewhat wider than the width of the shoulders. If a coat is what you are working on, the sides can now be drawn to the hipline with a slight inward curve for the waistline. Extend the side line straight downwards from hipline to hemline. Now establish the length of the sleeves by observing how great the difference is between the end of the coat and the end of the sleeves. You should also take a look at how the top of the sleeve is shaped. Is there a noticeable curve or is it rather flat? The width of the cuff provides another measurement.

Now you are ready to draw the shape. The external scaffolding of the garment is in place. Now tend to the details. A simple coat fastens with buttons. Buttons are always in the middle. Establish the number of buttons and the distance between them and draw them along the centre line. While you are working, you will discover that the front ends a few centimetres away from the centre line. That is called the front-panel overlap. It is important for making buttonholes. A button always slips towards the end of the buttonhole so you should also draw this in correctly. The first button is placed just below the collar. If the coat has notched lapels (as a coat or jacket normally tends to have), first establish the depth of the hole for the neck, then the width of the upper lapel, followed by the width of the lower lapel. Then take a look at the upper and lower points of the lapel. A lapel collar has what is called a reverse seam (the seam linking the two parts of the lapel). Be sure you note exactly how this runs. Now draw the collar. The buttons are then drawn in at regular intervals. There is usually a button at breast level and a button at waist level. If there are seams, pocket flaps, bar pockets or special quilting, these features must be drawn in now.

The same procedure is repeated for the back view. For the sake of clarity, I recommend always drawing the front view on the left and the back view next to it on the right on a slightly smaller scale. If there are invisible details, such as a zip beneath a pocket flap, you should make a detail drawing of this. In this case, the flap would be drawn turned up to show part of the zip.

Workshop drawings are line drawings. Use a felt-tip pen for the outer contour and seams and a fineliner pen for quilting. I recommend drawing quilting as an unperforated line. If a line of this kind is perforated, the quilting looks proportionately much larger than it is in reality. It is easy to show the difference between seams and quilting by using lines of different thickness. It is permissible for a workshop drawing to show very slight movement in the way back or side pleats are handled. You can also make use of colour by colouring surfaces or using coloured contour lines. Patterns are not usually drawn in: the cut of an article of clothing is not changed by colour or patterning. If a workshop drawing is also to be used as a presentation drawing, you are allowed to draw in the patterns on the cloth.

After you have drawn various articles of clothing and can master your material, it is best to do your workshop drawings with Illustrator software.

Creating workshop drawings always entails being in personal contact with a pattern maker. You have to inform the pattern maker of the measurements of an article of clothing in advance, for instance. Should that not be possible, you then work with **technical drawings.**

Articles of clothing are always drawn flat in a technical drawing. They have no colour or back and side pleats. Unlike a workshop drawing, measurements are given at every important point. For instance, the length of the arms is given, as are the length of the trunk, the width of the seam, the distance between the buttons and much more besides. Technical drawings are part of a production card that not only lists all details in writing but also includes data on the thread with which the article of clothing is to be sewn and on the lining. Production cards can differ slightly from company to company but the type of drawing as a rule does not.

Heads

[134 - 135] In a fashion drawing the head is the visiting card. The individual elements – eyes, eyebrows, nose, mouth, ears and hair – all tell a story. If the story is coherent, the viewer knows immediately what atmosphere is to be conveyed. This is particularly important for conveying the intention behind the clothing shown. To take one example, if you are drawing a sportswear collection but draw the heads in a romantic style, the message is not clear. Clarity on what you as an illustrator would like to communicate is the First Commandment!

Hardly anyone has a symmetrical face. Nevertheless, many illustrators doggedly persist in drawing perfectly symmetrical faces as soon as they have to do a fashion drawing. I find the results of their efforts quite dull.
A simple exercise for schooling your eye is look-ing at black-and-white photos. If the (fashion) photographer has not completely blotted out the face, you will discover that shadows are never identical. That should definitely be taken into account when drawing. And, while we are at it: shading on a face consists of blotches that are interlinked. Discover how exciting it can be when, for instance, the shadows of the nose and eyes blend into one another. But also bear in mind that the blotches are different on the left-hand side of the face to those on the right-hand side.

Noses: no wall sockets, no pigs.
Eyes: reduce eyelashes to a single stroke. You can't draw in every eyelash separately when a head is only 3 cm high.

Facial shading consists of many different nuances. It is a good idea to reduce them to three or four gradations at most. If you are drawing a face in colour, the colour of the paper represents the lightest gradation. If someone is wearing a red or green sweater, the colour is reflected on their face. You should definitely include this in your drawing. That will give it a distinctive touch.

The individual elements of a face offer the possibility of giving character to it. Sometimes all you need to do is add a little bump to a nose or make the ears stand out a bit. The main thing to remember is to design a portrait in such a way that it arrests the viewer's eye. You can also create good effects by emphasising a single element. In any case, avoid 'driving on automatic pilot' when drawing. That's what I call neglecting to observe a face really closely and instead just constantly repeating the same scheme.

Before starting to draw a face, either from the model or from a photo, you should screw up your eyes and look at your model through your eyelashes. All details disappear and you spot the main features at once. In a fashion portrait, it is important to pick one element of a face and emphasise it.

Trying out ways of changing the atmosphere of a face by varying your materials is a great exercise. It makes a great deal of difference whether a portrait is drawn only to the shoulder or is waist length. The latter type provides an opportunity for telling a bit more of a story. Backgrounds, of course, also play a major role. But be sure that the face remains the most important element in your drawing.
Hair should be drawn with great care. I often see drawings in which the face has been drawn with concentration but does not make an impact because the hair is an undefined blob.

Hair: neither a floor mop nor a silly headscarf.

Drawing all the hairs you can distinguish in a black-and-white photo is a good exercise. That takes patience but you discover how important the external form and the alignment of the hairs are. Later you can practise reducing the same hairstyle more and more to find out just how omission works. Incidentally, Laura Laine is an expert in drawing fantastic hair.
If you don't want to draw in each individual hair but prefer to work with surfaces, you should take a close look at the light and dark parts. Here, too, you'll notice immediately that there is no symmetry. The lightest colour is the colour of your paper; the other surfaces consist of three gradations at most. To bring the individual surfaces together, draw a few individual locks of hair.

Of course, there are other possibilities for representing hair: for instance, a cut-out or simply a contour.

You can create very good effects by working with a dry brush and watercolours that have been only minimally moistened. And don't throw away that big, old, seemingly empty Edding pen. It will still contain a drop of ink, which will be great for drawing marvellous hair.

To sum up: a face should have a distinctive expression, be it aggressive, dreamy, cool or extravagant. It should captivate the viewer and make the atmosphere of a drawing unequivocally clear.

[138 - 139] Another exercise for discovering how important it is not to simply draw without giving a thought to what you are doing. You can influence atmosphere enormously by using different materials or colours.

[152 - 153] Knowing your way around in current fashion trends is vitally important. Nonetheless, it can be fun on occasion to defy the prevailing ideal of beauty and develop a type of your own. These heads are inspired by the United Kingdom's Queen Elizabeth I. Beauty and ugliness are closely related. Both can be moving.

Styling drawings

[160 - 161] I am sometimes asked, 'What precisely is the difference between a styling drawing and an illustration?' There is no clear answer because the boundaries between the two are often blurred. Roughly speaking, a styling drawing must make clothing recognisable but an illustration need not do so.

There are two types of styling drawings. The first is done when a collection has been finished. These drawings are often used in production so they must be executed absolutely flawlessly. Drawings of this kind always represent reduction, the concentration on essentials. This applies to the pose: it should be simple and drawn both frontally and from the rear. The same holds for hairstyle and make-up: both should be very reticent. Forms must be represented with absolute accuracy. The proportions within an article of clothing must be meticulously translated to scale. The viewer must be able to tell what material has been used to make an article of clothing. Even when it is merely a line drawing. In this case, colour and patterns are not drawn in; they do not affect the overall design and cut. In a styling drawing, all details must be recognisable: How long is the article of clothing? How wide? What sort of pockets does it have? What does the collar look like? Does the article of clothing have four or six buttons? Are they concealed or not? Does it have pleats and, if it does, what kind of pleats? Creases, inverted pleats, box pleats, turned leftward or rightward? Or is it merely gathered? Every button, the width of each hem, must correspond to reality. Drawings of this kind also serve as quality-control checklists for articles of apparel once they have been produced.

The second type of styling drawing is also known as drawing trend lines. These drawings are meant for designers and provide them with information on the look of upcoming trends. Here what matter most are atmosphere, silhouettes, colours and materials. Atmosphere is expressed in attitude but the pose definitely must match the mood of an article of clothing. So no introverted poses if sporty clothing is concerned, similarly no extroverted attitudes if clothing is classic and understated. Silhouettes should be exaggerated in drawings to bring out a look clearly. Colours should for the most part correspond to reality. Nonetheless, you are permitted a certain degree of artistic licence, although an article of apparel must not appear brown when it is really black. Representing the tactile qualities of textiles is particularly challenging. (You should once again think about experiments with materials.) Here you definitely have to draw pre-existing patterns. Information on details is also of major importance here. Accessories, if present, should be carefully drawn. They provide important information on the look desired. Artistic licence is permissible with facial features and expression, with hair and make-up especially. Styling drawings like these are also used as advertising material by fashion firms (here you must be clearly aware of the target clientele and match the type accordingly) or as explanatory drawings in fashion magazines (here artistic licence knows virtually no bounds). Then there might also be a background to underscore the statement made by the article of clothing or the type.

Creativity

[180 – 183] Creativity defies labelling, is incalculable. There is no formula for it. Creativity is a package. We are given it at birth. One person will open his or hers; another ignores it. Some are overjoyed and play with it all their lives; others don't really know what to do with it.
You need curiosity, open-mindedness, tolerance. Don't be afraid of making mistakes. Or of trying out new things. Don't give up if something doesn't work out straight off. Question well-tried solutions. Transgress borders. Go ways that no one may ever have gone before.

Creativity is a sensitive thing. It is easily distracted, and if someone closes in on it, it is quick to retreat. Nor does it like to be laughed it; it is virtually defenceless. It is, after all, not measurable; there is no formula for it.
Sometimes it needs frantic activity, tension and drama. Sometimes it needs quiet, profound stillness and a great deal of room. Creativity needs space. But how can you measure how much space creativity needs? And what does this space look like? Is it an interior or an exterior space?
Oh, just let it be, creativity. 'Trust' is the key word. Only then can you take untrodden paths. Only then can you seek. Go left at times, go right at others. And when the road gets bumpy, just keep on going. Remove the stumbling blocks or simply go round them. That is what a creative person is like; you know no other way.

Before you are written off as a harmless eccentric, you should learn how not to drown in your own creativity. This process of learning how to swim is perhaps the only thing you can work on. There are many studies dealing with whether creativity can be learnt or not. Scientists do not agree on this.
As someone with a gift for inventiveness, the creative person should be distinguished by sensitivity to problems, inventiveness, flexibility and originality. A creative person should be curious, willing to think independently and capable of looking in different directions at once. He or she should combine things that actually do not fit together. They should defamiliarise what is familiar.
They should never take anything for granted. They should have the courage to resist prevailing norms and not accept established opinion. They should not shy away from conflicts and should also be able to overcome frustration. They should put out the inner Black Dog day after day, never give up, keep going, without stagnating or becoming fixated. They should be self-critical, not easily satisfied.
That takes hard work. It's as if you were swimming in a vast sea. The waves are beyond your control. Sometimes they even threaten to wash over you or drag you down into the depths. So learn how to swim.

In my experience, this is the most important thing: throwing away lifebelts, cautiously learning how to keep your head above water.
As a university teacher, all I can do is try to elicit by hook or by crook what is already there and hope that students will accept me as a swimming instructor, that we can swim a length together.
The first exercise on receiving an assignment is: 'Tell me what your gut feeling is. Try to describe your gut feeling'. In fact, allowing others to participate in the creative process or convincing them of an idea is premised on communication. When you have finished this first exercise, that means, embedded it in a societal, cultural and historical context and then completed it with your own approach to a solution, you have a concept. And you already know in what direction you are able to swim.

The second exercise deals with 'how to'. After a phase in which your imagination is boundless and teeming with ideas, my question is: 'What would happen if you took a step back? What is good and what is bad?' This detachment is necessary, not just for questioning ideas self-critically and checking whether originality is present but also for checking whether the orientation is still there.

The last exercise is metamorphosis. My question is: 'How will your idea become a product; what requirements must you meet?' In this phase, especially, it is of vital importance to concentrate once again where you are going, learn techniques or get help from third parties who master them. Now you can swim in perfect form.

My thesis is as follows:
Creativity cannot be taught nor can it be learnt. But it can be fostered or hindered.

Illustrations

[185] Apart from the items of information that a fashion drawing is supposed to convey, it is mainly expected to showcase a silhouette and details. Here the illustrator has virtually unlimited freedom. He or she can convey a personal take on things, work out a personal approach and thus develop a signature. On the other hand, I cannot emphasise it enough: you mustn't stand still. Fashion trends are constantly changing so an illustrator must avoid falling asleep on the job and being content with the momentary status quo.

You should look at as many fashion illustrations as possible. Linger over details, analyse what materials have been used, delve into what the signature features of a particular illustrator are.
Sometimes it's even a good idea to copy an illustrator just to hone your eye and get a feel for the work in your own hands. Your hand will do the rest.

At some point, however, enough is enough. By then you will have experimented and copied sufficiently. You have developed your own signature even though it should remain flexible and never be viewed as conclusive.

Illustration is the most free form of fashion drawing. Here atmosphere rather than details is what makes an article of clothing recognisable. It is up to you to decide what is most important – the silhouette, the colour, the look or perhaps the wearer. An illustration can be realised in infinite ways. There are really no rules because what come into play here are your own imagination, your own creativity and your own standards.

It isn't a matter of perfectly representing reality; it's all about capturing the essence. Don't lose sight of what you are really after. The atmosphere of a garment remains the most important thing. However, what is at stake is not so much imparting commercial information as enabling viewers to identify with a particular statement, awakening their dreams and desires.

Fashion images. Some observations

Anna Zika
For Lisa

[215–221] *Now he knows as well as I do that true fashion plates are less concerned about whether their journal is written in the Greek or Hebrew languages and that the copperplates are their chief concern.* [1]

In 1972 my godmother gave me a book for Christmas. It would be a year before I went to school and I could not even read. So I studied the pictures in that book all the more intensively. The book was called DIE MODE and was written by JAMES LAVER. It set me on course for my professional life. And still guides it.

As a child, I dreamed of becoming a 'fashion illustrator'. Representing fashions, bringing them to life in drawings, was more important than 'creating' fashions ('makers' of fashion were still termed 'fashion designers' in those days). Now I neither represent nor create fashion. But I have studied the history of fashion in depth to arrive at the following conclusion: the history of fashion is primarily a history of how it has been imaged.

The French word for fashion, *la mode*, in German Mode, has been used in the present meaning of the term since the seventeenth century. Derived from Latin *modus* (meaning 'manner or fashion in which') the term *la mode* covers the entire gamut of external appearance: from clothing and hairstyle through posture, manners, table manners and dancing to interior decoration and manners of locomotion (as in sport). The essential thing is that the range outlined above is subject to cyclical change. Change is what differentiates fashion from costume or custom. The causes of this change may vary – the whimsies of capricious princes or celebrities that inspire emulation or economic interests (such as those of individual businesses) or political regimes (think of 'Nazi chic') – are often irrational and may seem surprising. We are indebted to the fashion media, especially the print media in the form of fashion magazines, for enabling us to keep up with the constant changes in fashion.

Their earliest predecessors appeared in the seventeenth century. However, MERCURE GALANT (from 1724 MERCURE DE FRANCE), which reported *inter alia* on changes in fashions at the court of Versailles, had virtually no illustrations or only very few.

The earliest *illustrated* journals devoted to fashion appeared in print in the last quarter of the eighteenth century: GALÉRIE DES MODES, for one, consisted entirely of illustrations while CABINET DES MODES, which was renamed several times, was ultimately the closest to what we view as a fashion magazine today: every ten days it furnished readers 'precisely and promptly' with updates on 'new clothes & trimming for both sexes, new furniture, new objets d'art, interior decoration, new carriage models, trinkets, gold jewellery and in general everything that the prevailing fashion had to offer in the way of uniquely gratifying and interesting information in all areas.' [2] Each issue comprised eight pages in octavo format, with a supplement consisting of three hand-tinted copperplates. They usually featured a lady's dress, a gentleman's suit – or, more rarely, children's clothing – and two or three new hairstyles. Sometimes the third plate was reserved for representing furnishings and appointments, including elegant beds, clocks, table decorations and the like.

Those meticulously hand-tinted engravings are of a graphic quality that still must be regarded as exceptional: the figures depicted were given essentially individual, portraitlike features. Most of them are shown standing solemnly on a floor that is merely suggested by shadowy surfaces. Representation of backgrounds or all suggestion of an interior setting was eschewed even though the ladies and gentlemen depicted look almost 'lifelike'. This, then, is the origin of the type that persisted in fashion illustration on into the early twentieth century: they presented clothing, which was the focus of attention, on full-length figures depicted in frontal view. Extensive descriptions accompanying the copperplate supplements made men and women readers familiar with a wealth of technical terms for accessories, materials and colours.

The graphic style was immediately imitated, even outside France. A German journal, JOURNAL DES LUXUS UND DER MODEN (1786–1827), which was brought out by the Bertuch publishing dynasty in Weimar, resorted particularly frequently to borrowing illustration material from CABINET, which was often only slightly changed by the talented draughtsman GEORG MELCHIOR KRAUS (1737–1806). Kraus was one of the first distinguished fashion illustrators in the German-speaking countries – and among the best because his illustrations 'are almost all characterised by enchanting delicacy of form and loving treatment lavished on fashion details, such as ruffles, pleats, lace, bows, etc. and unusually careful highlighting. Even jewellery worn by his figures and minute polychrome patterns dotted on textiles stand out.'[3]

The manner of representing fashionable clothing in plates hardly changed at all over the course of the nineteenth century: no matter whether we open LE PETIT COURRIER DES DAMES, GALLERY OF FASHION, LADIES' MAGAZINE or ZEITUNG FÜR DIE ELEGANTE WELT – we almost invariably see ladies and/or gentlemen depicted standing in surroundings that are only minimally suggested. Occasionally a scaled-down reproduction of a model is depicted from behind to showcase an outfit in rear view as well. The fashion journal LA MODE (1829–1854; 1856–1862 as LA MODE NOUVELLE) employed PAUL GAVARNI (1804–1866), a brilliant draughtsman who had also distinguished himself as a satirist and caricaturist – after all, extreme elements of clothing, such as the crinoline or mutton-chop sleeves, the bustle or even the cloche hat, tended to be such ludicrously exaggerated forms that they verged on caricature. Gavarni's fashion plates feature ladies chatting while strolling on promenades, mothers and daughters engaged in needlework or young women leafing through their voluminous correspondence. The leading chronicler of the Second Empire age of the crinoline did not, on the other hand, work for any fashion journals: CONSTANTIN GUYS (1802–1892), lauded by CHARLES BAUDELAIRE as *the painter of modern life* (1863),[4] produced a great many drawings in which he lavished the same interest on *premières dames du monde* as he did on frivolous flirts in their rustling dresses at balls and in the Bois de Boulogne, in carriages or dining exclusively in a separate dining-room: 'Ladies and fashion belonged together in imagery whose primary function was to affirm and stimulate the masculine imagination'.[5] Guys's drawings in turn had an effect on fashions, whose protagonists came to take things more casually as the nineteenth century progressed, and provide some insights into how their real-life settings were staged (interiors or boulevards): here a little table, there a balustrade or lantern marked private, or public spaces, invariably retaining an air of elegance.

Developments in printing technology finally made it possible to insert fashion illustrations in the form of inexpensive wood engravings into the print space of newspapers – from then on it was no longer necessary to present an illustration as a supplementary page. That put an end, at least temporarily, to the primacy of those choice hand-tinted little works of art that were already hot collector's items in their heyday. From about 1850 the magazine market was dominated by cheap publications of mediocre quality, whose main selling point consisted in detachable pages of dressmaking patterns.

It was not until about 1910, with the emergence of extravagant bespoke haute couture represented in France by names such as PAUL POIRET and the achievements of the Wiener Werkstätte in the German-speaking countries that an artistic, indeed avant-garde take on fashion imaging was revived. From 1912 LUCIEN VOGEL was the visionary general editor of the GAZETTE DU BON TON, for which he hired the leading masters of their craft to publish the drawings they executed on hand-milled paper. Their approaches to draughtsmanship varied widely: GEORGES LEPAPE focused on fashion colours in brilliant tints, FRANCISCO JAVIER GOSÉ lent his figures a touch of the louche allure radiated by sultry silent-film divas and LOUIS-MAURICE BOUTET DE MONVEL told little stories in the *ligne claire style* favoured by cartoonists – every plate of his in the GAZETTE seems an elaboration of the tales told in gracefully poetic accompanying captions. No wonder CONDÉ NAST tried to headhunt such talent for VOGUE, their flagship publication. Nor was the competition in Germany slow off the mark: in 1915 Inter Arma-Verlag, a Berlin publishing house, launched KLEIDERKASTEN – unfortunately, only two issues saw the light of day. EMIL ORLIK, JULIUS KLINGER and ANNI OFFTERDINGER were among the graphic artists who guaranteed the quality of its illustrations. Like their French colleagues on the GAZETTE, they would frame their illustrations, which often look as if freshly sketched, in hand-drawn passe-partouts, comp-lemented by narrative titles: 'What jewels should I choose?' or 'Papa, a letter from the front!' – the dark blue afternoon dress was drawn in ink by LUDWIG KAINER, who had previously worked for the BALLET RUSSES as a set and costume designer. Thanks to such employment, which required of its practitioners the ability to design creatively while working independently and to realise designs thus produced with consummate craftsmanship, a man like KAINER had received the perfect professional training for fashion illustration. ALBERT REIMANN, head of a respected decorative and applied arts school in Berlin, had offered instruction in fashion design and illustration since 1910. His curricular concept, which advocated linking the two- and three-dimensional aspects of design, seems timeless: 'If an artist learns dressmaking and a tailor learns to draw, both will develop so much knowledge of each other's work that they can collaborate successfully.'[6] By about 1920 so many young women had already been students at the Reimann School that a dazzling array of superbly qualified women fashion illustrators became available. Some of them, including STEFFIE NATHAN and LIESELOTTE FRIEDLAENDER, worked for

STYL, an ultra-exclusive magazine published in Berlin between 1922 and 1924.[7] Like the GAZETTE DU BON TON, it featured high-quality hand-tinted fashion plates: they staged the little events of a carefree lifestyle devoted to beautiful and pleasing things. The mature and curvaceous feminine type favoured in the belle époque seems to have gradually grown younger, only to be ultimately displaced by the vivacious flapper. And since the ideal 1920s figure was very slender, the editors were only too happy to eschew showing upmarket fashion on real bodies. Those were the years that saw the emergence of photography as a medium for fashion illustration. However, immaculately made-up professional fashion models who could pose perfectly had yet to appear on the scene. Fashion photography did not attain a first aesthetic zenith until about 1930, but from then on it would gradually supplant the hand-drawn fashion illustration. For the time being, however, artists such as ERTÉ (real name ROMAIN DE TIRTOFF) dominated the fashion scene: his artificial figures look daemonic, medusas that seem to have been petrified in geometric poses matched by the cool art deco jewellery they are wearing on their heads and around their necks and wrists. Even as ADOLF LOOS was condemning ornament as 'a crime', ERTÉ continued to stylise female bodies into deco-rative arabesques as if he were intoning a mannered, morbid swansong to the declining era of sumptuous elegance.

The years before the First World War and between 1910 and 1930 saw the fashion drawing rise to the status of artwork in its own right. Even earlier, in the eighteenth and nineteenth centuries, fashion journals had been bought chiefly for their (few and far between) illustrations. Fashion copperplates were sometimes kept and even framed and hung on the wall. However, they hardly ever revealed a recognisable individual stylistic signature, let alone bore an appended artist's name. Their decorative function in middle-class sitting rooms and girls' bedrooms notwithstanding, historic fashion images were primarily commercial art: they were supposed to inspire the men and women who saw them to dress well in public and, moreover, to develop their personal taste. Dressmakers and tailors used them more or less as patterns for developing clothing and accessories: 'The fashion illustration is an all too short-lived work. If it is not put to use at once by virtue of having a dress made after it or by being reproduced in a magazine, it is obsolete in only a few months' time; the effort that went into making it was labour in vain,'[8] as ALBERT REIMANN summed it up retrospectively in 1918. In the twentieth century, on the other hand, fashion design was no longer the preserve of individual small businesses but had grown into a powerful industry that represented a major economic sector and, moreover, a 'world cultural mission', as PETER JESSEN, general editor of STYL, had already observed in 1916 in the publication MITTEILUNGEN DES VERBANDES DER DEUTSCHEN MODENINDUSTRIE.

Exponents of the fine arts inspired fashion and in turn drew inspiration from it. A prime example is the famous collaboration in the 1930s between the painter SALVADOR DALÍ and the fashion designer ELSA SCHIAPARELLI. The illustrations for Schiaparelli's creations were often the work of CHRISTIAN BÉRARD, who captured the quintessence of fashion in his abstract graphics.

The work that RENÉ GRUAU (born RENATO ZAVAGLI RICCIARDELLI DELLE CAMINATE, 1909–2004) produced as a fashion illustrator was even more highly stylised: his style of draughtsmanship epitomised the post-war New Look. The House of DIOR, in whose name GRUAU – literally – pushed the pen, condensed fashion silhouettes to typographic ciphers: CHRISTIAN DIOR's designs were based on, for example, the A, H and Y lines. In Gruau, DIOR found a kindred spirit in his mastery of reductionism, which brought those designs to life in just a few crisply contoured colour fields. Obviously inspired by the posters of HENRI TOULOUSE-LAUTREC and Japanese coloured woodcut techniques, GRUAU needed only a scattering of sinuous lines to capture the very essence of a fashionable outfit – just as JAN VERMEER VAN DELFT could merely jot down a dab of white paint and you saw the baroque pearl at a girl's ear.

At the same time, photography was rapidly gaining ground on drawing in fashion: a growing band of extremely talented photographers, exemplified by RICHARD AVEDON, IRVING PENN, HELMUT NEWTON, BOB RICHARDSON, REGINA RELANG and NORMAN PARKINSON, had since the 1960s vied with exceptionally talented fashion draughtsmen such as GRUAU, albeit at first only sporadically and on an individual basis. ANTONIO LOPEZ, for instance, was a Puerto Rican fashion illustrator based in New York who produced a voluminous body of work in the 1960s and 1970s, which, chameleon-like, mirrored contemporary art trends, most notably Pop art. He assiduously cultivated a pop-star image – photos taken of him at parties or in the legendary STUDIO 54 nightclub were as well known as his drawings.

By the 1980s *photography* had asserted itself to become the most widespread vehicle for depicting fashion in the print media. However, in the past three decades, *drawn illustration* seems to have once again become the source of enormously inspiring potential for innovation in the fashion scene. In the age of analogue photography, the *technically generated image* was, of course, subject to specific limitations as far as its relationship with reality was concerned whereas fashion illustrators could give free rein to their imagination – and certainly did. AURORE DE LA MORINERIE, to take just one example, has no qualms about atomising her subject matter: dresses and bodies are often almost unrecognisable as such because the artist has given them a mood-enhancing twist by resorting to spray cans and airbrushing, ink and the use of Ben-Day dots, and MATS GUSTAFSON and EDUARD ERLIKH have continued to develop the GRUAU abstraction process to the point where silhouettes are merely suggested in watercolours. FRANÇOIS BERTHOUD, on the other hand, devotes himself to surfaces and textile texturing as well as figure contours. Fashion illustration had a real comeback in *La Mode en Peinture*, a wonderful magazine published from 1982 until 1990, in which the editorial section featured only hand-drawn graphics.

The digitalisation of the designing process and representation strategies since the 1990s has ushered in a rapprochement between fashion illustration and fashion photography in as much as defamiliarising and unsettling elements have been integrated in fashion imaging – techniques and combinatorics seem to know no bounds: photographs are overpainted (by analogue or digital means) or embellished with graphic signs; photographic constituents are mounted in draughtsmanly visions to induce specific moods and atmospheres. There is also collaboration between distinguished photographers and graphic artists: NICK KNIGHT and PETER SAVILLE, for instance, collaborated as far back as 1987 on a campaign for YOHJI YAMAMOTO.⁹

Such diversity tallies with the fact that for years now there have been no prescribed styles or mandatory trends in fashion that we would have to follow with religious zeal. Instead pluralism populates the catwalks with a wide range of looks. Fashion as a contemporary '*identity play*'¹⁰ has overridden the link to our physical bodies: insinuating our imagination into art as projection surfaces, be they one-offs, printed or immaterial, makes everything possible.

That also means that specific articles of clothing are no longer of paramount importance to the fashion 'experience' – hence they no longer tend to be represented in fashion imaging: 'We now see clothing as image and not necessarily as something consisting of material, cut, hems and fasteners'.¹¹ The 'use' of fashion, finally, is revealed as the observation and appropriation of images in which we participate in our imagination. We draw our inspiration from those who produce fashion imaging – no matter what designer medium and techniques they employ.

Incidentally, I still enjoy dipping into JAMES LAVER's DIE MODE. By now I am able to read it, too.

---

¹ JOURNAL DES LUXUS UND DER MODEN, no. 4, 1792, p. 190, rebutting a suggestion made by Dr. Both in his 'Zeitschrift für Gattinnen, Mütter und Töchter'. Dr. Both had recommended publishing the journal in French to safeguard the lower classes from temptation.
² Author's translation of the preamble to the first edition in 1785.
³ Ruth Wies, 'Das Journal des Luxus und der Moden (1786–1827), ein Spiegel kultureller Strömungen der Goethezeit', doctoral dissertation, Munich, 1953, pp. 39–40.
⁴ Charles Baudelaire, 'Der Maler des modernen Lebens', in: idem, AUFSÄTZE ZUR LITERATUR UND KUNST 1857–1860, Munich, 1989, pp. 213–5.
⁵ Doris Kolesch, 'Mode, Moderne und Kulturtheorie', in: Gertrud Lehnert (ed.), MODE, WEIBLICHKEIT UND MODERNITÄT, Dortmund, 1998, pp. 20–46, here p. 40.

⁶ Albert Reimann, 'Die deutsche Modezeichnung', in: MITTEILUNGEN DES VERBANDES DER DEUTSCHEN MODEN-INDUSTRIE, 3.4.1918 (Berlin), pp. 71–3.
⁷ See Adelheid Rasche, Anna Zika (eds.), STYL. DAS MODEJOURNAL DER FRÜHEN 1920ER JAHRE, Stuttgart, 2009.
⁸ Albert Reimann (see note 6).
⁹ See Jan May, 'Grafik und Illustration', in: Adelheid Rasche (ed.), VISIONS & FASHION, Bielefeld, 2011, p. 193.
¹⁰ Adelheid Rasche, 'Die Bilder der Mode: Eine Einführung', in: idem (ed., see note 9), pp. 8–17, here p. 9.
¹¹ See Ulrich Lehmann, 'Modefotografie', in: idem (ed.), CHIC CLICKS: MODEFOTOGRAFIE ZWISCHEN AUFTRAG UND KUNST, Ostfildern, 2002, p. T12.

HOW TO GET THERE

[225] After finishing your studies, you leave the safe haven of college confronted with the vexing question: 'What now?' Advertisements for vacancies in fashion illustration have always tended to be few and far between. Commissions are usually given by word of mouth and potential employers begin to notice you. High time to make up a professional portfolio. Your portfolio should only contain your best work. After all, you cannot confidently stand behind work you don't feel one hundred per cent sure about. And you need self-assurance when you are confronted with a potential employer. You are the one to determine the arrangement of your portfolio: either in ascending order of development leading up to a high point or in a thematic arrangement. Whichever approach you choose, it has to be obvious. A potential employer is seeing your work for the first time and so must be immediately convinced that you are the right person for the job. Should you happen to know in advance how a potential employer works, it can be helpful to add a couple of new drawings in a similar style. This enables you to gauge immediately the reaction to your potential for the commission.

A portfolio must be constantly updated. What counts is showcasing your best work, and that is usually the most recent. Immediately after receiving your diploma, you will not have any professional commissions to include in your portfolio. But you may have submitted work to competitions during your studies, drawn posters for fashion shows at the college or even collaborated with a company while still a student. Work of this kind should definitely be included in your portfolio. It proves that you already have some experience in dealing with employers to their satisfaction.

A home page of your own, a digital portfolio, is a must for an aspiring fashion illustrator. While still at college, students tend to be helped out with a web page of sorts by friends or fellow students. Be sure that the website you do have is clearly structured without too much 'extraneous information'. Your drawings shouldn't be lost in a welter of verbiage. And your web page should definitely be user friendly. It is also important to be able to keep adding new work to your digital portfolio. If you're lucky, you might attract the attention of a fashion blogger and receive commissions from all over the world. Armed with a portfolio and a web page, you are ready to discover the world outside and to show that you are there. You just have to get out into it. First contacts are made by applying to fashion magazines.

Hunt out some fashion magazine articles and illustrate them. It doesn't matter if the articles are not current. What counts is showing how imaginative you are, what statement you make and what your signature is.

Visiting fashion fairs can also lead to commissions. The best time to do so is the last day of the fair because things tend to be much too hectic at the beginning so no one will have time to sit down with you and give your work the attention it deserves. In this case it makes sense to take business cards with you. You can also leave an illustration with people who have looked at your work. Choose good quality paper in A4 format and don't forget the copyright sign. Lifestyle businesses, for instance, the kinds that produce gift-wrapping paper or party napkins, are also potential employers for people starting out.

As a freelance illustrator you will discover how difficult it is to be your own boss. Not only do you have to know the fees you can charge and how to calculate them, you also have to be able to negotiate and, finally, know how to write up and submit your invoices. Doing all that takes self-assurance, a quality that is sometimes lacking. But so many people do learn how to cope with this aspect of freelancing. Everyone makes mistakes, but you should learn from them. Some people, of course, never learn from their mistakes, and there are agencies for handling all this (such as unit.nl). They are there to relieve clients of all 'tiresome' aspects of this kind of work, including negotiating with potential employers, calculating costs and writing up invoices. They take a cut when you have finished a commission.

Drawing for a living is not a nine-to-five job. You will not have a steady income. It is always uncertain whether you will land that commission or not. And yet! This is a job which offers limitless freedom. You are constantly working on the aesthetic plane. You can give free rein to your imagination. This keeps you mentally versatile. You will never be bored. When you see your work published for the first time, you know for certain that you would never want to be doing anything else!

Diploma project
[227] To simulate a real-life situation while you are still at college, you can ask fellow students who are taking a diploma in fashion design whether you might do the illustrations for their diploma project. You are highly likely to meet with an enthusiastic response. The advantage in this case is that you can accompany a collection from its inception. You can follow its development from the first sketch, the choice of silhouettes, the colours and the materials from the ground up. Since the designer may still be unsure about the type to be targeted by the collection, it is a good idea to do some sketches early on in order to have a basis for discussion. The concept often includes approaches to designing the staging.

This exercise shows how important a good briefing is. You should get used to jotting down the most important points in a conversation with a designer and then going through them again with him or her just to be sure you speak the same fashion language.

[226] Here a designer has rendered her own illustrations for her diploma project.

[228 – 229] This and the drawings on the following pages show how a diploma collection has been thematically built up around the subject 'fear'. The assignment was to develop four pages for an imaginary magazine. In this case, you would work with what is known as a blind text, enabling you to calculate how much space should be allocated to your drawing. In practice, the magazine would give you the live area (the space to be printed), the arrangement of a page with the text columns blocked in.

[232 – 233] The following pages show illustrations for graduates, which were presented in their respective collection books.

WILLEMINA HOENDERKEN
IN CONVERSATION WITH
ANNETTE GÖRTZ

[248 – 251] *Why did you decide to study at FH Bielefeld University of Applied Sciences and when did you begin your studies?*
During the orientation phase I considered three colleges in all: one of them Trier College, a private school in Hamburg and FH Bielefeld.
I opted for Bielefeld in the end because even then they practised a holistic approach to design and the departments collaborated well with one another.
The mix of photography, sculpture, printmaking, fine art and fashion is exciting and the individual assignments and projects benefit from it. I studied eight semesters in all at Bielefeld, from 1979 to 1983.

What did you do after finishing your studies?
I knew even as a student that I would be taking the step into self-employment after I finished. I have always attached great importance to realising my fashion ideas and presenting them. After finishing my studies I founded the Zic Zac label with a woman friend. The concept was considerably different to what it is now. It was more on the Ikea principle: we sold flat-pack fashion (sew it yourself). Unfortunately, my business partner fell seriously ill. When that happened, I had to reorientate myself.

When did you found the company?
Actually, that is hard to say precisely because I sold fashion under my own name even before the Zic Zac label was launched.
While I was still a student I supplied some boutiques with exclusive one-offs.
They were often very special garments, which sold well so I was able to partly finance my studies with such work.

How has the business developed over the years?
The fashion industry isn't an easy sector; it's highly competitive and you have to work hard to get a foothold. As a self-employed designer, you either have to learn to think like a businesswoman or you get help. Otherwise even the best design cannot be sold with any sort of profit margin. Profitable derives from profit ... or from pro? I learnt this just at the right time ... and later I also married. My husband, Hans-Jörg Welsch, who holds a diploma in business studies, had had some experience in the industry. Looked at today, the company has enjoyed healthy growth. Steady, slow growth has enabled the financial framework to grow along with it. There has been enough time for spatial, technical and personnel development. Design is just part of it ... production, quality control and distribution are equally important criteria.

What is the philosophy behind your business?
It has always been important to me to make a fair product, hence no production in the Far East. Treating employees on a par with management and a positive business climate also belong to my philosophy.

Where do you draw inspiration for your work?
Every day you are surrounded with all sorts of inspiration: forms, colours, light and shade are all part of everyday living. Fitting impressions together to form something new ... that's how inspiration turns into creativity.
The trick is to channel all those influences without getting confused, to guide your inspiration yourself and realise it in your own style. I enjoy what isn't commonplace, what is special.
One of the greatest sources of inspiration for me is travelling, when you soak up a foreign culture in entirely different surroundings.
Another indispensable source of inspiration for me is unrelated to the fashion industry. Architecture and art are important subjects for me.

What forms the way from an idea to a finished collection?

I start with the material; I let myself be inspired at textile fairs and usually have the basic framework of a collection in my mind. After a few years you know your clientele and know what materials and articles of clothing you have to have in your collection. Then you have to establish proportions and silhouettes.

I have always tried to keep my own signature, that way I think you transmit a statement and part of your own character.

A clientele stays faithful to a line if the line remains true to itself, and my aim for myself has always been to get a style across.

What is the status of art in your life?

It's an integral part of my life. In our private life, my husband and I are surrounded by a great deal of art of various kinds. Art is a companion. In our house, art is always in motion, is being rearranged so it is perceived more consciously.

Do you have a favourite artist? If so, who is it?

No, there would be too many of them. I change my favourite artist as often as my mood changes about what to wear.

Do you perceive a great difference in designing fashion and art?

Definitely. Fashion has a much shorter life span and in general is subject to rapid change. Fashion is very difficult because the materials and technical aspects have to result in a product that is ultimately useful and wearable. Art, on the other hand, is much freer; you can draw on a wide range of possibilities and abstract forms. Art doesn't have to fit perfectly; you can simply go on a rampage. Art is more self-assured and independent than fashion in the conventional sense.

How do you perceive your own work in relation to art?

The work of an artist and the work of a designer are related in kind but nonetheless very different. In both fashion and art you are concerned with producing a composition, combining materials, shapes and colours in an exciting way or emphasizing their differences. But art doesn't lay claim to trying to please. I don't view myself as an artist.

To what extent do you view illustration as a medium for expressing yourself and what importance do you attach to it?

To me, illustration is a medium for inspiration; I like looking at colours, seeing progressions that ultimately end in a form. Illustration isn't as difficult as art; instead, it's easier and makes a descriptive statement. Art is rather more serious, is often communicative in character. I find looking at illustrative drawings refreshing because shapes are exaggerated, colours that are completely alien to reality can be used and they show a world full of imagination. Illustration can be very exciting and describe fashion in a subtle way.

What do you judge design quality by?

Design quality is difficult to judge; it is always subjective and there are only a handful of objective criteria to draw on. I find it basically crucial to spot a common theme running through and to see a link to inspiration. I also always judge the overall picture.

What have we forgotten to ask you?

How long I want to keep on doing this?! :)

Illustrating a winter collection

[252 – 255] Görtz-Welsch Design, the fashion firm known for their Annette Görtz label, agreed to collaborate with a group of nine fashion illus-tration students. The assignment is to illustrate the 2013/2014 winter collection. This is a great opportunity for the group because it is the sort of routine commission professional fashion illustrators receive.

1st Briefing

- Explanation of the company philosophy
- Explanation of the colour range
- Targeting the right clientele
- Coming up with a new advertising strategy
- Viewing the collection
- Photographing a selection of six outfits
- Agreeing on deadlines for viewing the illustrations and a second briefing

In the first phase, the students are invited to visit the company and glean background information. Annette Görtz is in charge of design and is chiefly responsible for pattern cutting. All important preparatory work for production is done in-house.

Top quality materials are given very high priority at Annette Görtz: designs are strongly affected by the tactile qualities of materials and the way they hang. Materials worked with are expected to meet very high standards, so all textiles are washed before use at the company to ensure that they really live up to manufacturers' claims.

The palette ranges from black through various shades of grey to white in summer. Every season also has an additional key colour of its own.

This label targets down-to-earth women with a penchant for comfortable, classic and very stylish clothes who also appreciate materials with an exceptional feel and look.

The 2013/2014 winter collection consists of 180 items, including several coats, for instance, in alpaca and pure wool or boiled wool, coated with neoprene. There are rugged lambskin leather jackets as well as more formal jackets, in brocade, for instance. The collection includes dresses, blouses, trousers and skirts made of the finest silk organza or high-quality viscose.

To provide the students with the widest possible range to illustrate from the collection, six outfits made in widely diverse materials are selected.

The members of the illustration group are given an opportunity to photograph these outfits as worn by professional models. The photos serve as documentation of the clothing, including all details, and their exact shape. Moreover, the students may request specific poses. To simulate reality as authentically as possible, from then on each student works alone; there is no more communication with other members of the group.

Drawing type and format are not prescribed. Students are free to opt for illustrations, styling drawings, portraits, detail drawings or representations of materials. Drawings can be glamorous or abstract, in colour or black and white. A two-week deadline was agreed on for completion of the first illustration assignment.

When you receive a commission, it is of vital importance to become as well acquainted as you can with your client. Even before you have your first deadline, you should have collected all the information available. The

easiest way to do that is online. There you will find not just the current collection but also earlier collections. Some clients advertise in the print media so you should take a look at that, too. Information on companies can be gleaned from specialist periodicals such as Textilwirtschaft and Textile Mitteilungen. The more informed you are about your prospective client, the more professionally you can conduct yourself during your interview with them.

In the interview, it is important to stay alert and ask a few questions yourself. That shows you are interested and committed to your profession. From now on, you should stop revolving around yourself and daydreaming. Only one thing counts: your prospective employer! The ANNETTE GÖRTZ label targets women, not girls. Women with both feet on the ground, who are not romantics. Women who love being well dressed. Your illustration is supposed to convey all that. If you have had a foible for drawing very young women or a soft spot for quirky types, you will have to adapt your style. It is a balancing act but it can be done. The focus is on material properties so you should work experimentally in any case to accentuate the qualities of particular materials. Colour, too, plays a major role. A black article of clothing should not look brown. Shapes should be exaggerated although the form should not be lost.

2nd Briefing
- Viewing the illustrations
- Selecting finished works
- Suggestions for improving the rest of the work viewed
- Agreeing on a deadline

After the illustrations have been worked on for two weeks, they are shown to the client. Illustrations rendered by two of the students appeal immediately. One series is very aesthetic in feel, the other reveals a glamorous approach but with-out looking old-fashioned. Both series are also convincing because of the way the material has been handled. The other illustrations need improvement in details, be it in respect of form or of material, or because the heads do not match the client's expectations or the atmosphere is too romantic. It was also noticed that one outfit was only drawn once. However, comparison with illustrations of the other outfits clearly reveals the various students' signatures. After discussing the results, it was decided that everything should once again be redrawn.

Handling criticism is not always easy. You have done your best but your work has not been accepted without comments, let alone with enthusiasm. That is disappointing. But don't let this feeling linger. Not every drawing is right from the start and there are days on which anything you draw is only fit to be binned. Still, you shouldn't let yourself be discouraged. Do it again. It is a good idea to analyse where you went wrong. You might have to redraw the same thing two or even three times. But if you keep going, you can't go wrong.

The deadline is in exactly one week. In practice, three weeks are an unheard-of luxury; you often have only a week's time or even just two days. Even so, you should go through all the phases. Just accelerate your pace a bit.

INTERVIEW WITH PROFESSIONALS
AYSE KILIC

[274 – 285] *What was your first step after finishing your studies?*
I was fortunate in being able to work as an illustrator for two fashion magazines towards the end of my course so I'm still doing this work. I also had begun at the same time to sell cotton carrier bags I made with my own illustrations.

How did you make your first contacts and land jobs?
Mainly by being proactive. That means, while I was still a student, I simply applied via email to various magazines with my illustrations.

What inspires you?
Basically, I find inspiration in many different things. But above all, my source of inspiration is a sensuous female face. I like playing with facial expressions and reproducing certain expressions in my own style.

When you run out of ideas, what do you do about it?
As a rule, I browse in all sorts of magazines and, by looking at photos and pictures, try to form a new idea that I then capture in sketches. It might at first just be details that I later fit together in an illustration.

What does your working day look like?
Basically, the way my working day looks depends on the commissions I have at a given time. If I'm not under time pressure, I start off by sitting down at my work bench, also if I have a concrete idea for realising an illustration.
It isn't worth starting on anything before you have the idea. Because, when an idea is there, I may even work through on into the evening.

Is working as an illustrator very different to the idea you originally had of the profession?
No, not at all! On the contrary, I had always wanted to pursue my passion for illustration alongside my main profession as a fashion designer.

What status does the sketch book have in your working life?
It has tremendously high status for me. As soon as I have an idea, it's always conveniently there to hand so, basically, I use it every day.

What materials are indispensable for you?
I work a lot in watercolour. Be it in a paintbox or watercolour pencils as well. It's always fascinating to see that unplanned effects can also be created with it so that a picture goes in a surprisingly different direction.

How do you discover your own style as an illustrator?
I think that your own style, depending on your personal preferences as an individual, develops entirely of its own accord over the years. Since childhood, I have really loved drawing and then as a student I worked mainly with fashion illustration so that I developed far in that direction and hence was able to find my own style.

What is your advice for young people who want to become fashion illustrators?
What makes a fashion illustration special are distinctive personal features that make an artist's signature instantly recognisable, which make a drawing interesting to the viewer. That's why you definitely must have discovered or developed your own style at some point. In addition, I'd say you should work with as many different

materials as possible to be able to find out here, too, what your 'favourite tool' is.

Suki Kim (Soo kyung Kim)

What was your first step after finishing your studies?

For me, as a Korean woman, it was especially difficult to get a job in Germany. Initially I wanted to apply as an illustrator on a freelance basis with a view to being able to teach students in my home country, South Korea, in order to pass on to them my knowledge and the skills I had gained from my studies. After finishing in Bielefeld, I continued to study fashion illustration for a brief while in Hamburg. In general, I can say that you have to be willing to fight for a chance in life. You never know how many you'll have.

How did you make your first contacts and land jobs?

While still a student I received commissions for illustrations from numerous fellow students. Even after I graduated, they have remained clients of mine. My portfolio consists in part of those works. I tried online to land more jobs in South Korea with my portfolio online. I wanted to live there again. In the meantime, I have become an instructor in illustration at a fashion school in Seoul.

What inspires you?

Everything! When I listen to music, a colour chart immediately springs to mind to accompany it. But I'm usually inspired by fashion-related things, such as fashion magazines, fashion blogs and people in the street who are strikingly dressed. I don't just look at things superficially but go into them in depth and that's when the inspiration comes.

When you run out of ideas, what do you do about it?

Simply draw! Even if what I'm drawing doesn't exactly make sense, an idea for a new illustration often comes out of it.

Is working as an illustrator very different to the idea you originally had of the profession?

Well, I was totally aware that this wouldn't turn out to be an easy job. Missing commissions one month means that you're lacking a monthly salary, too. Time pressure is also a factor from which illustrators often suffer. Still my friends are a bit envious of me because the job I do is nothing less than pursuing my hobby and passion.

What status does the sketch book have in your working life?

My sketch book can be equated with a diary. Every sketch provides fresh material for new works and I often use my old sketch books to find inspiration for new jobs.

What materials are indispensable for you?

Indian ink and watercolour.

How do you discover your own style as an illustrator?

I'm still looking for my own style because I keep getting dissatisfied with my style and am always attempting to try out something new. Of course everyone has their own style in some form, which might be recognisable in their brushwork or in sketches, which simply flows from the fingertips. It's well worth working on that and developing it further.

What is your advice for young people who want to become fashion illustrators?

Never stop drawing. Practice makes perfect. Nowadays, how well you draw is no longer so important but that you bring a certain distinctive individual touch to your work instead. My tip is simply keep on drawing and some day the good drawing fairy will come of her own accord.

Lisa Höger

What was your first step after finishing your studies?

The first thing I did was to establish the basis for my work, my portfolio. I filled my portfolio with those illustrations and made a web page. Then came customer acquisition; that means, of course, advertising, writing emails, sending postcards and hoping for a positive response.

How did you make your first contacts and land jobs?

For starters, through my web page. Pictures circulate very rapidly online. But just remember that your name always has to be on them. Some addressees responded to my postcard advertising and, on the other hand, personal contacts also brought me jobs. Many commissions go by word of mouth, and creative, reliable work always pays, not least with new commissions. You should definitely cultivate good contacts to your clientele!

What inspires you?

Often a commission is very inspiring in itself because it usually concerns articles on fashion, portraits of interesting people or products. Researching on these subjects already provides many ideas and images. Fashion magazines are indispensable because designers, good photo series and texts are the best sources of inspiration. Besides, all ways of representing fashion are important for recognising trends towards particular colours, cuts and styling and making use of them for illustrations.

When you run out of ideas, what do you do about it?

Go out, leave my desk, definitely look at something else besides the empty sheet of paper in front of me. A quick way for me is always telling others about the commission because when you recap in words what is at stake, you figure out yourself more quickly what might work and what won't. And then: simply get to work. The picture usually develops entirely of its own accord.

What does your working day look like?

When I've landed a commission, I always take a whole day just to think about it, even when there's very little time. Sometimes you have three weeks, sometimes only a weekend. Then I jot down my first ideas, collect ingredients for collages and decide on mood, materials, form and colours. I always work analogue first; that takes the longest. Composing various backgrounds, retouching and changing colours takes place at the computer, just like digital adjustments. Many clients, for instance, have a special colour profile. Then I send the illustrations to my client, sometimes something has to be changed, usually everything is satisfactory. When everyone is satisfied, I write my invoice and not long afterwards comes the best bit: rediscovering my finished illustrations in the magazine.

Is working as an illustrator very different to the idea you originally had of the profession?

Actually it isn't. But what I had to get used to was that it's, unfortunately, a very lonely job, just my desk, my computer and me. And that clients might not even find the illustrations so great that I have put the most blood, sweat and tears and the most working time into. In my case, those are, for instance, my elaborate drawings in Indian ink or coloured pencil. Oddly enough, the relatively simpler collages are what sell best.

What status does the sketch book have in your working life?

My sketch book has been transformed into a book for collecting ideas. When I receive a commission, I write down all items of information and instruction in it straight off, then of course drawings are also added, as well as cut-out pictures, materials, words, colours I want to use and layout ideas. My sketch book contains many little mood boards, so to say.

What materials are indispensable for you?

Paper, pencils, Indian ink, scissors, glue, scanner, computer.

How do you discover your own style as an illustrator?

By drawing. And by thinking about your own work.

What is your advice for young people who want to become fashion illustrators?

Trust in your own style! Then get used to short deadlines, working fast and sometimes waiting a long time between commissions. Never market yourself and your illustrations for less than they are worth because, if you do, you'll find yourself working for starvation wages: this client will never pay you or any other illustrator more than just that. And most important of all: never lose your delight in drawing, keep developing, keep on trying out new materials and forms; it's wonderful to earn money with something that's such fun!

Rafael Erfurt

What was your first step after finishing your studies?

The first step after I finished my studies consisted in my becoming aware first of all of what exactly I expected from a future as a designer. I decided fast, and I opted for looking for a job that would provide me with a possibility of variety and freedom so I wouldn't be too narrowed down and would be able to work on my own things.

How did you make your first contacts and land jobs?

I have only one thing to say: being proactive is the motto. You can't just sit there and wait for the jobs to come to you.

What inspires you?

Almost anything that grabs me at a particular moment and arouses my attention can inspire me. My work often deals with personal experiences or views on particular subjects. However, the 'woman's world' theme has haunted me for ages so it's also the focus of my work, regardless of what other subject areas it might revolve around.

When you run out of ideas, what do you do about it?

It's important simply to become detached from everything, free up your thinking. I've always found it helpful to undertake something with friends. On the other hand, I have had the experience that rummaging about in your own personal archives can be enormously helpful because you're always coming across elements that may open up a new perspective to you.

What does your working day look like?

First of all, my working day starts with going into class with my students and working on the projects, of which I supervise three each term. Then I see to supervising students who are about to graduate. In addition, I teach the fundamentals of design. That means I'm confronted with drawing there, too. After class I have enough time to sink into chaos and work on my own things.

Is working as an illustrator very different to the idea you originally had of the profession?

I never had a concrete idea of the profession or thought about it. I don't let my work depend on employers. My works are what they are, and they only come about for this reason. Hence any notions I might entertain about this profession are irrelevant.

What status does the sketch book have in your working life?

The sketch book is the 'holy grail' for a designer, a compendium of ideas that represent vast potential for further work. Unfortunately, technology is assuming ever more status for many. Absolutely nothing is forbidden in a sketch book, even if it's a 'scrawl' on a napkin pressed between two pages.

What materials are indispensable for you?

Actually there's virtually nothing you couldn't use to illustrate. But if I had to name something that's indispensable to me, it would be my coffee, my cigarette and my ballpoint pen.

How do you discover your own style as an illustrator?

I think finding your own style takes quite a while. You keep trying things out to discover new approaches offered by a particular material and handling it. I don't believe that you can, or put differently, should, deliberately construct your personal style. It should develop of itself so that it's genuine and doesn't become a thought construct.

What is your advice for young people who want to become fashion illustrators?

1st point: Be clear about who you are and what you want! 2nd point: If you're clear on that, don't let anything lead you astray! 3rd point: Always keep Point 1 and Point 2 in mind because that is the only way you are going to ensure that your work and you yourself have personality!

Peggy Wolf

What was your first step after finishing your studies?

Rather bumbling, undefined but still very exciting. I rented a studio in Bielefeld with two friends and set out looking for jobs. Very early on I realised that I wanted to work on a self-employed basis. During the two years after college I freelanced for some magazines and worked for a trend office. After a three-day visit to London in 2006, I felt very inspired by the city and its people. Three months later I was standing in Liverpool Street with twenty-five kilos of luggage and my portfolio of illustrations and waiting for a bus to take me to my new home.

*How did you make your first
contacts and land jobs?*

I rang up the magazine I wanted to work for and asked for an interview. I found the job at the trend office through an online advertisement.

What inspires you?

Nature, women with expressive faces, interior design, books, films, travelling and my own feelings provide stimuli for new work.

*When you run out of ideas,
what do you do about it?*

When I run out of ideas, I try to spend a whole day relaxing, getting out into nature, going to an exhibition or spending a day with family and friends.

What does your working day look like?

No two working days are alike and it depends on what my projects are. On average, however, it goes as follows:

In the morning I read and answer my emails from clients, a process that also goes on intermittently throughout the day. I've got used to corresponding with most clients almost entirely by email and we hardly ever talk on the telephone or meet personally.

Then from ten o' clock I work on the commission with the closest deadline. After two or three hours I usually take a break and either work on ideas for a different project or I order prints from my printer in London. I have an online shop, where you can buy my illustrations as originals or prints. Shops from several countries order my prints in larger quantities for sale in their own shops. That means I have to deal with those things, too, and I go to the post office two or three afternoons a week to send off these orders. Towards four o'clock I go back to work on my commission. When I have a lot to do, some days can be very long indeed. But there are also other days which are not so hectic and then I can concentrate solely on illustrations.

Is working as an illustrator very different to the idea you originally had of the profession?

To be honest, the profession is even better than I had thought it would be. I personally find that I have a great deal of freedom and my clients are very easy going and open minded. This boosts my creativity so I also manage to discover new things in my work and to develop them. The commissions I receive from my clients and their ideas for realising them inspire me and constantly show me new approaches.

*What status does the sketch
book have in your working life?*

I used to keep sketch books while I was a student but since I have been self-employed, I have completely abandoned them. My ideas emerge while I'm discussing commissions with my clients and grow within the working process.

What materials are indispensable for you?

Paper, pencils and watercolours are very important to me.

*How do you discover
your own style as an illustrator?*

At first it was important for me to try out many different materials, be open minded and get involved with new things. It took several years for me to find my signature and my own expression in my work. Discovering your own style is a journey and a constantly changing process.

*What is your advice for young people
who want to becomrators?*

I would advise everyone to be brave, curious and open minded. Most beginnings are not always straightforward and sometimes you may land in a job that you wouldn't have imagined yourself doing. But you always learn something new and you can put this experience to very good use as an illustrator. You should look up companies you'd like to work for and then make contact with them. It's also important to have a web page on which you present your most important and best work. It needn't always be very extensive but it should contain enough to show what you are like as an illustrator so that companies can have a clear idea of your work and learn what is most important about you as a person. In conclusion, I advise everyone to have a lot of endurance and patience. At first you may get some job rejections and things don't work out quite the way you had imagined. Just keep on trying and don't give up!

CLAUDIA AREND

*What was your first step after
finishing your studies?*

I'll have to take a rather roundabout way to answer that. Before graduating, I spent some time in Paris, where I gleaned my first experience in a trend office. By that time I had had drawings published in a specialist magazine, followed by other work, and shortly before I took my diploma I was 'cast' by an agent. That opened the door for me to the profession, on one hand, but I also illustrated in other fields that had nothing at all to do with fashion. Still what I enjoyed about this was the variety. All those experiences sharpen your eye, go into your style and make your signature distinctive.

*How did you make your first
contacts and land jobs?*

Mainly through my agent but also through friends. Later on, professionally, always through my work itself.

What inspires you?

Life itself. My son. So the most inspiring artists I know ;-) I'm a person who's always observant and perceptive on very many levels. That's a gift but it can be exhausting at times unless you learn to close doors when it's appropriate to do so. Often all you need is quiet to be able to lap up ideas like sipping water. I have the feeling more and more frequently that everyone is increasingly taken up with babbling and shouting at the same time to reassure themselves constantly that they do exist and are important. That is as desperate as it is pointless. We are being swamped by visual and acoustic messages; hardly anything seems to be left to chance now. Subtlety is growing rare. Silence is golden. But it's important to be alert and on your toes both internally and externally. Travelling, exposing yourself to other realities, can be incredibly inspiring. Shifting your centre.

*When you run out of ideas, what do you do
about it?*

No matter what, come up to the surface for air in order to be able to plunge in again refreshed. Just taking a walk can help. Walking in itself sorts ideas that keep buzzing round and round in your head and provides a wealth of inspiration. Going out with good friends. When a picture 'has gone wrong' and I can't see my way, I also hold it up to a mirror to be able to analyse it afresh. That always helps.

What does your working day look like?
No two working days are alike. I'm freelancing, working on a commission – communication takes time – working in the office, working with paint-smudged hands in the studio, working at my Mac, teaching my students. I'm a 'multitasker'. My working day entails accommodating my child and my family, illustration, freelance work as an artist, and my professorship under a stylish hat. I don't know what it's like to be bored.

Is working as an illustrator very different to the idea you originally had of the profession?
I actually started out without such a clear idea. This profession is very complex, and illustration is really a broad field. So I didn't just saunter up and say to myself: 'Hey, what a cool profession, that's what I want to be too'. You don't get very far with that attitude. I believe that you have a calling, which you follow because that is your path. Or else not. Everyone experiences for himself in his own way how incredibly magnificent this 'vocation' is and at the same time how nightmarishly hard freelancing can be. You have to be able to stand that. People with romantically exalted notions are in absolutely the wrong place here.

What status does the sketch book have in your working life?
Sketch books are indispensable and my recommendation is that everyone should keep one. It should become an illustrated, described part of your life. Admittedly, sometimes the pages may remain empty. But I still view many of my sketches that have come into being in this way, under no constraints and aimlessly, as my best. First and foremost, your sketch book captures ideas and scenes. Otherwise you would no longer be able to retrieve many of your memories. The linkage between image and word and the diversity of motifs and ideas also make a sketch book a highly individual total work of art in its own right.

What materials are indispensable for you?
I can't give a blanket answer to that because I use and combine such a wide variety of colours and materials. It's the combinations, sometimes also the conflict between materials that generates friction and tension. You must literally hear something crackling. I am very fond of working in oils, with Indian ink, graphite, pencils of all kinds. Illustrator, Photoshop, ballpoint pens, half-empty marker pens and a camera are also very appealing and indispensable tools.

How do you discover your own style as an illustrator?
If you're lucky, the style will find you. But it also has something to do with not being uptight in your attitude to your work, a mixture of meticulousness, sensitivity and brutality. And above all, with work, work, work and, once again, work. You have to learn to welcome mistakes as opportunities. Style is perched at the summit of a mountain of torn-up paper. But the way to it goes on and on and you never really come to rest on that summit.

What is your advice for young people who want to become fashion illustrators?
Believe in yourselves. And in beauty.

KONTAKTE / CONTACTS

Mitwirkende Illustratoren / Contributing Illustrators

Alöna Leis	alonaleis@googlemail.com
Andrea Scholz	andrea.scholz89@gmx.de
	www.andreajung.npage.de
Christin Lohmann	christin.lohmann@gmx.de
	www.ugly-perfection.de
Dominik Plassmann	domi.plassmann@gmx.de
	www.blackyboy-illustration.com
Elisabeth Grosse	ellison@gmx.de
Jan Müller	jan.mueller1990@yahoo.de
Joana Pertl	joana.pertl@googlemail.com
	www.talenthouse.com/joanapertl
Jula Buchwitz	noel_23@web.de
Julien Kurtin	julienkurtin@web.de
Katja Skoppek	kasko90@gmx.de
Kirsten Fiebig	kirsten.fiebig@yahoo.de
	www.graduatefashion-germany.com
Leonie Barth	info@leoniebarth.com
	www.leoniebarth.com
Lisa Dominicus	e.dominicus@web.de
	www.elligant.com
Marcellina Kemper	info@marcellina-illustration.de
	www.marcellina-illustration.de
Melinda Weber	melindaweber@web.de
Okan Zafrak	okanzafrak@hotmail.com
	www.okanzafrak.com
Patryk Sniecinski	Vincent-Graphit@gmx.de
Rabia Celik	rcelik90@yahoo.de
Raisa Hirsch	raisahirsch@hotmail.de
	www.raisahirsch.de
Sarah Brieden	sara.brieden@t-online.de
Stephanie Höcker	steffi.hoecker@gmail.dcom
	www.stephanie-hoecker-fashion.de
Susan Krug	Sakura310790@gmx.net
Susanne Küstner	s.kuestner89@gmx.de
	www.susikuestner-illustration.de
Tatjana von Elverfeldt	telverfeldt@gmx.de
Vera Ickler	ickler.vera@gmail.de
	www.cargocollective.com/vera
Vitalli Peters	Vitalli.peters@gmx.de

Interviews - Absolventen / Former Students

Ayse Kilic	info@ayse-kilic.de
	www.ayse-kilic.com
Claudia Arend	contact@claudia-arend.de
	www.claudia-arend.de
Lisa Höger	mails@lisahoeger.de
	www.lisahoeger.de
Peggy Wolf	peggywolfdesign@gmail.com
	www.peggywolf.com
Rafael Erfurt	rafa.e@gmx.de
Suki Kim	suki0318@googlemail.com
	www.sukiillustration.tumblr.com

Weitere Kontakte / Further Contacs

Annina Hannas	annina.hannas@fh-bielefeld.de
Christina Falke	post@artbestimmt.de
Eva Begemann	eva.begemann@fh-bielefeld.de
Eugenie Koch	www.eugenie-koch.com
Jan Trussner	mail@jantrussner.de
Juri Wunder	juri.wunder@gmail.de
Pascal Niebur	pascal@annettegoertz.com
Svenja Hemke	www.svenjahemke.de
Tobias Kunkel	www.tobias-kunkel.com
Prof. Dr. Anna Zika	anna.zika@fh-bielefeld.de
Prof. Uwe Goebel	uwe.goebel@fh-bielefeld.de

IMPRESSUM / IMPRINT

© 2013 Willemina Hoenderken, ARNOLDSCHE Art Publishers, Stuttgart, und die Autoren / and the authors.

Alle Rechte vorbehalten. Vervielfältigung und Wiedergabe auf jegliche Weise (grafisch, elektronisch und fotomechanisch sowie der Gebrauch von Systemen zur Datenrückgewinnung) – auch in Auszügen – nur mit schriftlicher Genehmigung der ARNOLDSCHE Art Publishers, Liststraße 9, D-70180 Stuttgart.

All rights reserved. No part of this work may be reproduced or used in any forms or by any means (graphic, electronic or mechanical, including photocopying or information storage and retrieval systems) without written permission from the copyright holder ARNOLDSCHE Art Publishers, Liststraße 9, D-70180 Stuttgart.
www.arnoldsche.com

HERAUSGEBER / EDITOR
Prof. Willemina Hoenderken
IDEE UND KONZEPT / IDEA AND CONCEPT
Prof. Willemina Hoenderken
ART-DIREKTION / ART DIRECTION
Prof. Uwe Göbel
GESTALTUNG / DESIGN
Tobias Kunkel, Svenja Hemke, Eugenie Koch
MITARBEIT / ASSISTANCE
Eva Begemann, Annina Hannas

AUTORIN / AUTHOR
Prof. Willemina Hoenderken
BEITRAG / ESSAY
Prof. Dr. Anna Zika
INTERVIEWS
Annette Görtz;
Claudia Arend, Rafael Erfurt, Lisa Höger, Ayse Kilic, Suki Kim, Peggy Wolf
ENGLISCHE ÜBERSETZUNG / ENGLISH TRANSLATION
Joan Clough, Castallack
ENGLISCHES LEKTORAT / ENGLISH COPY EDITING
Wendy Brouwer, Stuttgart
FOTOGRAFIE UND BILDBEARBEITUNG / PHOTOGRAPHY AND IMAGE EDITING
Jan Trussner, Juri Wunder, Christina Falke
REDAKTION / EDITING
Vera Ickler, Marcellina Kemper, Susanna Küstner, Julien Kurtin, Christin Lohmann, Pascal Niebuhr, Dominik Plassmann

DRUCK / PRINTED BY
Gorenjski tisk storitve, Kranj, Slovenia
PAPIER / PAPER
Arctic Volume White 1.1, 130 gsm

Bibliografische Information der Deutschen Nationalbibliothek
Die Deutsche Nationalbibliothek verzeichnet diese Publikation in der Deutschen Nationalbibliografie; detaillierte bibliografische Daten sind im Internet über www.d-nb.de abrufbar.

Bibliographic information published by the Deutsche Nationalbibliothek
The Deutsche Nationalbibliothek lists this publication in the Deutsche Nationalbibliografie; detailed bibliographic data are available in the Internet at www.d-nb.de.

ISBN 978-3-89790-395-1

Made in Europe, 2013

KONTAKT / CONTACT
Prof. Willemina Hoenderken
Fachhochschule Bielefeld / University of Applied Sciences
Fachbereich Gestaltung, Mode
Lampingstrasse 3, 33615 Bielefeld, Germany
willemina.hoenderken@fh-bielefeld.de

ARNOLDSCHE Art Publishers
Liststrasse 9, 70180 Stuttgart, Germany
art@arnoldsche.com
www.arnoldsche.com

Dank

Das Redaktions- und Grafikteam hat hervorragende Arbeit geleistet, dafür möchte ich allen danken. Uwe Göbel und Anna Zika, geschätzte Kollegen, haben ohne Wenn und Aber ihre Unterstützung zugesagt. Danke für euer Engagement.
Ohne Diethard Sawicki wären die Texte nicht deutsch und nicht niederländisch gewesen. Danke für deine korrigierende Hilfe. Birgit Grommel ist Expertin für das Programm Illustrator. Danke für deine wertvollen Tipps. Elisabeth Groth, Lena Meder, Katharina Schöne und Lena Heiler danke ich für die Ermutigung und die freundliche Kritik.
Dirk Allgaier und Wiebke Ullmann von den Arnoldschen Art Publishers danke ich für das Vertrauen und die großartige Umsetzung von einer Idee zu einem Produkt. Joan Clough hat die Texte ins Englische übersetzt. Danke für das Finden der Worte.
Ohne die Großzügigkeit von Annette Görtz und Hans-Jörg Welsch hätten wir aber erst gar nicht anfangen können. Dreimal danke!

Auch meinem Sohn, Alexander Heils, danke ich für die Unterstützung und das Verständnis. Es ist nicht immer leicht, eine Mutter zu haben, die oft so in Gedanken versunken ist. Ihm widme ich dieses Buch.

Acknowledgements

The editorial and the graphic team have done splendid work and I want to thank you all. My esteemed colleagues, Uwe Göbel and Anna Zika, promised their unconditional support and kept their promise. Thank you for your unwavering commitment.
Without Diethard Sawicki there would have been no German and no Dutch texts. Thank you for your helpful corrections. Birgit Grommel is an expert in Illustrator. I am thankful to you for those valuable tips. My thanks to Elisabeth Groth, Katharina Schöne and Lena Heiler for their encouragement and constructive criticism.
Thank you to Dirk Allgaier and Wiebke Ullmann from Arnoldsche Art Publishers for your trust and your superb realisation of an idea as a product. Joan Clough translated the texts into English. Thank you for finding the right words. But without the generosity of Annette Görtz and Hans-Jörg Welsch, we couldn't have even begun. Thanks thrice!

To my son, Alexander Heils, I am indebted for his support and understanding. It isn't always easy to have a mother who is so often lost in thought. This book is dedicated to him.